W9-AVH-728

<u>Playbook for Manhood</u>

A Game Plan for Being a REAL Man

~ The Condensed Version ~

© 2010 Frank DiCocco.
All Rights Reserved. All content, ideas, and logos contained in this book are the sole property of Frank DiCocco. The contents, ideas, and images contained in this book may be duplicated and used; however, they may not be reproduced or used for profit, without the formal written consent of Frank DiCocco or REAL Man LLC.

Condensed Version
First Edition
Printed April 2010
Produced by REAL Man LLC.

For Information, Contact:
Frank DiCocco
REAL Man LLC
(860) 543-9683
(860) 674-1366
fdicocco@gmail.com

DEDICATION
To all the young men whom I have been blessed to work with over the years:
I am proud to be called your coach.
To all the people who have influenced me throughout my own life:
I am blessed to share this world with you. Your words live on in the pages that follow.

Forward
Playbook for Manhood
A Game Plan for Being a REAL Man

I have had the privilege of working with young people for the better part of the past decade, dating back to my undergraduate days of coaching high school football while still a student at Boston College. During that time, I have been doing my best to help provide our nation's young men with the guidance and wisdom that they so desperately need. As part of my whole-hearted commitment to fostering the positive development of our world's young people, I have written the first edition of *Playbook for Manhood: A Game Plan for Being a REAL Man* in order to help steer so many of our uncertain young men in the right direction.

The Playbook presents a powerful message about what it means to be a real man in today's society, by outlining the virtues and characteristics that make up a responsible, respectful, and respectable man. The book provides a very valuable and important message to today's young people: it is a message about respect, honor, commitment, and integrity. It is a message that very much needs to be heard, understood, and most importantly, *lived out*, by today's young men.

~ **The Playbook** ~

In sports and in life, a young man receives all kinds of instructional manuals and materials, everything from playbooks to textbooks to resource guides. A young man will receive a set of instructions on how to do and become just about everything in life. The one thing, however, that a young man never receives, is a manual for how to be and become a man. No young man ever receives a manual that teaches him how to be a *real* man. **Until Now.**

Playbook for Manhood: A Game Plan for Being a REAL Man provides a complete game plan for how to be a REAL Man in today's world. It offers information, insights, and advice on how to be a real man, by spelling out the four main components of what truly constitutes a "real man" in today's society—or, to put it in sports terms: *The 4 Quarters of Manhood* that make a person a "REAL Man."

~

The *Playbook* is meant to be a resource for you to use as you grow through both adolescence and adulthood. Whether you are a young man, or a man of any age, *Playbook for Manhood* will offer you the advice to help you lead a successful and meaningful life. In the pages that follow, you will find valuable life lessons, countless pieces of priceless advice, and hundreds of practical tips for living the life of a *real* man. Use them as a source for knowledge, wisdom, and advice on your journey through this world, and take the book— and the lessons you learn from it—with you wherever you decide to go in life.

~

Wherever you go,
and whatever you do…
Always be a REAL Man!

Stand up and stand tall: be a REAL man!
~ Coach Frank DiCocco

TABLE OF CONTENTS

INTRODUCTION

INTRODUCTION

What does it mean to be a real man?
Every young man goes through each day attempting to figure out the answer to one question: *What does it mean to be a **real** man?* In other words, what does it mean to be a real man… in the eyes of my teachers, in the eyes of my coaches, in the eyes of my parents and my family members, in the eyes of my friends, in the eyes of my girlfriend, and in the eyes of society?

What does it mean to be a real man?
It is a question that every young men struggles to answer, each and every day.
In truth, it is a question that all men—of every age—constantly wrestle to determine.
It is a question that not only occupies the fascination and focus of our culture,
but one that burdens every aspect of the society in which we live.

What does it mean to be a real man?
Perhaps no other question is so difficult to answer, and perhaps no other question is so vitally in need of being answered. For, it is not until we can accurately and completely identify what attitudes, actions, and character traits truly comprise a real man, that we can begin to address the many and severe consequences that grow out of our society's current inability to express what it means to be a man.

Not until we can distinguish what makes a man a *real* man—and not until we can provide that definition in an explicit fashion to our world's young men—and not until we can actively live out that definition through every word we speak, every action we take, every expectation we effect, and every standard we set, can we finally begin to make a *real* difference in our communities, our society, and our world.

Then, and only then, will we finally be able to bridge the gap between what we presently are as a society, and what we are fully capable of becoming. Then, and only then, will we be able to bring about real, positive and lasting change. Then, and only then, will we be able to help create a better and more complete world for all of us to share.

~

"If we do not help boys become men,
then we really won't be able to fix anything else in this country."

~ *Joe Ehrmann*

WHAT IT MEANS TO BE A REAL MAN

There are a lot of myths in our society about what it means to be a real man. Contrary to popular belief, being a man is not about how strong and muscular you are; it's not about what kind of car you drive; it's not about how much money you have, or about how many women you can use.

Life is not about money, cars, fame, physical appearance, and women. It's about who you are as a person; it's about the way you live your life; and it's about how you treat other people. When it comes right down to it…

Being a **REAL** man means that you:

    R-espect all people,

      E-specially women.

        A-lways do the right thing.

          L-ive a life that matters.

~

"The great aim of our living and striving should be to become better men."

~ David Bancroft Johnson

~

BEING A REAL MAN

What Does It Mean to Be a REAL Man ?

Deep down, we all yearn to be good men. But how exactly do we define what it means to be a good man… to be a *real* man? What makes a man a real man? How do you define one? How do you know if someone is a real man? How do you know if *you* are a real man?

A lot of times in our society, we are given the wrong definition of what it truly means to be a real man. We get images from the media that stress the importance of money, clothes, cars, status, promiscuity, and personal success … as if all these things are what give a man his true value as a male.

~

What Defines You As a Man ?

Contrary to popular belief, what defines you as a man is not about how attractive you are or about how strong and muscular you are; it's not about what kind of car you drive or about how big your house is; it's not about how many material possessions you have or about how popular you are with the ladies. What defines you as a man is who you are and how you live your life.

~ **What defines you as a man is *who you are* and *how you live your life*.** ~

What defines you as a man is not your individual wealth, but your personal worth. It is not about how much money you can make or your financial status.

What defines you is not how many possessions you can amass, or how many people you can surpass; it is how much respect and admiration you can earn, and how much you can do to help others. What defines you as a man is not what other people think about you, but what you think about yourself. It is not about who other people think or say you are, but about who you know deep down that you really are.

What defines you as a person is who you are on the inside. What defines you is the way you carry yourself. What defines you is the way you live your life. When it comes right down to it, being a *real* man is about… respecting all people, especially women, always doing the right thing, and living a life that matters.

~

Be a **REAL** man!
Respect all people, **E**specially women.
Always do the right thing. **L**ive a life that matters.

Being A REAL Man

When it comes right down to it…
Being a REAL man is not about possessions, but about principles.
It is not about image, but about integrity.
It is not about circumstances, but about character.
It is not about being a character, but about having character.
It is not about style, but about substance.
It is not about financial value, but about personal values.
It is not about net-worth, but about self-worth.
It is not about being honored, but about having honor.
It is not about selfish gain, but about selfless service.
It is not about serving yourself, but about serving others
And being part of something that is larger than yourself.
It is not about living only for your own wants and desires,
But about living for something beyond yourself.
It is not about taking whatever you can get and living beyond your means,
But about leaving a legacy and living beyond your years.

~

Being REAL Is A Lifestyle

Being REAL is about the way you carry yourself.
Being REAL is about the way you treat people.
Being REAL is about what you stand for.
Being REAL is about what you do with your life.

Being a REAL man is about respecting all people, *especially women*,
always doing the right thing, and living a life that matters.

~

There Is No Substitute

There is no substitute for being a good person.
There is no substitute for the real thing.
There is no substitute for being a real man.

R~espect all people,
   E~specially women.
      A~lways do the right thing.
         L~ive a life that matters.

The 4 Quarters of Manhood

When it comes to the world of sports...
In order to win in any contest, you have to learn to play a complete game.
In other words: you have to play hard and play well for *all four quarters*.

~

When it comes to the world of manhood:
In order to win at being a man, you have to learn to become a complete individual.
In other words: you have to understand and live out *all four quarters* of manhood...

~

THE 4 QUARTERS OF MANHOOD

Respect all people

Being a *real* man is about treating *all* people with respect and dignity. The golden rule is simple enough, and true enough that virtually every religion and ideology in the world deems it one of its most important values. Treat everyone the way you'd want to be treated…period. You can tell virtually all you need to know about a man by the way he treats others.

Especially women

Being a *real* man is all about treating women with respect—plain and simple. Be a gentleman at all times, and always be respectful. You can tell just about everything you need to know about a man by the way he treats a woman.

Always do the right thing

Being a *real* man is about having principles and living by those principles. It is about having something called "consistent character," which means that you have the same principles, regardless of the circumstances. It is incredible how much good you can do, and how many difficult situations you can make it through in life if you just live by five simple words: *Always do the right thing.*

Live a life that matters.

Being a *real* man is about striving for excellence in every aspect of life. It is about always doing your very best to reach your full potential in this world: to make the most of your talents, opportunities, and potential to impact others in a positive way. Being a *real* man is about investing yourself in your own success, and more importantly, in the success of others.

Be a *REAL* Man!

R

Respect
All People

Respect All People

Respect All People

Being a REAL man means treating *all* people with respect and dignity, without exception. It means understanding that everyone is worthy of respect, and that all people deserve to be treated respectfully. A REAL man shows respect to all people, at all times, in all ways… without exception.

The Nature of Respect

Respect is all about treating people right: regardless of who they are, what they say, or how they act. Respect is about treating others the way you would want to be treated, at all times and in all situations. Being respectful means extending to others the patience, courtesy, kindness, and politeness that you, yourself, would want to receive.

The Reason for Respect

All people are entitled to be treated with respect. All people inherently possess basic human dignity, and that dignity is to be honored at all times by respectful treatment. Everyone has the spirit of divinity in them—including one's self—and therefore, we should regard everyone in such a way. Each person is a sacred and divine being—including one's self—and therefore, we should treat everyone as such.

Being Respectful to Others Will Lead
Others to Be Respectful to You In Return

How you treat others directly and indirectly affects the way that you are treated in return. The way you treat others affects peoples' attitudes toward you and their opinions of you. It determines the perception they have of you, and ultimately, the manner in which they treat you.

How you treat other people directly influences those peoples' moods and mental states, which directly influence what they say and how they say it, as well as the actions and behaviors they direct at others. Therefore, always be mindful of the way you act toward others. Be careful to always treat others with respect, patience, and civility. Because ultimately, the way you treat others will, to a large degree, determine the way that they treat you in return.

The Way You Treat Others Is The Way Others Will Treat You

Treat people the best way you can treat them, and treat everyone the way you'd want to be treated. Because, the way you treat others is most likely the way that other people will treat you. Don't believe me? Think about it: if you are nice to someone, they likely will be nice to you. If you are kind to someone, they likely will be kind back to you. If you yell at someone or tell somebody off, they probably won't be very nice to you in return.

Whenever you are speaking with, spending time with, or dealing with another person, keep in mind that the way you treat that person is most likely the way that they will treat you back in return.

Not sure what I mean? Think of it as bouncing a ball against a wall. When you throw a ball against a wall, it will come back to you in a similar manner in which you first threw it. If you throw the ball hard, it will come back at you hard. If you throw it softly, it will bounce back at you softly. If you throw the ball with some spin on it, it will come back to you with some spin on it.

Ultimately, the way you throw the ball will dictate the way that it comes back to you. How you toss the ball will determine how it bounces and returns to you. And so it is with the attitudes and behaviors you exhibit toward others.

Much of what you think, say, and do will be returned to you through what other people think, say, and do. Everything that you send out into the lives of others will come back into your own; and everything that you put into the world around you will return back to you as well.

~

You have a large degree of influence over the way that others treat you. If you are initiating the conversation or interaction, then being kind, calm, and respectful likely will produce those same behaviors in the other person. If they initiate the conversation— and they do not do so in a respectful or kind way—then by reacting calmly and by being nice to them, you greatly increase the chances that they will change their approach and begin speaking and acting more along the lines of the way that you are.

~

Treat people the way you want them to treat you …
Because ultimately, the way that you treat people will determine
the way that they treat you in return.

~

"Treat all people with respect and dignity."

~ George Allen

~

The Benefits of Being Respectful ~ A Thing Called Karma

The Nature of Karma: What Goes Around... Comes Around

The notion of Karma states that what goes around comes around, and that we all get what we have coming to us sooner or later. Call it Karma, or call it common sense. But whatever you want to call it, the truth of the matter is that it makes perfect sense logistically.

~

The more negative things you do, the more negativity you add to the world. The more negativity there is in the world, the more likely your chances of feeling the effects of that negativity.

Conversely, the more positive things you do, the more positivity you add to the world. The more positivity there is in the world, the more likely your chances of reaping the benefits of that positivity.

Every time you do something bad, you make the world a worse place; and therefore, you increase the chances that something bad will happen to you. Every time you do something good, you make the world a better place; and therefore, you increase the chances that something good will happen to you.

~

If you do good things, good things will come back into your life.
If you sow seeds of goodness, you will reap the rewards of goodness.
Be good to people, and people will be good to you.
Do good things, and good things will happen to you.
This is the true essence of Karma.

~

What goes around, comes around. So be careful what you make "go around." Do good, and good things will happen. Do bad, and bad things will happen. Remember that, eventually, it all catches up to you in the end.

~ You will get what your works deserve. Whether it is good or bad, you will get what you deserve... either in this world or the next. Send goodness out into the world, and goodness will return into your life. Send evil and rottenness out into the world, and those same things will return into your life. Essentially, Karma is a philosophy of cause and effect. Therefore: Do Good and Be Good... and all will be good.

~

What goes around... comes around.
Therefore: treat all people, at all times, the way that you
yourself, would always want to be treated.

~

There is a destiny which makes us brothers;
None goes his way alone.
All that we send into the lives of others
Comes back into our own.

~ Edwin Markham

Always Be Respectful, and Always Be Civil

Being civil means simply being courteous to other people, regardless of who they are or what the situation is. Whether you want to be respectful or not, is irrelevant. Being civil means that you extend courtesy to all people, at all times. To put it in another way, it means being polite and treating people right.

~

You don't have to walk up to everyone and hug them; you don't have to agree with everyone's decisions and philosophies of living; and you don't have to be best friends with everyone you meet. You do not even have to like any of the people that you meet… But you do have to treat them with respect and politeness, and you do have to be civil.

You don't have to agree with others, you just have to be respectful to them.

You don't have to agree with people's beliefs, you just have to be respectful *of* them, and of that person's right to believe in whatever they choose to believe in.

You don't have to agree with other people's lifestyles, you just have to be respectful of them, and of that person's right to live however they choose.

~

Being civil means being polite and treating people right.

Be Tolerant and Accepting of Others

Tolerance has been defined as: "Learning to accept others as **valuable** individuals, regardless of their traits or beliefs." In other words… Tolerance means putting individual differences aside and embracing collective similarities. It is about recognizing that differences exist, and then choosing to put those differences aside. It means recognizing that differences exist, but then realizing that they do not matter as much as the things we all share in common.

Tolerance is the realization that others—though they may look, act, speak, or worship differently than us—are our equals. It is the realization that our bond to these individuals is not to their differences, but to that part of them which brings us all together: it is to the common threads that weave us all into one intricate web of humanity—it is to the universal commonality that binds us all into one collective human family.

~

All People Are Equal Members of the Same Team and the Same Family

All people are equal members of the same team; all people are equal members of the same family. Regardless of our race, religion, gender, ethnicity, financial worth, or social status… each of us belongs to the same group, the same greater whole. When you strip away all the categories, the terms, and the titles… we are left with only one name that matters… *human.*

All people are part of the same team and the same family—the *human* team and the *human* family. Therefore, all people deserve to be treated in a respectful and dignified way, just as the members of *any* team and *any* family deserve to be treated in a respectful and dignified manner. All people are *equal* in their membership to the team and family, and therefore, all people are entitled to *equal* amounts of respect and regard.

~

**"I'm not concerned with your liking or disliking me…
All I ask is that you respect me as a human being."**

~ Jackie Robinson

Victory Should Be Earned,
But Respect Should Be Given

Respect should not have to be won by any means. Rather, it should be granted without condition, for the sole reason that all members of a team—and all members of a family—should be treated with equal amounts of respect and esteem, simply for the reason that all are equally a part of that team. There should be no distinctions drawn, no discriminations exercised, and no exclusions made.

~

Respect should not have to be *won* by any means, at any time, by anyone.

~

When it comes down to it, whether the discussion is about a sports organization, a business, a family, or all of us collectively as a human race: the fact of the matter is that **we are all equal members of the same team**; we are all equal parts of one greater whole. As such, each of us deserves to be regarded with an equal amount of respect and treated with an equal amount of dignity… regardless of any differences or distinctions, and without any other required conditions.

~

Respect and esteem should be granted to all: no exceptions and no exemptions.

~

~ The Human Team ~

We all wear the same uniform, we all play for the same team;
Each of us may have a different position, each of us may play a different role,
and each of us may wear a different number on his jersey…
but all of us—*each and every one of us*—belongs to the same great-big team:
and that team is the one, and the only team really, when it comes to it…
The Human Team.

~

~ Everyone Is Equal; Each Is Unique and Important ~

"Everyone is equal in God's sight. There is no distinction on the basis of race, religion, or social position—or first, second, or third string on a football team. We are all of equal value. I tried to see each player as unique and important… and tried to treat him accordingly."
~ *Tom Osborne, former Head Coach, University of Nebraska*

Live by the Golden Rule

The Golden Rule

The golden rule is simple enough, and true enough, that virtually every religion and ideology in the world deems it as one of its most important values. Treat everyone the way you'd want to be treated…plain and simple. Live by the golden rule, and always show respect to others. You can tell virtually all you need to know about a man by the way he treats other people.

The Golden Rule is a foundational principle of many of the world's major religions and philosophies. Below are versions of the rule from some of the various belief systems and cultures in this great world of ours.

Judaism
"What is hateful to you, do not do to your neighbor:
that is the whole of the Torah; all the rest of it is commentary." ~ *The Talmud*

Christianity
"In everything, do unto others as you would have them do unto you;
for this sums up the Law and the Prophets." ~ *The Gospel of Matthew 7:12*

Islam
"Not one of you is a believer until he loves for his brother what
he loves for himself." ~ *The Fortieth Hadith of an-Nawawi 13*

Hinduism
"This is the sum of duty: do naught unto others
that which would cause you pain if done to you." ~ *The Mahabharata*

Buddhism
"Hurt not others in ways you yourself would find hurtful." ~ *Udana-Varga, 5:18*

Zoroastrianism
"That nature alone is good which refrains from doing unto another
whatsoever is not good for itself." ~ *Dadistan-I-Dinik, 94:5*

Jainism
"A man should wander about treating all creatures
as he himself would be treated." ~ *Sutrakritanga 1:11:33*

Western Tradition
"Treat others the way that you yourself would want to be treated."
~ *The words of parents, teachers, and mentors everywhere*

~

Do good to all. Do harm to none.
This is the formula for achieving harmony in life.

Some Other Important Rules

The Golden Rule states that you should treat others the way you would want others to treat you. But the Golden Rule, however, is not the only important rule that there is. Here are a few additional rules to consider for treating other people with respect:

The Silver Rule

If the Golden Rule states:
Treat others the way that you would want to be treated.
— Or —
Do unto others as you would have others do unto you.

Then the Silver Rule complements it by stating:
*Do **not** do unto others as you would **not** have others do unto you.*
— Or —
*Do **not** do to other people, what you would **not** want them to do to you.*
To take it one step further: Do not do—or say—to other people what you would not want them to do, or say, to you.

~

"What is hateful to you, do not do to your fellow man."
~ Hillel the Elder

The Bronze Rule

The Bronze Rule states:
*Treat others the way you would want the person you **loved most** to be treated.*
— Or —
*Treat others the way you would want your **favorite person** to be treated.*

We all have people whom we care about deeply, and whom we respect highly. Whether it is a mother, a father, a favorite teacher or coach, a sister, a girlfriend, a best friend, or a relative… the fact is that we would never want anyone to do or say anything that might hurt that person in any way.

If you would treat other people as if they were the one person you cared about most in this world… then you would be upholding the spirit of the Bronze Rule.

If you would treat other people—even the person who cuts you off at the traffic light, even the telemarketer who calls you during dinner, even the annoying person who asks you the same question or who nags you about the same thing over and over again… If you were to treat all people as if that person (up in that car ahead of you, or on the other end of the phone line, or on the other side of the conversation) were the person you loved and respected most… then you would be helping to make the world a better and more pleasant place for all of us.

The Titanium Rule

Finally, there is the Titanium Rule.
The Titanium Rule gets its name for one reason: because,
like the strong alloy known that it is named after, the Titanium Rule is *bulletproof*.
Meaning, that if you follow it, then you cannot help but to act respectfully toward others.
The Titanium Rule states: *Treat other people the way you would want your own **mother** to be treated.*

~ Live By The Rules ~

In any sport, the best way to play the game is to play it fairly, squarely,
and by the rules. It is to play with complete and total respect for the game,
the opponents, the officials, and everyone else involved with the experience.
When it comes to the game of life, the best way to live it is with class, honor, virtue,
and excellence. The best way to do this is simply to live by the rules. It is to have
complete and total respect for the nature of life and for the world in which we live, the
people who share this world with us on our journey through life, the Creator who made it
all possible, and everyone else whose path we may come cross along the way.

~

Below are brief summaries of the most important rules of life:

The Golden Rule
~ Do unto others as you would have them do unto you. ~

The Silver Rule
~ Do not do unto others what you would not have them do unto you. ~

The Bronze Rule
~ Do unto others that which you would want done unto your favorite person. ~

The Titanium Rule
~ Do unto others that which you would want done unto your own mother. ~

~

"How fine it is at night to say:
'I have not wronged a soul today.'"

~ *Edgar A. Guest*

The Most Important Person You Will Ever Meet

When your time in this world ends, and you are called up to your inevitable appointment at the entrance to the Pearly Gates (or wherever your afterworld may be), there is going to be someone standing there to greet you. That someone is going to be sitting there patiently waiting to ask you a single question. Your answer to that question is going to determine the rest of your eternity… because you see, that one person holds the key to the Gates, and he or she alone gets to choose whether to let you in or not.

The only catch is this: the person standing there is going to be the exact opposite of you in every way. They are going to be short if you are tall; they are going to have blond hair if you have dark or red hair; they are going to be fat if you are skinny, or be skinny if you are overweight.

That person is going to be black or Asian if you are white, or perhaps Middle-Eastern if you are Hispanic. They are going to be homosexual if you are straight. They're going to have a lot of tattoos or body piercings if you don't have any; they are going to be foreign or an immigrant if you are an American. They are going to be Muslim, or Atheist, or Hindu, or Jewish if you are a Christian; they are going to be devoutly religious if you are not. They are going to be a Boston Red Sox fan if you are a New York Yankees fan; they are going to be a Democrat if you are a Republican, or vice-versa. They are going to be poor if you are rich, or vice-versa. They are going to be a woman if you are a man, or vice-versa.

And when you arrive at the entrance way to Heaven (or to whatever afterlife you may believe in), the person that you meet there is going to look you squarely in the eye and ask you one thing… and one thing only…

How did you treat me?

~ Let's try to keep that in mind as we pass through this world with one another.

~

"Do not judge, or you too will be judged.
For in the same way you judge others, you will be judged…"
~ The Gospel of Matthew 7:1-2 (from the Christian Faith Tradition)

———————————————

Treat everyone as if they were the most important person
you were ever going to meet … because ultimately, they very well may be.

———————————————

"If you judge people, you have no time to love them."
~ Mother Theresa

All People Are Entitled
To Be Treated With Respect & Dignity

You are entitled to one great thing in this world: to be treated with respect and dignity…
for the sole reason that you are a human being; and all members of the human family
deserve to be treated in such a way.

~

Regardless of personal preferences and individual differences, everyone is a
member of the same team… the *Human Team*. And although some people may have
different roles than others, and while some roles may be bigger or smaller than others, it
is important to understand that everyone is an equal member of the group. As such,
everyone is equally significant. Therefore, everyone is important, and everyone matters.
Every person counts, and indeed, every person contributes.

~

All People are Equal and
All People Deserve Equal Treatment

Everyone is important, and everyone matters.
We are all of equal value, whether we like it or not, and therefore,
we are all deserving of equal respect.

~

Everyone Is Important

Everyone you meet is important.
Everyone deserves to be treated with respect and dignity.
Everybody matters. Everybody is somebody.

~

"Everyone, everywhere … deserves your respect."

~ Ewan McGregor

~

"Men are respectable only as they respect."

~ Ralph Waldo Emerson

~

A real man respects others
and is respected by others in return.

Respect All People, Especially…

Respect all people…

Especially those who are different than you—those people who look differently
than you, those who think differently than you, those who act differently
than you, and those who believe differently than you.

Especially women—at all times.

Especially yourself—in all ways.

Especially those who don't like you.

Especially those whom you don't like.

Especially those who disagree with you.

Especially those with whom you disagree.

Especially those whom you do not feel deserve it.

~ Whether you feel they do or do not deserve it doesn't matter, because all
people deserve to be treated with respect and dignity; and nothing you think,
say, or do will be able to change that.

Especially those who are disagreeable and not easy to get along with.

Especially those who don't treat you with respect to begin with.

Especially those who don't treat you with respect in return.

Especially those who mistreat you.

~ It is no worthy accomplishment to be respectful to those who
are respectful to you. What is worth distinction is to treat <u>all</u>
people with respect: not only those who are easy to be
respectful to, but to everyone else… *especially* to everyone else.

Especially when you don't feel like it.

~ It is no worthy accomplishment to be respectful to others only
when you feel like being respectful to others. What is worth
distinction is to treat all people with respect at <u>all</u> times: not only
when you feel like it, but even when you don't feel like it…
especially when you don't feel like it.

~

Treat all people with respect… even those who make it difficult to do so:
Especially those who make it difficult to do so.

~

"Why were the saints, saints?
Because they were cheerful when it was difficult to be cheerful; patient when it was
difficult to be patient; and because they pushed on when they wanted to stand still, and
kept silent when they wanted to talk; and because they were agreeable when they
wanted to be disagreeable. That was all.
It was quite simple, and always will be."

~ Miriam C. Hunter

~

Respect <u>all</u> people, at <u>all</u> times, and in <u>all</u> ways.
This is the true essence of respect.

~

~ A REAL man respects all people, at all times, and in all ways. ~

The Most Important Lesson That Competitive Sports Teaches Us

The world of competitive team sports teaches a great number of valuable life lessons. Perhaps the single most significant of all these lessons—even more important than the virtues of hard work and perseverance, sacrifice and commitment; even more valuable than the process of learning to set goals; even more vital than developing the necessary skills for achievement—is the importance of treating other people with respect.

In order for a team to be successful, every one of its members must learn to accept, respect, and value one another. No team can ever be successful without first having respect as a basic foundation. No group can ever be great unless its members have mutual respect for one another and treat each other respectfully.

The first and most valuable lesson that sports teaches is the importance of treating others with respect: players must respect other players; players must respect coaches; coaches must respect players, and coaches must respect coaches.

~

The importance of treating other individuals with respect is the foundational lesson of team sports. Without respect, success is not possible. Period.

Come Together and Work Together

One of the first things that every member of a team must learn, is that everyone must come together and work together, in order for the team—and everyone on it—to be successful. You have to learn to understand the importance of viewing your teammates with dignity—of accepting them and valuing them for who they are and for what they are capable of contributing. And you must learn the importance of treating your teammates with respect at all times, and in all ways.

You have to learn to do these things in order to coexist on the same field, and in the same huddle with one another. You have to learn to coexist before you can learn to come together; you have to learn to come together before you can work together, and you have to learn to work together before you can ever hope to accomplish anything special together. And you can do none of these things unless you first learn to treat each other with respect; and unless you first learn to see all your lives as connected, all your goals as linked, and all your destinies as one.

Come Together, Work Together, Achieve Together

As members of a team, you have to realize that you do not have to like each other, but that you do have to treat one another with respect. You do not have to be best friends with one another, but you do have to be civil toward each another. You must be respectful toward each other; you must be civil to one another; you must come together and learn to work together in order to achieve success together.

~

"The game has no prejudices, and neither do I."
~ Jim Calhoun

All In The Same Huddle

When you step into a huddle, you step out of your own individual world and into the collective world of the team. When you look around at the other sets of eyes in that huddle, you realize that everyone is all of a sudden pulled together in the pursuit of one dream, of one hope. At that point, you realize that, while everyone's histories may be uniquely different, everyone's future is entirely one. And at that point, it doesn't matter who you are, what you look like, where you come from, or where you've been. All that matters is that everyone comes together and begins working together; all that matters is that every member of the team is headed in the same direction.

~

It doesn't matter where each of us has come from, but where all of us are going.

~

You may not be from the same background, you may not have the same beliefs, but you have to understand that you are all part of the same team. You may not share anything in common in terms of your personal lives or your beliefs, but you all share a common purpose and a common goal.

When a group of teammates enters a huddle, they may all enter from different places, at different positions, and from different directions. When that group walks into the huddle, they do so as individuals. When that group breaks the huddle, however, they do so in unison. And when that one team breaks the huddle to run to the line, they all run together in the same direction.

All In The Human Huddle

In the game of life, we are all part of the same team; we are all members of the same unit, the same group. We may all come from different places, we may all be at different positions and in different situations, we may all look upon life from different perspectives… but ultimately, we all walk in the same direction.

~

We are all part of the same team.
As such, we all have a stake in one another's success, because everyone's success is linked together. I cannot succeed if my brother fails, nor can he succeed if I fail.
All of us are connected. All of our lives are intertwined.

~

One Team. One Family.

We are all part of the same team, regardless of race, ethnicity, financial rank, personal status, social class, religious beliefs, and gender. We all wear the same uniform, and we all play for the same organization. We may each have different numbers and play different positions, but all of us—*each and every one of us*—belong to one team… *The Human Team.* We all share in the great huddle of humanity, we call the same great field of this world our home, and we find common ground in our common bond—our unmistakable and undeniable link as members of the human chain of life.

~

"The bond that links your true family is not one of blood, but of respect…
Rarely do members of one family grow up under the same roof."

~ *Richard Bach*

~ Would It Really Matter, and Would You Really Care ~

Foxholes and Football...
& What Really Matters At the Moment of Truth

If you were in a foxhole in the middle of a battle, and you had to risk your life and run across the battlefield, and you had to count only on the person next to you in that foxhole to provide cover for you—essentially, to keep you alive... would you really care what color that person was? Would you really care what religion that person subscribed to? Would you really care what social circles that person was a part of? Would you really care what sexual orientation that person was? Or would you only care about whether or not he or she kept you alive?

All the terms and titles in the world go out the window as soon as the bullets start flying; and all the semantics a man can come up with seem to disappear the moment those bullets start flying *at you.*

~

If you were a running back, and you were going to be carrying the ball up the middle of the field on an "Iso" play, and *Ray Lewis* was the linebacker who was supposed to get "Iso"-blocked, and you had to rely entirely on your fullback to throw the key block—essentially, to keep you *alive*... would you really care what color that fullback was? Would you really care what religion your teammate subscribed to? Would you really care what social circles he belonged to? Would you really care what sexual orientation he was? Or would you only care about whether or not he made that block?

It's funny how all the terms and titles in the world go out the window as soon as the defenders start flying to the football; and it's comical how quickly all the semantics seem to disappear the second that those defenders start flying to the football...when *you are the one who has the football.*

~

If something matters at the moment of truth, then shouldn't it always matter?
Also, if something *doesn't* matter at the moment of truth, then shouldn't it never really matter at any other time?

~

There lies before us, if we choose,
continual progress in happiness, knowledge, and wisdom.
Shall we, instead, choose death,
Because we cannot forget our quarrels?
We appeal as human beings, to human beings:
Remember your humanity, and forget the rest."

~ Bertrand Russell

We Are All In This Together

Whether we like it or not, we are all in this world together. Just like in sports, where we may not get to pick the team we are on, or the members of the team whom we must play alongside with, so too in life we also do not get to pick the team we belong to.

We are born into this world as human beings, and therefore, we are drafted onto the one enormous team that is humanity. We, along with everyone else in the world with us, is a part of the same great organization, and we must all learn to embrace the team-concept as a result.

Regardless of whether we want to be on the team or not, and regardless of whom we want to share that team with, we must learn to accept our place in this world and on this team. We must learn to accept both our place and our teammates' places on it as well. In order for this world, *and this team*, to run smoothly, then all of us—each and every one of us—must buy into the team concept. We must accept it, we must embrace it, and we must buy into it wholeheartedly.

~

To return to the "foxhole" analogy: If you were in a foxhole in the middle of a war, dodging enemy fire and fighting for your survival… and all of a sudden you had to run out of that foxhole, and get to another one just a little bit ahead… and you had to count on the one other guy sitting there with you in that bunker to provide cover for you—to return enemy fire and give you a chance to make it to that next bunker…to KEEP YOU ALIVE … I ask you this: Would you really care what color that guy was? Would it really matter, honestly, what religion he was? Would you really, honestly care about which state he was from, or who he voted for in the last election, or whether he was a Democrat or a Republican? Would it really matter? At that moment, would you truthfully be concerned about what his ethnicity was, or what his sexual orientation might be? Would it make any difference if he were a North Carolina or Duke fan, or a Red Sox or Yankees fan? Honestly, would it *really* matter… and would you *really* care?

The answer to all of those questions is NO. And the reason for that is because, when the bullets are whizzing by your ear and your life is on the line, the only thing you would care about is whether or not *you could count on that person to keep you alive*. In other words, all that stuff about "personal differences" and "alternative beliefs" goes right out the window when the bombs start blasting and the bullets start flying. It's funny how, when your life begins to flash before your eyes, you quickly lose sight of all the irrelevant things that don't have anything to do with what's important.

~

When it comes to this life of ours, and when it comes to this world of ours…
We are all in this together.

> Accept it.
> Embrace it.
> Buy into it.
>
> … Because it is 100 percent true.

Accept It: "Whether you're a hawk or a dove, you're just a bird living in the same environment, in the same world." ~ *Jesse Jackson*

Embrace It: "We are not going to be able to operate our Spaceship Earth successfully, nor for much longer, unless we see it as a whole spaceship and our fate as common. It has to be everybody or nobody." ~ *Buckminster Fuller*

We are all in the proverbial bunker. For as long as we live in this world, we will always have the proverbial bullets flying by. None of us is beyond the grips of Fate, and therefore, none of us can get through this world unscathed. We need one another.

Buy Into It: "We must learn to live together as brothers, or perish together as fools." ~ *Dr. Martin Luther King, Jr.*

~

"So long as we live among men, let us cherish humanity."
~ *Andre Gide*

Life Is Color-Blind ... Shouldn't We Be Too?

Life does not care about race, creed, color, or ethnicity… neither does Death, for that matter. Life doesn't care about material wealth or social status; nor does it care about orientation or political views. Life does not care about any of these things, and neither should we.

Life, itself, has no prejudices… and neither should we. Life, itself, does not discriminate on the basis of anything: not gender, not creed, not financial worth, not social class, not race, and not color… and neither should we.

Life is color-blind. Or, should I say, *living* is color-blind.
~ Shouldn't we be too?

~

The sooner we realize that **we are all people**, the better off we will all be.

~

It Makes No Difference *Up There*, So Why Does It Matter Down Here?

"Nothing is precious except that part of you which is in other people,
and that part of others which is in you. Up there, on high, everything is one."

~ *Pierre Teilhard de Chardin*

"In the sky, there is no distinction of east and west;
people create distinctions out of their own minds
and then believe them to be true."

~ *Buddha*

Live As One, Play As One, Win As One: Victory Together Is All That Matters

We all play for the same team; we all have the same name on our jersey; we all have the same goal on our mind. Winning is color-blind, and victory does not discriminate. If we will put the differences of the past behind us, and focus on the dreams of the future ahead of us, if we will come together and work together, if we will search for the one thing that all of us want… we will find that the rest of it does not matter, that most of it makes no difference. For in the game of life, much like the world of sports, the one thing that matters is winning, and victory is its own reward.

~

It Makes No Difference To Me

Your race, your color, your credit, your creed:
It makes no difference to me.
Respect in word, and honor in deed;
These, and Victory, are all that I seek.

I care not what color it is that you bleed:
It makes no difference to me.
So long as you spill it in toil—not for you nor me, but *we*.
These, and Victory, are all that I seek.

Your height, your weight, your leap, your speed,
It makes no difference to me.
Your will to strive, your effort to reach,
These, and Victory, are all that I seek.

I care not for what language you speak,
It makes no difference to me.
A bond not meek and a word not weak,
These, and Victory, are all that I seek.

Whose works, whose gain, whose fame may peak,
It makes no difference to me.
I long for honor and glory—not yours or mine—but *ours*, you see.
These, and Victory, are all that I seek.
…

Victory and Honor, are what matter you see.
The rest of it makes no difference to me.
Your word and your bond—not a grand applause;
Your best and your most, for a worthy cause;
Your head and your heart, and the truth that they speak…
These, and Victory, are all that I seek.

The Human Ocean

I was looking out at the ocean one day and I wondered to myself, "I wonder how many drops of water are in that whole thing?" My first immediate thought was "A whole lot… hundreds of thousands of millions of bazillions." But then I thought about it for a second, and I realized that there were two answers to my question: *A whole lot…* or, simply: *one.*

As many gallons of water as there might be in an ocean, they are all part of the same body of water. As many millions of drops of water as there might be in an ocean, they are all part of the same powerful wave.

When each of those millions of drops is in the ocean, they are all connected— their movements, their histories, their futures, and their fates. Upon realizing this, I thought to myself, "Wow, that sounds a lot like us as people: There are millions of different people, people of all different shapes and sizes, people of all different races and beliefs, people of all different types and kinds… but we are all part of the same body."

~

We are all part of the same body, all members of the same family.
We are all drops of the same ocean, all part of the same wonderful wave of humanity…
known simply as *the Human Ocean.*

~

"We are the leaves of one branch, the drops of one sea."
~ Jean Baptiste LaCordaire

One Heartbeat

One group. One unit. One vision.
One squad. One family. One mission.

One team. One dream. One goal.
One head. One heart. One soul.

One present. One future. One story.
One fate. One fortune. One glory.

One body. One arm. One hand.
One hope. One bond. One band.

One note. One rhythm. One harmony.
One melody. One symphony. One destiny.

One tone. One tune. One drumbeat.
One song. One sound. One heartbeat.

"He who experiences the unity of life
   sees his own self in all beings,
      and all beings in his own self."
   ~ Buddha

Respect Yourself

Self-Respect

Having respect for *all* people means also having respect for yourself. First and foremost, true respect for others must begin with genuine respect for one's self. At the heart of a true sense of self-respect is a clear and healthy understanding of a person's own self-worth.

Realizing that each of us has an incredible amount of inherent value—based solely on the fact that each of us is a human being, and therefore, that each of us deserves to be treated as such and each of us owes it to ourselves and others to act as such—is the first step in developing self-respect.

Having Self-Respect

Having self-respect is about always carrying yourself with class. It means always acting with class, always talking with class, always walking with class, and always living with class.

Having self-respect is about recognizing your true value and inherent dignity as a human being. It is about realizing that all people, including yourself, are important and deserve to be regarded as such.

Having self-respect is about striving to be your best self at all times. It is about believing in, and working toward, your absolute full potential; it is about striving for personal excellence in all that you do. Essentially, self-respect is about always doing your best to be your best and to become your best.

"People with self-respect exhibit a certain toughness, a kind of moral nerve; they display what is called <u>character</u>—the willingness to accept responsibility for one's own life."
– Joan Didion

"Self-respect is the cornerstone of all virtue."
~ John Herschel

Self-Respect Starts With You

Self-respect starts with you.
It starts with the way you think about yourself, the way you carry yourself, the way you talk about yourself and others, and the way you present yourself to others.

~

Self-respect continues with you.
It continues with the way you continue to regard yourself, it continues with the way you continue to treat others, and it continues with the way that you carry yourself.

~

Self-respect will only end with you.
Your self-respect will only end if you decide to make it end.
No one can take away your self-respect, and no one can take away your dignity.
You are in control of your own level of personal excellence;
you are the one who determines the level of class you show;
you are the one who dictates the amount of positive pride you have for yourself;
you are the one who decides the manner in which you live your life.

~

Self-respect starts with you; self-respect continues with you; self-respect will last as long as you preserve it, and it will only end if you allow it to. Preserve your dignity.
Always keep your self-respect.

~

Self-respect starts with you.
If you don't take yourself seriously, then no one else will either.

~

~

"Respect yourself
if you would have others respect you."
~ Baltasar Gracian

Always Carry Yourself With Class:
Take Pride In Who You Are

~ Be Somebody ~

The late, great Eddie Robinson summarized the nature of self-respect in a
slogan he constantly preached to his student-athletes. Always one to stress the importance
of carrying one's self with class, Coach Robinson
tirelessly exhorted his young men:

~

Look like Somebody.
Act like Somebody.
Talk like Somebody.
BE Somebody.

~

Look Like Somebody: Take care of your overall appearance. Dress well, wear
clothes that fit, wear your pants where they're supposed to be worn. Make a good
first impression. Make a good lasting impression. Take pride in the way you look.

Act Like Somebody: Carry yourself with class at all times. Be respectful to all people,
and be respectable in all situations. Do what is right, do what is best, and never accept
anything less. Always be yourself, always take the high road, and always show class.
Take pride in the way you act.

Talk Like Somebody: Speak appropriately; speak respectfully; be polite; use proper
grammar. Talk like a respectable person, and people will think of you as a respectable
person. Speak like an intelligent person, and people will think of you as an intelligent
person. Speak properly and speak respectfully. Take pride in what you say, and in how
you say it. Take pride in the way you talk.

Be Somebody: Strive to be your best in all that you do. Strive to give your best to others
at all times. Become someone you can be proud of. Become someone others can be
proud to know. Be somebody. Take pride in the way you carry yourself.
Take pride in who you are. Take pride in who you are becoming.

~

Look like Somebody. Act like Somebody. Talk like Somebody.
BE SOMEBODY.

~ **Always Carry Yourself With Class** ~

The Essence of Class

Class has nothing to do with what kind of clothes you where, what kind of car you drive, or how many possessions you have. Class is about how you carry yourself, how you think, and how you act. You can be broke and have all the class in the world. And you can have all the money in the world and still not have an ounce of class.

The Essence of Classy People

You can tell who classy people are, because they are the ones you look at and think to yourself, "Now there's a person who carries himself the right way: he always takes the high road and says the right things, he always acts like the better man and does the right things, and he always handles situations in the right way." Classy people are the ones you look at and think to yourself, "Now there's someone I admire, there's someone I respect, there's someone I want to be like; and… if I had a daughter, there's someone I would want my daughter to marry.

~

Your actions echo your character;
they are for others the greatest representation
of who you truly are and what you really believe in.

~

"Success—*the real success*—does not depend upon the position you hold,
but upon how you carry yourself in that position."

~ *Theodore Roosevelt*

~

~ **A Great Thought On Self-Respect** ~

"Self-respect is a sense of a reasonable measure of pride and dignity toward oneself.
Possessing self-respect makes one more confident, competent, and courageous.
Self-respect gives one the ability to live up to the highest of personal values.
Respect is a key virtue we should practice in life, and we should always treat
people with the respect that we would want in return. Self-respect is the key to
making the right decisions in life. Learning to respect ourselves and to carry
ourselves with class, will no doubt help us to make the right choices
when we are faced with adversity in life."

~ *Mary Kathryn Mason*

Your Worth As A Man

The Source of Your Self-Worth

In order to have a healthy and accurate sense of yourself, it is necessary first to understand the nature of your self-worth. In order to develop a positive and healthy self-image, you must first recognize the source of your self-worth—in other words, where it is that your worth as a person comes from. Both a positive sense of self and a healthy self-image are vital to developing and maintaining a proper self-respect.

In order to establish a sound sense of respect for yourself, you need to recognize and understand what it is that gives you value as a human being. You must realize what does and what does not determine your worth as a person. In other words: you must understand which things do—and do not—contribute to determining your value as a human being.

So, where exactly does your self-worth come from? What is it that actually contributes to determining your overall value as a human being? What exactly does and doesn't determine your worth as a person? Let's start with what it is that *doesn't* determine your worth as a person, and then we will take a look at what it is that actually does.

~

What *Doesn't* Determine Your Worth as a Person

There are a lot of things we use to assess how important we think we are, how valued we think we are in the eyes of society, and how we feel about ourselves overall. Unfortunately however, many of these so-called self-worth "barometers" are inaccurate gauges of our true value as individuals. Before we can understand where our worth as human beings comes from, we first must learn to recognize which things do not help constitute our value as people.

Your Worth Isn't Determined by Others: Your worth is not determined by what other people think of you, what other people say about you, or how other people treat you.

Your Worth Isn't Determined by Society: Your worth is not determined by how much money you make, what kind of clothes you wear, or what kind of car you drive.

Your Worth Isn't Determined by Your Career or Your Workplace: Your worth is not determined by the type of job you have, the number of sales you make, the size of desk you sit at in your office, whether or not you get that promotion, or whether or not you have a corner-office.

Your Worth Isn't Determined by Your Physical Prowess: Your worth is not determined by how attractive you are, how popular you are with members of the opposite sex, how much you can bench press, how much you look like the model on the cover of a magazine, or how you measure up to society's ideal body image.

Your Worth Isn't Determined by Your Athletic Prowess: Your worth is not determined by how many touchdowns you score, passes you complete, or tackles that you make on a Friday night. Your worth is not determined by how many times you get your name in the newspaper or by how many pats on the back you receive in the hallways at school. It is not determined by whether you play every play, both ways, as a starter… or, if you never get the chance to get in the game at all. (This may diminish your *recruiting* value, but it doesn't have anything to do with determining your value as a human being.)

Your Worth Isn't Determined by Your Status: Your worth is not determined by your accomplishments, nor is it determined by your lack of accomplishments. Your worth is not determined by your weekly tee-time at the local country club, nor is it determined by the type of school you go to, or by how prestigious of a school your children go to. Your worth is not determined by your place in the proverbial "pecking order" at work, at home, in school, at the country club, or any place else.

~

What *Does* Determine Your Worth as a Person

~ If none of the previous things determines your value as a human being, then what exactly is it that *does* determine your worth as a person? When it comes right down to it, the answer to that question is very simple…

Your Worth Is Determined By Your Birth: Simply by being born into this world, you possess an incredible and undeniable value as an person—a value that can never be diminished in any way, by anything or by anyone.

Simply by being born into this world as a human being, you have an enormous and awesome worth as a person—a worth that can never be lessened in any way, and a worth that can never be taken away from you by anything or by anyone.

Your *worth* is determined by your *birth*. When you are born into this world, you bring with you an incredible amount of value as a human being. You enter this world with an enormous worth as a person, and that worth can never—and will never—decrease in its value. Nothing anyone says or does can lessen or take away your value as a person.

~

"None of us come to this earth to <u>gain</u> our worth; we brought it with us."
~ *Sherri Dew*

Look The World Straight In The Eye

Look people straight in the eye when you talk to them and shake hands with them. Looking a person in the eye shows that you respect and value that person's presence and dignity. Looking someone in the eye shows that you respect and value yourself as well, and that you are fully aware of your own worth as a human being. Look upon others with respect and dignity; look upon yourself with respect and dignity as well. Look the world—and everyone in it—straight in the eye.

Look people in the eye when you talk to them: it shows people that you have enough respect for them to give them your full attention and focus, and it demonstrates to them that you have enough respect for yourself to know that you are equally deserving of that same amount of attention and focus.

~

Have enough respect for others, and for yourself,
to look people in the eye when you talk to them.

~

Look people in the eye when you shake their hand: it shows that you have enough respect for that person to look upon them with dignity and consideration. It also demonstrates to that person that you have enough respect for yourself to know that you are deserving of dignified and considerate treatment.

Look people straight in the eye: don't look above them, and don't look below them. Look them eye-to-eye. If you were to look up above someone's eye-level, it would show that they aren't important enough to you—that you view yourself as superior to them, and that you look at them as being inferior to you. If you were to look over someone's eyes, it would implicitly tell that person that you are *over-looking* them.

If you were to look below someone's eye-level, it would show them that you view them as superior to you—that you view yourself as inferior to them and to other people as well. If you were to look down at the ground, or around at other things below the other person's eye-level, it would implicitly tell them that you don't think highly enough to hold your head—and your eyes—high enough to at least be on the same level as other people. It would tell that person that you don't think of yourself as equal to others, or as deserving of as much respect as everyone else.

(*Note: Some people may be much shorter or taller than you, so you may have to use your neck a little bit. Fortunately for you, however, your neck and your eyes are capable of moving and adjusting... so make sure that you move and adjust them as much as you need to, in order to be able to look other people—and the world—straight in the eye.*)

~

Have enough respect for others, and for yourself,
to look people in the eye when you shake their hand.

~

"Never bend your head. Hold it high.
Look the world straight in the eye."

~ Helen Keller

Who You Are Is More Important Than What You Have

At the end of the day—and during every single minute of it as well—who you are as a person is infinitely more important than what you have for possessions. Who you are as a man, what you believe in and what you stand for, how you carry yourself, and how you treat others is of much greater consequence than what you have in terms of material possessions.

~

Your self-worth is more valuable than your material worth;
your value as a person is more important than your value as a purchaser.

~

"Your self-worth is more important than your net-worth."
~ Joe Ehrmann

Your self-value is more important than your material value; the value of your self-worth is more important than the value of your financial worth.

Your Personal Statement Is More Important Than Your Financial Statement

Your *personal* statement—what you believe in and what you stand for—is much more important than your *financial* statement. Your principles and your priorities are more significant than the price tag on anything that you, or money, can buy.

Your Personal Account Is More Important Than Your Bank Account

Your *personal* account—the way you carry yourself and the way you treat other people—is much more important than your *bank* account. Your words and your actions are more significant than any deposit that can be made or any amount that can be written on a check.

Your *Qualities* Are More Important Than Your *Quantities*

The qualities you possess as a person are far more important than the quantities of material things that you possess. What you stand for, what you believe in, the manner in which you carry yourself, and the manner in which you live your life are of far greater value than what you have and what you can buy.

~

The *quantities* a person possesses are nowhere near as important as the *qualities* a person possesses.

~

Be more concerned with the qualities of your life rather than with the quantities of it. Be more concerned with *who you are* and with *the way you are living your life* rather than with the number of material possessions that you can buy, or with the value of the price tags on the things you can afford.

~

Always remember what really counts. Always remember what really matters.

"Not everything that counts can be counted, and not everything that can be counted counts."
~ Albert Einstein

It's Not *What You Have*, But *Who You Are*... That Really Matters

Life is not about what you have; it's about who you are. What matters in this world is not what you have, what you can buy, what you can get, and what you can do for yourself. What matters in this world is *who you are, what you believe in and what you stand for, what you can do for others*, and *what you can do for the world you live in*.

It's not about what you have; it's about who you are...

It's not about what you have,
    But about *who you are*.
It's not about what you obtain in terms of possessions,
    But about what you maintain in terms of *principles*.
It's not about what you possess in terms of goods,
    But about what you possess in terms of *qualities*.
It's not about what you choose to invest in,
    But about what you choose to *believe in*.
It's not about what you are able to pay for,
    But about what you are willing to *stand for*.
It's not about what you can do for yourself,
    But about what you can *do for others*.
It's not about what you can get for yourself,
    But about what you can *give of yourself to others*.
It is not about the success you can attain in your own life,
    but about the *significance you create in the lives of others*.
It's not about what name you can make for yourself,
    But about what *difference you can make for others*.
It's not about what kind of reputation you can create for yourself,
    But about what kind of *character you can build for yourself*.
It's not about what type of fame you can acquire for yourself in the present,
    But about what type of *legacy you can leave for yourself in the future*.
It's not about where you're from or where you've been,
    But about *where you are going* and *who you are becoming*.
It's not about what may or may not be, or what others think or say you are,
    But about who you *really* are, and who *you* think and say you are.
It's not about the amount of wealth you can acquire around yourself,
    But about the amount of *worth* you learn to recognize *within* yourself.

~ It is not what you have, but **who you are**, that *really* matters.

What Really Matters In Life: What It's Really All About

It's not about what you look like, or how popular you are; it's not about how much money you make or how much you can afford to buy with that money; it's not about the value of your possessions, or about how much you value those possessions.
It's about your own value as a person. It's about how much you value yourself. It's about how much you accept yourself. It's about how much you respect yourself.
Deep down, it's not about the amount of your material worth.
It's about the value of your self-worth.

~

It's not about your reputation, but about your character.
It's not about what other people think or say you are, but about who you really are.
It's not about what other people think or say about you. It's about what you think of yourself, and what you know to be true about yourself.

~

It's not about trying to be like someone else, but about doing your best to be yourself.
It's not about being better than anyone else, but about trying to be the best *you* that you can be. It's not about trying to please everyone and be like everyone else.
It's about being true to yourself. It's about being the best *you* that you can be.

~

It's not about how many people you can get to like you, but about how much you can learn to like yourself and the person you are becoming. It's not about how many women you can get to love you or be with you. It's about how much you can learn to love yourself, and more importantly, to Respect Yourself.

~

Respect Yourself for Who You Are; Respect Yourself for Who You Can Become

"Self-respect is the cornerstone of all virtue." ~ *John Herschel*

~

Self-respect is the one virtue that gives a man a reason and a desire to develop all other virtues. It is this developmental process by which a man not only becomes the best that he is capable of becoming, but the most honorable that he is capable of becoming as well.

~

True self-respect exists when a man respects who he is, and more importantly, who he can become. A man possesses true self-respect when he realizes that he owes it to the world to develop himself to his full potential and to have the maximum impact which he is capable of having. A man also comes to have true self-respect when he understands that he owes it, first and foremost, to himself… to see how great he can become, how much he can accomplish in his lifetime, how much he can do and contribute in this world, and how wonderful a masterpiece he can make of his life.

~

To have true self-respect is to value yourself and your potential as a human being.

Value Your Dignity, and Protect It At All Costs

No One Can Take Away Your Dignity: It Belongs To You, and You Alone

There are certain characteristics that we all possess—undeniable traits that each of us is born with and that no one can ever take away from us. One of these traits is **DIGNITY**. Your dignity is your self-respect and your sense of self-worth. It is the knowledge that you are positively unique, that you have your own special talents and abilities, and that everyone in this world is worthy of respect, including you.

Dignity revolves around the realization that all people deserve to be treated with humanity and fairness—that no one is any better or any worse than anyone else. Dignity is the proud but humble understanding that *you, yourself,* are no better than anyone else, nor are you any worse than anyone else either.

No one, and no set of circumstances, can strip you of your self-respect: it belongs to you, and you alone. You came into this world with your dignity. You should do everything you can to leave this world with it as well.

~

"One's dignity may be assaulted, vandalized and cruelly mocked,
but cannot be taken away unless it is surrendered."

~ Michael J. Fox

~ No one can take away your dignity: it belongs to you, and you alone. ~

Your Self-Worth Never Changes, Just Your "Sense" of Self-Worth

Your true self-worth never changes. It cannot be diminished, and it cannot be increased because it is already as great as it could be. Your self-worth is fixed and abundant. It's your *perception* of your self-worth, that sometimes changes. Your "sense" of self-worth can change. However, you must always remember that your *actual* self-worth will never change. Your actual self-worth remains the same, no matter what happens. Your "sense" of self-worth, however, is what changes. Your true self-worth is what you are born with: it's who you are and what you are. Your *"sense"* of self-worth is how *you think about* your value as a person—it's how you see yourself and how you perceive your own worth.

Our true self-worth—our real self-worth—is constant. It never changes.
Our actual self-worth as a human being is always the same. It's inherent, and
nothing that happens to us, through us, or in us, can ever change it.

When you find yourself thinking negatively about yourself or talking down to yourself, when you find yourself feeling down or discouraged, always remember that your self-worth is as great as anyone else's. Understand that you may be thinking or feeling differently—your sense of self-worth may be suffering or low—but your true worth is still as high and as great as the greatest of people. Just because your perception of your personal value may be low, does not change the fact that you are as valuable a human being as has ever lived.

Priceless Worth: What the Value of a $20-Bill Can Teach Us About Our Own Value

(A story from an unknown, but very wise author)

A well-known speaker began one of his seminars by holding up a $20.00 bill. In a room of close to 200 people, the speaker asked, "Who would like this $20 bill?" As you could imagine, about 200 hands went up. The speaker continued by saying... "I am going to give this $20 to one of you but first, let me do this."

He then proceeded to crumple up the $20 dollar bill. The man then asked, "Who still wants it?" Still, 200 hands went back up in the air.

"Well," the speaker replied, "What if I do this?" And he dropped it on the ground and started to grind it into the floor with his shoe. He then picked it up—now crumpled and dirty—and asked... "Now, who still wants it?" Still, the hands went up.

The speaker then began to deliver the moral of his story. "My friends, we have all learned a very valuable lesson. No matter what I did to the money, you still wanted it because it did not decrease in value. It was still worth $20."

~

Many times in our lives, we are dropped, crumpled, and ground into the dirt by the decisions we make and the circumstances that come our way. We feel as though we are worthless. But no matter what happens, no matter what already has happened, and no matter what will happen in the future... none of us will ever lose our value as a person.

A $20-bill might get walked on, it might get stepped on. That bill might feel putdown and neglected. It might feel hurt and upset. It might go through tough times and feel down and discouraged, and even worthless. But, no matter what happens to it, deep down on the inside, that $20-bill still possesses the same worth that it began its life with. No matter what it looks like, no matter what has happened to it, and no matter what other people think of it, that $20-bill still has the same value that it always had. It's still worth $20.

Dirty or clean, crumpled or neatly-folded, stepped on or straightened: *you* are still a priceless human being. After all, your worth as a person comes not from what you have, what you do, what you look like, or who you know. Your worth comes from who you are.

Your Self-Worth... It's Not Like The Dow Jones: It Doesn't Go Up and Down

Your self-worth is not like the stock market: it does not rise and fall with the economy. It doesn't go up and down each day; it doesn't go back-and-forth between good and bad. Your self-worth does not bounce up and down based on external forces, it does not rise and fall with your bank account, it does not change with your income statement, it does not fluctuate based on your mortgage rate, and it does not change with the interest rate or with your retirement plan. *Your self-worth is constant: it is always as high as it can be.* **And that will never change.**

~ We Are All Part of the Same Team ~

We are all part of the same team, and therefore, we are all teammates.
We are all part of the same family, and therefore, we are all related in some way.
We are all linked together, whether we like it or not, as members of the human family.
That is the nature of life. That is the essence of humanity.

In the world of sports, each team has rules, and chiefly among those rules is to treat all members of that team with respect: coaches, players, managers, trainers, starters, back-ups, benchwarmers, and mascots... *all* members.

In the world in which we live, there are rules that each of us must follow and abide by. Chiefly among those rules, as is the case with sports, is to respect all members of the network of people who call this Earth home, just as we do: men, women, young people and old people... *all* members.

Whether you agree with the rules or not, is irrelevant. You are here, you are a member of this team, and therefore, you must abide by the team's rules. None of us gets to make the rules; we simply get drafted onto this great big *team* of ours and then try to play it as well as we can. It is our job to do our best to abide by the rules of life. It is our task to do our absolute best to live our own lives the best way that we possibly can, and to help everyone around us live their lives as well as they can at the same time.

~ Respect all people.

The success of a *team* is built on a foundation of respect.
The success of a *family* is built on a foundation of respect.
The success of a *society* is built on a foundation of respect.
The success of our *world* is built on a foundation of respect.

~ Now it is up to us to do the building.

Build A Better World

Choose to Help Build a Better World

When you choose to show respect to all people, you in fact are choosing to help make this world a better place. With every good word you speak, with every good choice you make, and with every good action you take, you are making this world a better and brighter place to live.

Choose A Lifestyle Of Respect

Rather than being judgmental, choose to be tolerant.
Rather than being critical, choose to be accepting.
Rather than being disagreeable, choose to be understanding.
Rather than being angry, choose to be patient.
Rather than being bitter, choose to be forgiving.
Rather than being disparaging, choose to be encouraging.
Rather than being conceited, choose to be humble.
Rather than being offensive, choose to be courteous.
Rather than being rude, choose to be polite.
Rather than being harsh, choose to be kind.

~

**Choose a lifestyle of respect. Choose to be respectful to all people.
Choose to be respectful at all times. Choose to be respectful in all ways.**

R. E. S. P. E. C. T.

R ~ Recognize and appreciate the divine dignity that every human being possesses.

E ~ Embrace the wonderful differences and diversity among all people, and also make the effort to understand the many similarities we all share.

S ~ Smile and say hello to people in passing, reach out to others, and lend a helping hand whenever you can.

P ~ Practice patience, understanding, and forgiveness toward others…even when you don't feel like it… *especially* when you don't feel like it.

E ~ Educate yourself about other people's cultures, ethnicities, religions, and backgrounds.

C ~ Care for and about others by showing genuine concern and consideration at all times.

T ~ Treat people the way that you, yourself, would always want to be treated; and treat everyone you meet as if they were the most important person in the world at that time.

~

**Make respect an attitude.
Make being respectful a way of life.**

Some Questions To Consider

Is a school better when its students and teachers show mutual respect to each other?
Is a team better when its players and coaches all show mutual respect for one another?
Is a neighborhood better when its members show mutual respect to each other?
Is a society better when its people show mutual respect for one another?

~ If "Yes" is the answer to each of these questions, then shouldn't we all do more
  to show respect to one another and to treat each other with respect?

~

Let us always strive to treat one another with respect. By being tolerant, civil, and respectful to all people at all times, we make the world a better and more pleasant place. By treating others the way that we, ourselves, would want to be treated, we will make this wonderful world of ours a much more peaceful and enjoyable place in which to live.

"Show proper respect to everyone"

~ *1 Peter 2:17 (from the Christian Faith Tradition)*

The Respect Rules ~ A Simple Set of Instructions

+ Treat all people with respect.
+ Be positive and encouraging toward others. Lift people up; don't put people down.
+ Work to resolve conflicts while being respectful.
+ Treat everyone as if they were a member of your own family.
+ Treat all people, at all times, the way that you would always want to be treated.

~

"All that we call ethics simply spring from
the one great principle of *non-injury and doing good.*
Don't injure any, do good to all that you can …
and that is all the morality and ethics there is."
~ *An idea taken from the Jainis Faith Tradition*

~

We must make respect more than just a nice word—more than merely a noble ideal.
We must make respect a way of life.

~ Develop An Attitude of Respect ~

+ Develop an attitude of respect, and make respect a way of life.
+ Cultivate as much respect, in you and around you, as you possibly can.
+ Show the utmost respect for yourself and for others; extend the highest amount of respect to yourself and toward others.

~ <u>Go Beyond Tolerance</u> ~

We should not only tolerate each other,
but we should seek to learn about and appreciate one another as well.
We should not merely try to coexist,
but we should understand and respect one another as well.
We should not be satisfied with simply putting up with each other,
but we should seek to enjoy and value one another's company in this world.

~

"If it is possible, as far as it depends on you, live at peace with everyone."
~ Paul the Apostle: Romans 12:18
(from the Christian Faith Tradition)

~ <u>Respect Has No Borders, and Kindness Has No Boundaries</u> ~

You make your own life better when you do things to make other people's lives better.
And the most basic way to do that is to start by treating everyone you meet with respect…
regardless of who they are, regardless of where they are from,
and regardless of where they are going.

~

"My country is the world, and my religion is to do good."
~ Thomas Paine

~ <u>Go Beyond Respect</u> ~

We should begin with tolerance, but then we should go beyond it to respect.
We should continue with respect, but we should not stop there.
We should go beyond respect and strive for kindness.
We should go beyond respect and aim for compassion.

~

Be Tolerant. Be Respectful. Be Kind.
Be Compassionate.

~

"My religion is very simple. My religion is kindness."
~ The Dalai Lama

We Have an Important Obligation to
Help Raise Other People's Quality of Life

The world will bring a lot of circumstances into our lives—some good, some bad, and some indifferent. The world certainly will bring each of us our share of heartache and pain to deal with as well. The one thing that we *don't* need in our lives, is for other people to go out of their way to make things even harder on us than they already are. Along those same lines, the one thing that *other* people don't need in their lives, is for us to be making things any harder on them either.

Life is hard enough for all of us to begin with; we don't need to go out of our way to make it any harder on each other. **What we need to do is go out of our way to make it *easier* and *more pleasant* for one another.**

In this life of ours, we have to take advantage of every opportunity we have to do positive things for one another. People don't need us to add any hardship to their lives; instead, they need us to add a little joy and happiness to them. They need us to help balance out all the negative situations in their life; and they need us to help add to the number of positive experiences, in order to outweigh all the difficult moments they already have to deal with.

We all have our struggles, and some of us have more than others. The daily obstacles we all face will give us each enough reasons to be upset, discouraged, saddened, and disappointed. We don't exactly need to go adding any more of those types of reasons to each other's lives. Instead, we have to do all that we can to give people a reason to *smile*, a reason to be *happy*, and a reason to *feel good about themselves*. **We have an obligation to help raise other people's quality of life.**

Ultimately, it is our responsibility to create as much joy and happiness for others as we possibly can. Any opportunity that we get to do something good for someone—whether it's a big thing, or just a little thing—we have to take advantage of, and we have to go out of our way to do it. After all… no one's life is so perfect that they couldn't use a little bit of kindness or encouragement from someone else.

We all have our struggles, and some of us have more than others. The daily obstacles we all face will give us each enough reasons to be upset, discouraged, saddened, and disappointed. We don't exactly need to go adding any more of those types of reasons to each other's lives. Instead, we have to do all that we can to give people a reason to *smile*, a reason to be *happy*, and a reason to *feel good about themselves*.

Ultimately, it is our responsibility to create as much joy and happiness for others as we possibly can. Any opportunity that we get to do something good for someone—whether it is a big thing or just a little thing—we have to take advantage of, and we have to go out of our way to do it.

Life is hard enough for all of us to begin with; we don't need to go out of our way to make it any harder on each other. **What we need to do is go out of our way to make it *easier* and *more pleasant* for one another.** No one's life is so perfect that they couldn't use a little bit of extra kindness and encouragement from someone else.

~

*"The greatest responsibility each of us has
is to raise the life condition of everyone we touch."*

~ Lou Holtz

Choose to Make the World a Better Place

Everything you choose to do—from the words you say and the things you do, to the things that you tolerate others to say and do in your presence—either make our world a better or worse place in which to live. Every good word that you speak, every good decision that you make, and every good action that you take, ultimately makes our world a better place. Conversely, every mean or disrespectful word you utter, every selfish choice you make, and every bad action you take, ultimately makes our world a worse place in which to live.

~

Choose to make the world a better place.

~

You can improve the world you live in,
by improving the way you treat the people you live in the world with.

~

With every decision you make, you have the power to improve the world in which we live. At any given moment, in anything you do, and in everything that you do, you are choosing to make this world either a better or worse place in which to live. Choose to speak good words, choose to make good decisions, and choose to perform good deeds. Choose to do all the good that you can do. Choose to make the world a better place.

~

You can improve the quality of the world by improving the quality
of the choices you make and the actions you take.

~

We all live in a world we help create.

Elevate Yourself and Elevate Your World

We all are capable of making the world a better place, because we all are capable of becoming better people. By working to elevate ourselves, we can elevate the lives of those around us, and we can lift up the world in which we live.

~

Choose to Live a Better Way.

Choose to Create a Better World.

~

"We must build a new world, a far better world—
one in which the eternal dignity of man is respected."

~ Harry S. Truman

We Don't Have to Wait Until We Get to Heaven to Love One Another

I think we all imagine Heaven as this great place where everyone loves each other, and where everyone treats each other with kindness and compassion. We think of it as a place where all people—regardless of race, ethnicity, and social background—live together in perfect harmony... *one day.*

The truth is, though, that we don't have to wait for some perfect afterlife to treat each other with love and compassion. We can get started on that right here and now. The world is not perfect, and none of us in it is. But we have to do our best to make it as positive a place as we can. Life is not about enduring until we finally get to Heaven; it's about doing the best we can to make this world as good a place as we can…because, for the time being, we all have to live here with one another. The only thing preventing us from living in harmony with one another *in this world*, is our own bias.

~

> **Choose to live with an attitude of respect.**
> **Choose to live with an attitude of kindness.**
> **Choose to live with an attitude of love.**

~

"We don't have to wait until we get to Heaven to love one another."
~ *Author Unknown*

Let's Work to Create Heaven Right Here On Earth

Patience should be a virtue that we all seek to cultivate. However, if we were going to be impatient about anything, it should be about experiencing our version of Heaven.
We should be too impatient about wanting to get to paradise that we do our best to try to create Heaven right here—on Earth—in the meantime.

~

> **Don't merely try to live in a way that will get you into Heaven.**
> **Your approach should be to live in such a way that you**
> **will be creating Heaven right here on earth.**

~

"Be such a man, and live such a life, that if every man were such as you,
and every life a life like yours, this earth would be God's Paradise."
~ *Phillips Brooks*

E

Especially
Women

Respect All People, Especially Women

Treat Women with Respect

Being a REAL man is all about treating women with respect— plain and simple.
Always be respectful and always be a gentleman. You can tell just about everything you
need to know about a man by the way he treats a woman.

~

Respect and Treat Women As Equals

"To call woman the weaker sex is a libel; it is man's injustice to woman.
If by strength is meant brute strength, then, indeed, is woman less brute than man.
If by strength is meant moral power, then woman is immeasurably man's superior.
Has she not greater intuition, is she not more self-sacrificing, has she not greater powers
of endurance, has she not greater courage?
Without her, man could not be."

~ Mahatma Gandhi

~

Love and Respect a Woman

"Love and respect a woman. Look to her not only for comfort,
But for strength and inspiration and the doubling of your intellectual and moral powers.
Blot out from your mind any idea of superiority; you have none."

~ Giuseppe Mazzini

All People – Men and Women Alike – Are Equal Members
Of the Same Team... The Human Team

Contrary to what society may tell us, and despite what our culture may suggest... women are not merely objects that exist for the pleasure and personal gain of men.

Contrary to the messages our society gives us, and despite the images our culture presents us with... women are not inferior to men, and they are not subservient to them.

Women are equal to men.

All women are members of the same team—the human team—that all men are a part of. All women are equally a part of the same family—the human family—that all men belong to. And therefore, all women deserve to be treated with equal respect.

All women possess the same amount of basic human dignity that men do. And therefore, all women deserve to be treated with the same amount of respect and esteem that men are treated with. As a matter of fact, not only do women deserve equal regard and respect... they are entitled to it, as *all* human beings are.

~

We are all part of the same team, regardless of race, ethnicity, financial rank, personal status, social class, religious beliefs, *and gender*. This is not a bad thing. Rather, it is a good thing. Actually, it is a *great* thing. After all, the human team is the greatest team known to man, and to be a part of it is not a burden, but a privilege. To be associated with your fellow man and your fellow woman is not an insult, but a compliment of the highest regard.

Like any sports organization, you should consider it a privilege to be a part of your current team. More importantly, you should be proud to be a part of that team, and you should show that pride through your respectful treatment of both yourself and others—*all others*. You should be proud of your team, and you should be proud of your teammates. You should value your team, and you should value your teammates. Finally, you should respect your team, and you should respect your teammates.

We all wear the same uniform, and we all play for the same team. We may each have different numbers and play different positions, but all of us—each and every one of us—belong to one team... the human team. We share the great huddle of humanity, we call the same great field of this world our home, and we find common ground in our common bond—our unmistakable and undeniable link as members of the human chain of life. We are all related, whether we like it or not, as members of the human family. We are all equal, whether we like it or not, and therefore, we are all equally deserving of respect. Regardless of race, religion, background, status, and gender. Especially gender.

~

In the world of sports, each team has rules, and chiefly among those rules usually is to treat all members of that team with respect: coaches, players, managers, trainers, starters, back-ups, benchwarmers, and mascots... *all* members.

In the world in which we live, there are rules that each of us must follow and abide by. Chiefly among those rules, as is the case with sports, is to respect all members of the network of people who call this Earth home, just as we do: men, women, young people and old people... *all* members... and *all* genders.

~ Respect all people, *especially women.*
That is the first rule of being a part of this team.

~ **A Real Man** ~

A Real Man treats women with respect.
A Real Man always acts like a gentleman.
A Real Man is always polite, courteous, and considerate of women.
A Real Man opens doors, holds umbrellas, and pays honest
Compliments when they are due.

A Real Man always carries himself with class.
A Real Man always speaks respectfully to women.
A Real Man always speaks respectfully *about* women.
A Real Man is never rude or offensive to women. He never uses
Derogatory language, nor does he tolerate others to do so either.

A Real Man listens to women.
A Real Man especially listens to his mother.
A Real Man takes care of his mother and all the women in his life.
A Real Man protects his sister, watches out for his girlfriend,
And takes care of his women friends.

A Real Man respects the strength, courage, and intellect of women.
A Real Man treats women as equals, not as subservient inferiors.
A Real Man treats women as human beings,
Not objects for his own personal gain or pleasure.

A Real Man always does right by the women in his life: whether
They are his family, friends, girlfriend, or wife.
A Real Man always does right by his family.
He is there to be a father to his children,
He sets a good example for the next generation,
And he invests himself fully in his personal relationships.

A Real Man always makes time for what is important,
And he always makes time for *who* is important.
A Real Man helps make the world a more respectful place
By his words and his deeds.
A Real Man helps make the world a safer place for women.
A Real Man makes the world a better place for all people.

A Real Man makes the world a better, safer, more honest,
And more respectful place in which to live.

~

A Real Man respects all women at all times.

~

"The way you treat women will impact every other area of your life at some point."
~ *Tony Dungy*

~ Show Respect Through Your Words ~

Speak Respectfully *To* Women; Speak Respectfully *About* Women.
Speak respectfully to women. Speak respectfully about women. Avoid making disparaging comments about women, and do not say inappropriate things to women. Don't use derogatory words like "hoe," "slut," "bitch," "whore," or worse when talking to or about women. Do not use disrespectful terms when referring to women, and do not use demeaning names when talking to or about women.

Words perpetuate attitudes and facilitate actions. If you speak disrespectfully about women, it reinforces disrespectful attitudes toward them, and it leads to disrespectful treatment of them.

Understand that every girl and woman is someone's daughter, someone's sister, someone's girlfriend, or someone's best friend. How would you like it if someone called your sister a "hoe" or a "whore?" How would you like it if someone called your mother a "slut" or a "bitch?" How would you like it if someone called your girlfriend, or your best friend, something like that?

Chances are, you probably wouldn't like it, would you?

~

If you wouldn't want any of those things said to—or about—your sister, your mother, your girlfriend, or your best friend… then don't say any of those things to or about someone else's. Don't call someone else's sister, mother, girlfriend, or best friend any derogatory names; and don't say anything disrespectful about women. It isn't respectful; it isn't classy, and it isn't what a REAL man does.

~

Remember:
We all came from a mother,
and we probably all will have a daughter.
Keep that in mind.

~

Think Before You Speak, and Be Careful What You Say:
Take the Test Before You Open Your Mouth
Before you say something derogatory about a girl, ask yourself this:

*"Would I want someone to say it about **my sister** or **my best friend**?"*
*"Would I want someone to say it about **my mother** or about **my grandmother**?"*
*"Would I want someone to say it about **my girlfriend** or **my wife**?"*

If the answer is "no," then don't say it. Period.

~ **Show Respect Through Your Deeds** ~

Please read the following section, entitled "The Ground Rules,"
to learn more about how to show respect for women through your actions.

~

~

Be respectful in every word and deed.
Speak respectfully about women, and act respectfully toward women.
Show respect to all women, at all times, and in all ways.

~

~

"A gentleman never makes himself the center of attention.
His goal is to make life easier, not just for himself but for
his friends, his acquaintances, and the world at large.
Because he is a gentleman, he does not see this as a burden.
Instead, it is a challenge he faces eagerly every day."

~ John Bridges

The Ground Rules
The Basic Guidelines & Minimum Expectations of a REAL Man

Simple Advice for Treating Women with Respect

The following is a list of basic guidelines and expectations for how a REAL man should act toward women. It is a set of the basic minimum requirements for treating women with respect. The following actions are what you are ***expected to do***, without being asked to do so, and without earning any "extra points" for doing them:

+ Be on-time for a date. Be on-time for a date; in fact, be a few minutes early. Show a woman that you respect her time by not wasting it. Be on-time, every time, all the time.

+ Call if you are going to be late. If you are ever going to be late for a date, or even just a meeting with a friend, call ahead of time and let the young lady know you will be late. That is just common courtesy. Do your best to be on-time or early, but if you can't be, then at least have the class and manners to call and let her know that you are running late. And make sure that you call to let her know *before* you are actually late, not after you already are.

+ Go to the door. If you have to go to a girl's house or apartment to pick her up for a date, don't ever pull up and honk the horn and expect the girl to come out. Don't sit in your car and call the girl and tell her to come out either. Shut the car off, walk up to the door, and knock or ring the doorbell. Be a gentleman and go to the front door, especially if her parents are going to be home.

+ Call if you say you are going to call. If you tell a young woman that you are going to call her, then call her. If you don't intend to call her, then don't tell her that you will.

If you say you are going to call a girl, then call. Otherwise, don't say it. That is basic courtesy. More than that, however, it is a matter of keeping your word as a man. Whatever it is: if you say you are going to do something, then follow through and do it. That is what a stand-up guy does. That is part of what being responsible is all about. A REAL man keeps his word; it is that simple. If you say you are going to call, then call. It is simply the respectful thing to do.

+ Call *when* you say you are going to call. If you say you are going to call a girl, then call her. If you tell a girl that you are going to call her at a certain time or on a certain day, then call her at that time. That is simply a matter of being reliable and dependable. Beyond that, it is about keeping your word as a man.

If, for some reason, you can't call (for example, if it is too late): text her and tell her that you will call her the next day or sometime soon. Apologize for not being able to call, and let her know that you will do so when you are able to.

+ Open doors. Open doors… all doors: car doors, house doors, restaurant doors, etc. Open doors: all of them, all of the time. Hold all doors open, and allow a woman to pass through the doorway first. Whether you are entering a restaurant, a coffee shop, a classroom, a store, or anywhere else: always open the door for a woman, and always allow her to pass through the entrance first.

+ Pay for dinner. Always pay for your date's meal… always. Pay for all meals, all the time. Pick up the check. Whether it is dinner, lunch, breakfast, brunch, coffee, tea, a bagel, or even a vending machine… always pay the bill. Whether it's a fancy restaurant, a fast-food joint, or just a coffee shop, does not matter: a REAL man never, ever lets a woman pay for a meal or a drink.

+ Pay for dinner… and don't expect anything in return. Always pay for your date's meal… and never expect anything in return. A woman does not owe you a single thing for picking up the check. Paying for dinner does not entitle you to anything. Buying a drink or a meal does not give you the right to anything in return from a woman. Pick up the check, and don't you dare expect any type of favor or service in return. Ever.

A REAL man pays for dinner or a drink because he is a gentleman, and because it is the respectable and classy thing to do… not because he wants something in return. A REAL man never, ever expects anything in return—of any kind—for picking up the tab. Pay for all meals, at all times, and expect nothing for it. The only thing you are ever entitled to… is the food you are purchasing. That's it. Period.

+ Pay attention to a woman when she speaks. If a woman tells you something, it is because she thinks it is important. And if she thinks it is important, then she will expect you to think it is important as well. Show her that you value what she is saying and that it is important, by giving her your full and undivided attention. If you expect anyone to pay attention to and listen to *you*, then you have to pay attention and listen to them first.

+ Listen to a woman when she talks. Show respect and consideration to a woman by paying attention to her when she is speaking. When a woman speaks, make and maintain eye contact with her. When you are out to dinner, take the seat facing the wall—and not the window, the television, or the rest of the room—so that you can focus on the woman you are with and what she is saying. By doing this, you will remove any distractions to the conversation. By listening to a woman, you show her that you value her time and words. By showing a woman that you value her time and words, you show her that you respect and value her as a person as well.

+ Make and maintain eye contact. Make eye contact… ***with her EYES***.
Don't check-out a woman while she is talking to you. It is extremely disrespectful and rude. A woman is a human being, not an object. Show respect to her by showing her that you respect her as a person.

Make and maintain eye contact… with her eyes. Do not treat a woman like she is a piece of meat by checking her out while she is speaking. Keep your eyes at eye-level. A woman is a human being, and she deserves to be treated—and respected—as such.

+ Keep your eyes on the woman you are with. When you are out in public with a woman—whether in a restaurant, walking through town, or at a game or performance—don't check out other women that you pass by or that are at another table. That is extremely disrespectful: both to the woman you are with, and to the woman you are checking out. Keep your eyes on the woman you are with; and keep your thoughts and your attention on her too.

+ **Remember what a woman tells you.** If a woman tells you something—anything—it is because she wants you to remember it. If a woman tells you something, it is because she thinks it is important. And if *she* thinks it is important, then she will expect *you* to think it is important as well. More importantly, she will expect you to act like it is important by remembering it.

+ **Know a woman's favorite *anything*.** Know a woman's favorite type of anything: her favorite restaurant, her favorite meal, her favorite type of coffee, her favorite kind of flowers, her favorite type of animal, her favorite type of stuffed animal, her favorite movie, her favorite book, her favorite color, her favorite *anything and everything*. Remember any and every "favorite." Write it down if you have to, but always remember those things.

+ **Allow a woman to pick the movie.** Let her pick the movie once in a while—if not more often than you—and do not complain about the movie that she chooses. If you don't like it, then keep it to yourself and at least try to learn something valuable from something in the movie.

+ **Allow a woman to pick the music.** When you are in the car, ask her what kind of music or what radio station she would like to listen to. Put that station on or that CD in.

+ **Share the remote control.** Watch her favorite TV shows. And don't complain about having to watch them or about how bad you think they are. Suck it up. It won't hurt you to watch her favorite show. Take advantage of an opportunity to spend quality time with her; and feel good about the fact that you are helping to make her happy. When she is happy, you should be happy too. It should make *you* feel good to make *others* feel good.

+ **Appreciate a woman's presence.** Show appreciation for a woman's presence, and let her know that you value her company. Thank her for watching a sports game with you, or for hanging out with the guys, or for making dinner or planning an evening together. Never take her presence for granted. A woman chooses to either spend time with you or not. Make her want to spend her time with you. Don't make her feel like she is wasting her time.

+ **Appreciate a woman's contributions.** Show appreciation when appreciation is due. Pay compliments when compliments are due; show her you appreciate her for who she is and for what she does. Say kind and thoughtful things, tell her you love her (if you actually do love her), tell her you enjoy spending time with her, compliment her on all the things you like about her, and show appreciation for all the positive things that she says and does.

Make her feel good about herself. Tell her what you like about her, tell her what you appreciate about her, tell her what you love about her… and tell her often. You do not have to get overly-sappy and romantic: simply let a woman know that you value and appreciate her, and make sure that she knows it.

+ Remember important dates and events. Remember birthdays, anniversaries, and holidays. If a woman remembers them, it means that she expects you to remember them as well. Remember and celebrate important dates. You do not need to make a big production or spend a lot of money, but you should sincerely acknowledge the occasion and do something thoughtful to commemorate it. You do not need to do anything grand or big: you can do something kind and simple. Just make sure that you do *something*.

Also, you do not need to wait for special occasions to say or to do something special. You can perform thoughtful acts and show appreciation to the woman in your life at any time, on any occasion. If you value having that woman in your life, then let her know it. If you appreciate having that woman in your life, then make sure you show it. Don't ever make her have to wonder.

+ Pay honest compliments. Be on the lookout for every opportunity to pay a genuine compliment. If a young lady looks nice, tell her. If she smells nice, let her know. If she has something insightful to say, praise her for her intellect. If she does something that you appreciate, thank her and tell her that you appreciate it.

Compliment the woman you are with on her smile, her eyes, her outfit, her shoes, her hairstyle. Compliment her on an intelligent or insightful comment. Compliment her on the way she says or does something. Make her feel good about herself.

+ Be careful what you say, and be careful how you say it. Be polite and considerate at all times. Never make fun of a woman, even if it is in sarcasm or in jest. Don't hurt her feelings, and do not, under any circumstances, insult her.

A woman may forgive you, but she will not forget the way you made her feel. Never give a woman a reason to remember anything bad about the way you treat her. A woman will not forget what you say or do; she may, however, forget you.

+ Be positive and be thoughtful. Point out positive things whenever you have to make a criticism of any kind. Praise a woman's positive features and attributes before drawing attention to something that is not as appealing.

Never joke about a woman's physical appearance. Never make fun of how a woman looks or is dressed. If a woman asks you a question that is tough to answer (such as: if an outfit looks good on her when it does not, or if she has gained weight when she has): try to be as polite and delicate as possible with your words. Choose your words carefully, and make sure to always point out something positive before providing any form of criticism. Always try to soften any critical remarks as much as you possibly can. Your words should serve to help, not to hurt.

+ Be positive and be encouraging. Never make fun of a woman's dreams, and never belittle a woman's aspirations. For some people, their dreams and aspirations are their only hope. Use your words to affirm and build up others, not to tear them down.

+ Be polite and respectful to a woman's family. Be polite to a woman's family, especially her parents and immediate relatives. Speak respectfully to, and about them. Never make fun of a woman's parents and family. They are the people she loves most in the world. Show respect to her by showing respect to the ones she loves.

+ Be polite and respectful to a woman's friends. Be polite to a woman's friends, especially her best friend and close friends. Speak respectfully to, and about them. Never make fun of a woman's friends. They are some of the people she cares about most in the world. Show respect to a woman by showing respect to her friends.

+ Offer your jacket or sweatshirt to a woman when she is cold. Offer your jacket or sweatshirt to her if it is cold outside—or if she looks like she is cold—if she does not have a jacket of her own. Offer your jacket or sweatshirt to a woman if she already has one but still appears to be cold.

+ Offer your raincoat to a woman when it is raining. Offer your raincoat to her if it is raining outside if she does not have a coat of her own.

+ Share your umbrella with a woman when it is raining. Share your umbrella if it is raining outside. If your umbrella is not big enough for two people to fit underneath, then give your umbrella to her.

+ Offer to carry a woman's bags. Offer to carry a woman's grocery bags, shopping bags, and other heavy objects. Offer to carry your girlfriend's books or backpack through school or to class. Offer to carry her duffel bag when traveling. Offer to carry or roll her suitcase when flying somewhere. Do not let a woman have to struggle carrying something heavy. Be a gentleman and offer to carry her bags.

+ Offer your seat to a woman. If you are on a bus or a plane, if you are in a classroom or in a meeting room, or if you are anywhere else where there are seats: if there is a woman who needs a seat, offer her yours if there are no others available. Stand up and be a real man… by standing up, literally.

+ Go get the car and pull around to the front. If it is raining or snowing, if it is extremely cold outside, or if you are parked very far away from the entrance: go to your car and pull around to the front door. Pick up the woman you are with at the entrance. Do not make her walk out to the car in the rain, snow, or cold. Do not make her walk a long distance to the car either, especially if she is dressed nicely or is wearing high heels.

+ Pump the gas for a woman. Never let a woman pump her own gas. Don't make her stand outside, especially in the cold or rain, and have to pump her own gas. Don't make her stand outside and have to smell the fumes or possibly get dirty from pumping gas either. Get out of the car yourself and pump the gas… even if it is not your car, and even if you are not the one driving. Whether it is your girlfriend, your wife, your friend, your mother, or your sister…does not matter. Do not let the woman you are with have to pump her own gas. Be a gentleman, get out of the car, and pump the gas for her.

+ Stand up when a woman leaves the dinner table. When you are out to dinner and she gets up from the table, stand up as well. Stand when your date leaves the table; stand once again when she returns to the table. At a formal dinner or event, stand when a lady leaves the table; stand once again when she returns to the table. This is a very classy gesture: it is old-fashioned and extremely respectable. Once again: stand up and be a real man… by standing up, literally.

+ Be a gentleman, and be a *gentle man*. Be a gentleman in *all* ways. Always be respectful of a woman's physical rights. Always allow a woman to choose whether or not a situation proceeds. Always allow a woman to choose how a situation advances, if she decides that she would like it to advance. Never force a woman to do anything she does not want to do. Never try to coerce or convince a woman to do anything she does not feel comfortable doing.

+ Never attempt to intimidate a woman. Never threaten to harm a woman. Never attempt to psychologically or emotionally hurt a woman. Never try to physically impose yourself upon a woman. Always be respectful to a woman, and always be respectful of a woman's body and personal space.

+ Be tender and delicate, never forceful. When it comes to being physical or intimate, do not be forceful. Be tender, be respectful, and be considerate. Always take "no" for an answer, and never force a situation.

+ Never raise your voice in anger at a woman. Always be polite and considerate: not only in what you say, but in how you say it. If you are in an argument, remain calm and be patient. Never raise your voice in anger, and never try to "win" the argument by insulting a woman or by hurting her feelings. Always remember that words, once spoken, can never be taken back. Remain calm and be considerate.

+ Never harm a woman in any way. Never physically hurt a woman. Never put your hands on a woman in an aggressive or unwelcome way, even if you think you are just playing around. Never, ever, under any circumstances, hit a woman. No exceptions. No excuses. Period.

+ Date one woman at a time. Show respect to the woman you are dating by making her the only woman of interest in your life at that time. Do not be a player. Date one woman at a time.

+ Be faithful to the woman in your life. Be faithful to your girlfriend or the woman you are dating. Do not cheat on the woman you are with, under any circumstances. There is never a valid reason for cheating, and there is never an excuse for running around on your girlfriend. Be true to the woman you are dating. Be respectful to her by being true to her. Be faithful to the woman you are with, even if she is unfaithful to you. If she indeed is unfaithful to you, however, then you should not be in that relationship in the first place. You should have enough self-respect not to allow yourself to be treated like that by anyone else.

+ Be true to the one woman in your life. If you are married, then make sure you uphold your marriage vows. Honor your vows and honor your wife. Live by the commitment you made on your wedding day. Cherish your wife, and treasure your marriage. Honor your vows. Honor your wife.

~

A woman's company is a privilege. It is to be cherished, and never taken lightly.
A woman's presence is a blessing. It is to be treasured, and never taken for granted.

Be A True Gentleman, and Always Have Class

Being a true gentleman is not about using the proper fork or observing the most grandiose regulations of etiquette; rather, being a true gentleman is about showing every person genuine concern and treating all people with the utmost respect.

Being a true gentleman is not about following peculiar rules or wearing a tuxedo and cummerbund; rather, being a true gentleman is about carrying yourself with class at all times. It is about having the most sincere of intentions at all times, and it is about putting the rights and considerations of others ahead of your own desires at all times.

Being a true gentleman is about who you are and how you act. It means living with honor, respect, class, and decency. It means treating all people, especially women, with complete and total dignity.

~ Be a Nice Guy & Be a Good Guy ~

The truth of the matter is, being a gentleman is not rocket science.
Being a gentleman requires a little logic, a bit of forethought,
and a great deal of consideration for others.
It is not about complicated rules and convoluted instructions.
Instead, it is about trying to make life easier for other people.
It is about honestly and sincerely being a nice guy.

~ John Bridges ~

~ Be a Giver & Not a Taker ~

Always Give of Yourself, and Always Give to Others

Give more to others than you take from them.
Be a positive presence in the lives of others.
Add something positive to the lives of others.
Make a positive contribution to the lives of others.
Put more into the lives of others than you take out of them.

Give more to this world than you take from it.
Be a positive presence in this world while you are here.
Add something positive to this world while you can.
Make a positive contribution to this world while you have the chance.
Put more into this world than you take out of it.

~

"A gentleman is one who puts more into the world than he takes out."

~ George Bernard Shaw

Be Polite and Be Considerate

Be polite and be considerate of others. Show respect to other people, be kind and courteous to those you meet, and always do your best to do a little more than is necessary to help brighten someone's day, and to help make someone's life better in some way.

Considerate Behaviors

What follows is a series of considerate things you can say and do, to help make other people's lives better in some way. In a sense, it is a list of kind behaviors that you can perform to help improve the quality of life for other people… and for yourself as well.

What you can do to help make other people's lives better:

~ Smile and say hello to people you pass by. Send a quick smile and a kind word to people you see in your classes, in the hallway, in the lunchroom, or on the way to the bus. Smile and say hello to someone you pass by in the office, or in the grocery store, or on the sidewalk while you are out jogging, or in the park while taking your morning walk.

~ Strike up a conversation with someone who seems down or lonely. Start a polite dialogue with a friend, classmate, or co-worker who seems lonely, by saying something like *Hi there, how are you doing?* or *Hello, are you doing alright?* A little time and attention can go a long way toward making somebody feel better about their day and about themselves. A few minutes and a few kind words can do a lot to help make another person's day… even if you don't realize it at the time.

~ Eat lunch with a new student, a classmate, a co-worker, or someone who you don't normally see often or talk to; sit down next to someone who is sitting by themselves and who looks like they could use company.

~ Take a few moments to pass along a kind word or thoughtful note to a friend. Send a thoughtful e-mail, write an encouraging note, or send a quick text message to one of your friends who is having a bad day. Take a moment to wish someone luck with a test or a meeting that they might have coming up later in that day.

~ Be there for a friend in need; listen to them and let them know you care and are there for them… whether they need a little bit of help, or just someone to talk to.

~ Be there for anyone in need. Stick up for someone who is being picked on. Stand up for someone who may not be able to stand up for themselves.

~ Do little things, so that other people won't have to be inconvenienced by having to do them: flush the toilet, wipe the seat, pick up trash that missed the garbage can, pick up something you drop, clean up something you spill. Put your dishes away after you finish eating, unload the dishwasher without being asked to do so. Take out the trash without having to be told to do so. Take the dog out for a walk—even if it's not your turn; fill up the gas tank in the car if you notice it is running low, put the left-over food back in the refrigerator—even if you weren't the one who took it out; bring the mail in the house when you get home, put your things away when you're done using them, put your toys away when you're done playing with them (no matter what age you are). Push in your chair when you are done at the desk or at the dinner table. Clean up after yourself wherever you go.

~

If you don't do it, someone else will have to.
Be considerate of others: go through the trouble so that other people don't have to.

~

~ Do little things that take a minute, but that will be appreciated by others: wash your hands after using the restroom, use your turn signals when in the car, don't tailgate the person in the car ahead of you, turn off your high-beams when other cars are coming toward you so that you don't temporarily blind them.

~ Let other people go before you: put others ahead of yourself… *literally*. Let someone go ahead of you in line at the checkout; let someone go ahead of you in line at the deli counter or at the cash register. Allow someone to pass through a door before you. Hold the door for others, especially women and elders. Let another person go ahead of you in line at a store, especially women and elders.

~ Pass up the closest parking spot in the parking lot, and take another one a little farther away, so that another person can eventually pull into that space. You never know who might be coming into the parking lot after you who may need to park close—an older person, someone with an injury, or maybe even someone who is going to buy something heavy and have to carry it out to their car. What's walking a few extra feet, if it will help make someone's day a little bit easier?

~ Help lighten other people's burdens in life… *literally*: Offer to help carry a heavy object or grocery bags for someone else. Offer to help carry a friend's books or bag. Offer to help carry someone's luggage or to momentarily hold something while that person tries to do something else.

~

"What do we live for, if it is not to make life less difficult for each other?"

~ George Eliot

~

~ Pick up something that another person drops. If someone drops something without noticing it, get their attention, and then pick up that something and give it to them.

~ If you find something that belongs to someone, find that person and return it to them. If you cannot find that person, then turn whatever you found into someone who may be able to help find that person: a teacher, a coach, a secretary, etc.

~ If you find money that belongs to someone else, return it to that person. No one likes to lose money or valuables; so if you see someone leave either behind, make sure you return it to them… no matter how tempting it may be to keep it. Do the right thing. Do the considerate thing. Always.

~ Say simple words like "please" and "thank you." Say "you're welcome" and "no problem" as well. Say respectful words like "sir" and "ma'am" when speaking with elders or authority figures. Showing respect to others makes those people feel good about themselves in little ways. Saying words like "young lady" and "miss" … when said with a smile… can brighten an older woman's day and make her smile herself.

~ Take your hat off in-doors. Remove your cap when entering someone's home or a house of worship. (If it is a religious custom to wear a hat or head-covering in a place of worship, then make sure to do so.)

~ Show your love and appreciation for your friends regularly. Tell your friends that they are important to you, send them a quick text, or give them a phone call to let them know you appreciate them.

~ Give an old friend a call who you haven't talked to in a while. Resolve a wounded friendship or repair an injured relationship… especially if you were the one who did the damaging… or even if you were not. When two people rebuild their friendship, both people win: after all, both gain a friend as a result of the process.

~ Give people your time and attention. Go out of your way to strike up a conversation with others; do your best to hear what others have to say; allow people the time and opportunity to discuss what is important to them.

~ Listen to people who are talking. Really listen. Actually pay attention… *full* attention. Show respect to that person by treating what they have to say as important. When you really listen closely to another person, it lets them know that you value their words and, more importantly, it lets them know that you value them. Showing someone that you think their words are important, shows them that you think they are important as well. This will make everyone you speak with—and listen to—feel good. After all, everyone likes to feel important. Everyone wants to feel valued and appreciated.

~ Give people the benefit of the doubt, and look for the good in everyone you meet. You never know who might be having a rough day, who might be at their wit's end and be really frustrated, or who might just be a little misunderstood. So go out of your way to be a little kinder than you think is necessary; go out of your way to be a little more patient than you think you need to be; try extra hard to be understanding of others. Believe that each person you meet has good intentions at heart, and believe that everyone you meet is doing their best with what they have to work with in life. Be understanding. Be even more understanding. Be kind. Be patient. Be forgiving. Continue to be forgiving. Give people the benefit of the doubt, and look for the best in others.

~

*"You can easily judge the character of others
by how they treat those who can do nothing for them or to them."*
~ *Malcolm S. Forbes*

~

~ Do something good for other people, regardless of who they are: Do something good for a stranger. Do something good for someone who you'll never see again. Do something good for someone who will never have the opportunity to pay you back. Do something good for *anyone*, without seeking *anything* for yourself in return.

~

"You can't live a perfect day without doing something for someone who will never be able to repay you."

~ John Wooden

~

~ Do something good for someone who will never know about it: Sometimes, people never realize how others might have improved their lives—often by doing something that another person would not themselves have to do in the future.

~

"Real generosity is doing something nice for someone who will never find out."

~ Frank A. Clark

~

~ Do something good for someone who will never know *who* did it: Sometimes, people realize that others have done something kind and helpful for them, without knowing who the person was who performed the kindness. What matters is not the recognition you receive for doing good things for other people; what matters is the good things themselves, and the positive effect that those actions have on other people.

~

"This is the final test of a gentleman: his respect for those who can be of no possible service to him."

~ William Lyon Phelps

~

~ Compliment a stranger about something that he or she is wearing, or about their smile or hairstyle, or about something you see them do. Everyone likes compliments, because compliments make people feel important… and, everyone of us likes to be made to feel important. Compliment someone you know about something—about anything.

~ Do something to positively affect someone's life each day. Don't look for a *reason* to do something good for someone else. After all, you don't need a reason to do something good for another: doing good for others is reason enough.

~ Do something to make someone else's day. Don't look for a reason… look for an opportunity. Don't search for an excuse to do a good deed for someone else… be proactive and look for something good to do.

~

"Wherever there is a human being, there is an opportunity for kindness."

~ Seneca

~

"With great care and love, we can make the world a better place."

~ Constance Morin

~ Always say hello and smile to people you pass by. You don't have to hug or high-five everyone in the world, but you also don't have to walk right by them like they don't matter; you don't have to look right past them as if they don't exist. Acknowledge other people, even if you don't know them. Send them a quick smile, say a simple *hello*, or even just give them a polite nod of the head. But never, however, walk right by someone without saying or doing anything to acknowledge them. If you do, you make people feel unvalued and unimportant; you make them feel unworthy and undeserving of respect. And we are all worthy and deserving of respect. Make sure you understand that, and make sure that other people understand that as well.

~

"Be nice and smile to everyone you meet.
You don't know what they are going through,
and they may need that smile, and treasure it."

~ Christine M. Huppert

~

~ Say hello and strike up a quick conversation with toll-booth workers. After all, those hard-working people sit in a cramped booth all day, and have little-to-no meaningful interaction with others. Studies show that saying six words or more to a toll-booth employee, can increase their self-esteem and positive attitude by almost double. Studies also show that speaking six words or more can decrease a person's suicide rate by half. Six words are easy to say, and they do not take more than ten seconds to speak.
When you pass through a toll, make sure to take the time to say something like:
Hello, how are you doing today? or *Hi there! Have a great day*!

~

Kind words don't cost a lot, but they do count a lot.
"Simple courtesies may seem trivial and old-fashioned, but they are foundational in a civil society. Courtesies don't cost a penny, but they are priceless ways of showing respect, and making others feel special and valued." ~ Judi Vankevich
Caring words do not take much, but they indeed help much.

~

~ **Always Do More; Never Do Less** ~
When it comes to performing acts of kindness…
You can always do more, but you should never do less.
If you were ever charged with being a good person,
would there be enough evidence to convict you?
Do your best to make sure that there would be.

~

"The power of kindness is immense.
It is nothing less, really, than the power to change the world."

~ Daphne Rose Kingma

Find Time to Do Good Things for Others…
And If You Can't Find Time, Then MAKE TIME.

We are all busy, we are all trying to do a million things, we all have concern for our own welfare…but we're here on this earth to help one another, and that's more important than any meeting or agenda, or selfish concern that we might have.

Forget about what it may cost you in terms of time or convenience, and go out of your way to help someone in need. The chances are that the other person needs your kindness and compassion, more than you need those five minutes that it would cost to go out of your way. The chances are that the other person's life needs your consideration and positive impact, more than you need the couple of moments it would take to influence someone's life for the better.

~

Our true importance in this world lies not in what we do for ourselves,
but in what we do for others. The contribution we make to those in need
is the true measure of our significance in this lifetime.

~

Open your eyes, open your ears, open your mind, and open your heart. Go out and make a difference. Don't worry about the cost, and don't avoid doing a kind deed because it's inconvenient. Do what is right, do what needs to be done, and do what other people need you to do. As former United States president, Woodrow Wilson, once said: "If you will think about what you ought to do for other people, your character will take care of itself."

It bears repeating that, when it comes to performing acts of kindness…
you can always do more… but you should never do less.

Be On The Lookout For Opportunities To Perform Acts Of Kindness

Be on the lookout for opportunities to pay compliments to others.
Be on the lookout for ways to make people feel better about themselves.
Maybe someone has a new hairstyle that looks nice. Maybe someone lost a few pounds. Maybe someone did a great job on something big. Maybe someone did a great job on something small. Whatever the case may be, there is always something positive you can point out, there is always something positive you can say, and there is always something positive you can do for others.

~

Be on the lookout for opportunities to spread kindness.
Be on the lookout for opportunities to pay sincere compliments.
Be on the lookout for opportunities to make other people feel important.
Be on the lookout for opportunities to make other people feel appreciated.
Be on the lookout for opportunities to make other people feel good about themselves.
Don't wait for reasons to come and find you; go out and look for good things you can do for others. Good deeds won't just happen on their own: they need you to go out and make them happen. Be proactive in your approach to kindness. ***Don't wait for good things to start happening. Go out and make them happen.***

Find A Good Woman

Find a good woman: find a woman who is both classy and respectable. Find a woman who is intelligent and ambitious. Find a woman who is responsible and reliable. Find a woman who has a good personality and a good sense of humor. Find a woman who has direction in life; a woman who is going somewhere in life, find a woman who wants to do something special with her life. Find a woman who wants to be somebody special, and find a woman who wants to be with someone special.

Find A Good Woman, and Treat Her Well: Be a Good Listener

If another person takes the time and effort to tell you something, it is only natural that they would expect you to listen to what they have to say. More likely than not, that person is discussing something with you because they think it's important—if not to you, then at least to them. Chances are, they want you to care about what's important to them, and ultimately, they want you to care about *them*, as well.

When someone tells you something, no matter how casually they mention it, and no matter how unimportant it might seem to be at the time, make a point to remember it. If someone is telling you something, especially if it's about a preference of theirs—a specific date, a past experience, or something of sentimental value—do all you can to commit that piece of information to memory…and not just short-term memory, but long-term, useful memory.

~

If a woman ever tells you something…
whether she is a friend, girlfriend, potential girlfriend, fiancé, spouse,
or even a relative of yours… if a woman tells you something:
Commit It To Memory.

~

If she is telling you, it means she wants you to remember it, and she probably would love it if you acted on that knowledge in the future. (Favorite colors, important dates, favorite anything's, likes/dislikes, future goals, events, good things, bad things… anything: if she tells you, you better make a mental note of it—or a physical one if you have to—and store it away in your memory for future use.)

So, when someone is talking to you… Be a good listener. Actually listen to what the other person has to say, instead of just waiting for your turn to talk. Pay attention to what she or he is saying, instead of thinking about what you are going to say next. **If someone tells you something—anything, it is for a reason: it is because they want you to remember it.**

~

**"The most basic and powerful way to connect to another person is to listen.
Just listen. Perhaps the most important thing we ever give each other is our attention."**

~ Rachel Naomi Remen

Find a Good Woman, Treat Her Right, & Do Your Best To Hold Onto Her

Priceless Advice On Women

This is the best advice I can give you for if you're trying to get a young lady to date you, to be your girlfriend, or one day when the time comes, to marry you. As best as I can state it, there are four things that you need to do in regard to the young lady:

~

1. **Make her laugh and smile**: A woman has to enjoy being around you and spending time with you. If you're not fun to be with and talk to, then why would she want to?

~

2. **Make her feel like a lady**: Be a gentleman. Just be polite and courteous; hold the door for her, carry her stuff, etc. Also, don't make sarcastic jokes about her, and don't make fun of her even if it's just in jest. Little things make a big difference with women; and if it's a negative thing, they will be hurt by it.

   You had better be a gentleman to the parents too—make sure you look the father in the eye when you shake his hand, and give him a good firm handshake. Don't break eye-contact during the handshake until he does.

~

3. **Make her feel special**: Make her feel like you treat her better than anyone else could. You have to distinguish yourself from other guys. You have to give her a reason to want to be around you/with you, as opposed to anyone else…If you don't distinguish yourself from other guys, then she doesn't have a reason to choose you.

~

4. **Be able to dance, and actually like doing it from time to time (if not often)**: Women think guys who don't like to dance are rigid and boring…and if you're boring, then you're not fun to be around. And like I said, if you're not fun to be around, why would she want to be with you?

~

~ **Be a gentleman, and be a *gentle man*.** ~
Find a good woman, and always treat her right.
Be a gentleman at all times. Be a gentleman in all ways.

~

~ **Be a Good Man** ~

If you want to find a ***good woman***, you first have to become a ***good man***.
The best way to find a ***good woman*** is to start by being a ***good man***.

~

Whatever character traits you wish to find in a woman,
Start by developing in yourself.
If you want to find a good woman: be a good man.
If you want to find a classy woman: be a classy man.
If you want to find a respectable woman: be a respectable man.
If you want to find a real woman: be a REAL man.
If you want to find a good woman: start by becoming a good man.

~

The best way to find a good woman is by being a good man.
The best way to find a REAL woman is by being a REAL man.

~

Be a Good Man.

~

~

**The first step toward finding the right kind of person
is becoming the right kind of person yourself.**

~

**"Make a list of the traits of the type of spouse you would like to marry.
Then make a list of the traits you would need to attract that type of person.
Then throw away the first list and work on the second.
Don't just look for the right one—become the right one!"**

~ Author Unknown

Find a REAL Woman

In this playbook, we have discussed what it means to be a REAL man—what a REAL man thinks like, talks like, walks like, and looks like. But what exactly does a REAL *woman* look like?

First and foremost, a REAL woman is someone who respects herself. She accepts herself, values herself, feels good about herself, and has high expectations for herself. She values others as well as herself, and she sets high standards for herself and for the people she surrounds herself with.

A REAL woman is someone who cares about others and who takes care of herself as well. She respects other people and does right by them, and she is never afraid to be herself in front of anyone, at any time. A REAL woman is respectful and respectable at all times, and she is classy and honorable in all ways.

A REAL woman is someone who respects herself and who can take care of herself. She is someone who has direction and ambition in life. She is someone who is classy, respectable, responsible, and driven to be successful. Above all, a REAL woman is someone who… respects all people, especially herself; she is someone who always does the right thing, and who does her best to live a life that matters.

A REAL woman understands and lives by the creed:

> R~espect all people,
>   E~specially yourself.
>   A~lways do the right thing.
>   L~ive a life that matters.

Be a REAL Man

It takes a king to be with a queen, and it takes a REAL man to be with a REAL woman. If you want to find a good woman—a respectable, classy, intelligent woman—then you first must become a good man. If you want to find a REAL woman… then you first must become a REAL man.

No matter where you go, and no matter what you do… Always be a REAL Man.
No matter where you go, and no matter what you do… Always act like a REAL Man.
Make sure that you always live out the creed:

> R~espect all people,
>   E~specially women.
>   A~lways do the right thing.
>   L~ive a life that matters.

Always Remember That, One Day…
You Are Going To Have A Daughter.

One day, you are going to have a daughter; and one day, you are going to have to send her out into a world that you helped create. Whether it's good or bad, she is going to have to live in that world. The important thing to understand is that you help shape that world, by both your attitudes and your actions.

What you say and do, and, as importantly, what you tolerate other people to say and do—how you let other men talk about or treat women—creates the atmosphere in which our society's women have to live.

One day… you are going to have a daughter, and there is going to come a point in time when you have to send that daughter out into a world you helped to create. Will you be sending her into a safer, better, and more respectful world?

~

Always remember that every woman is someone's daughter.

~

One day… you are going to have a daughter, and when that happens, the Law of Karma is going to play itself out. Karma is the doctrine that states that what goes around, comes around. So, what you did with and to—and what you said about and to—women when you were young, is what will be said and done toward your daughter in the future. Remember that.

Don't Use Derogatory Language About Women, &
Don't Tolerate Derogatory Language About Women Either

When you talk about women in a disrespectful way, and when you allow other people to do so without addressing them about it, you send the message that it's okay to talk about women in that way. Implicit in that message is the idea that it's okay to treat women in a negative way.

~

The truth is… *it's not okay*. And you had better wake up and do something about it. You had better care about it, because the women who are affected by it aren't objects, pieces of meat, sources of male pleasure, or subordinate beings. They are your sisters, your mothers, your cousins, your best friends, and one day, your daughters.

~

One day, you are going to have a daughter of your own.
Always remember that, and don't ever forget it.

Be Respectful At All Times, In All Ways

When it comes to being intimate, always be gentle and always be careful.
Never push a situation, and never do anything hurtful. Be appropriate, be smart, and be respectful. If there is ever any uncertainty in a situation, do not push the boundaries. Be responsible and be respectful; treat women as equals, not as pieces of meat.

The worst thing you can do as a man is to take advantage of or force yourself on a woman. That is not what being a man is about. Imposing your will on a woman does not make you more of a man. In fact, it actually makes you less of one. If you do those types of things, then you are not a real man at all: instead, you are a piece of trash.
When it comes to women, always remember:

> *No* means **no**.
> *Maybe* means **no**.
> *I'm not sure* means **no**.

Remember that every young lady you meet is someone's daughter and someone's sister. If you have a sister of your own, then I don't even need to tell you what that means. And one day, at some point in your life, you are going to have a daughter of your own.
Keep that in mind.

~

**The choices we make, the words we speak, and the actions we take
not only shape our own futures; they shape the futures of everyone we know and love,
and they shape the future of the world in which we all live.**

~

Respect a Woman's Strength and Courage

In order to have respect for a woman's strength and courage, all you need to do is think about one thing: the process of giving birth. Child labor is perhaps the most difficult and painful experience known to mankind. And yet, the majority of women do it during the course of their lives. Never, however, has a man ever done it.

It takes tremendous strength and courage to give birth to a child. If you do not have respect for a woman, and for her ability to give birth… then you had better go home and apologize to your mother.

It may take a man's presence to make a baby…
But it takes a **woman's strength** to *have* a baby.

You Can Tell a Lot About a Man

You can tell a lot about a man by what he says;
You can tell even more about him by what he does;
And you can tell everything else you need to know about him
By what he tolerates others to say and do in his presence.
You must never mistreat a woman, or stand by and see another to do so."
~ Liam Neeson, from the movie Rob Roy

Respect Women. Protect Women.

Some Alarming Statistics

~ More than 650,000 incidents of rape are *reported* by women each year in the United States of America. It is estimated that the amount of actual incidents of sexual assault is far more than 1 million, and more likely closer to 2 million.

~ 1 of every 5 women will be the victims of attempted rape in their lifetime. That means that, if you know at least 5 women, the chances are that one of them will likely be assaulted at some point in her life. If you know more than 5 women—and the chances are that you do—then more than one of those women will become victims of some form of violence.

~ 1 of 5 *teenage* relationships involves some type of physical or sexual force. Not all incidents of rape and sexual assault are committed by strangers. As a matter of fact, the overwhelming majority of sexual assaults are perpetrated by men whom the victim knows, including a boyfriend, spouse, or an acquaintance. Approximately 75% of assault victims know the person who rapes them.

~ 1 of every 3 women in the world is the victim of abuse and some type of assault: either physical, emotional, or sexual. That statistic bears repeating: *1 of every 3 women in this world.* That is an *entire third* of the world's population.

These Statistics Are Disturbing.

What is more disturbing is that there are many more just like them—and many even worse. The facts listed above are only a short list of eye-opening figures about the dangers affecting women in this world today. All these statistics are equally alarming, equally disturbing, and equally *unacceptable*. It's time we do something about them.

It's time we put an end to this type of behavior; it's time we put a stop to this type of treatment of women; it's time we stand up for what is right… it's time we stand up for the rights and respectful treatment of women, and it's time we stand up *against* anything less than what the women in our lives deserve.

There is a saying when it comes to making good decisions and putting yourself in good situations: "Don't become another statistic."

When it comes to making good decisions toward women, putting yourself in good situations with women, being respectful of women, and being proactive in your protection of women… it must be said: "Don't allow another to become a statistic."

After all, it's not just a woman's problem; it doesn't just affect young ladies and girls. We are all members of the same team, and therefore, we all walk through this world together. And so, always remember that… ***What affects one of us, affects all of us.***

It's Our Problem Too

Mistreatment of women is not only a *woman's* problem: it is a *man's* problem also.

Not sure what I mean? Think about it…

More than 99% of physical and sexual violence toward women is perpetuated by men. That means that, as men, we are the source of the problem. To say that violence toward women is a woman's problem—making an analogy to the sport of football—would be like saying that poor blocking is a running back's problem. In reality, bad offensive line play is not a running back's fault: it is an offensive line's fault. The running back does not cause the violence that occurs from being tackled by numerous defenders; he is merely a victim of the circumstances. The cause of the problem lies up front, where the offensive linemen are concerned. The running back is not the cause of the problem; he is merely the one who suffers the effects of that cause.

In much the same way, women are not the cause of the violence that occurs at the hands of men; they are merely the victims of that violence. The source of the problem lies, first and foremost, with men. The bad news is that we, as men, are the main cause of the problem. The good news is that we, as men, are also the potential source of the solution to that problem.

As men, we have created many of the problems that women are forced to deal with. As the perpetuators of these problems, however, we also have the potential to bring about positive change and to create a solution to the issues of our time. We hold in our hands the keys to a better world. It is up to us whether we will use these keys—and both our heads and hearts—to unlock the door to a safer and greater world.

~

As men, we have an incredible obligation to act responsibly and respectfully toward women. Beyond that, we have an incredible opportunity to improve the world in which we live; we have the opportunity to help build a more positive world for ourselves, and to help create a safer culture for the women whom we share this life world with.

As men, the simple fact of the matter is that we have yet to uphold this obligation, and as of yet, we have not taken advantage of our great opportunity. The women we spend our time with, the ladies we share our lives with, and all the women with whom we walk through this world… they all want us to do a better job of being men. They all *need* us to do a better job of being men.

As a gender, we must find a way to do a better job of treating women. We are capable of so much more, we owe so much more, and the women of this world deserve so much more. To put it simply … we *can* do better; we *must* do better. We *can be* better; we *must be* better. Our women need it, our communities need it, our society needs it, and our world needs it.

~

What affects one of us, affects all of us. That is the nature of a team; that is the nature of a family. That, whether you like it or not, is the nature of the **Human Team** and the **Human Family**. And so, if something is affecting one of us, then all of us had better do something about it. It is no one person's problem; it is no one gender's responsibility. The problem affects all of us—men and women. Therefore, all of us must work to bring an end to the causes of that problem. We have an obligation to help improve other people's quality of life, and we have an obligation to help improve the quality of our world. The responsibility belongs to us… *all of us.*

<u>One Day, and Today…</u>

Always remember that, one day… you are going to have a daughter.
Keep in mind that, *today*… you already have a mother, a sister, an aunt, a cousin,
a girlfriend, a best friend, a grandmother, and other women you are fond of.

~

Work to create a better and safer future for your own daughter *one day*.
Do your part to help make a safer and better present
for every woman that you know *today*.

~

~ What affects one of us, affects all of us. ~

~

A

Always Do
The Right Thing

Always Do The Right Thing

Always Do the Right Thing … Always

Being a REAL man means seeking to determine what is right, desiring to do what is right, and following through and actually doing what is right. Always say the right thing. Always do the right thing. Always stand for the right thing. Do what is right, *because* it is right. And do it all the time.

It is incredible how much good you can do, and how many difficult situations you can make it through in life if you just live by 5 simple words: *Always do the right thing.*

There is never a wrong time to do the right thing, and there is never a right time to do the wrong thing. Therefore, always remember… *You can never be wrong if you always do what is right.*

Uphold your honor. Guard your dignity. Protect your integrity. Live by your principles, and not other people's perceptions or opinions. Keep to your convictions. Being a REAL man is about having principles and living by those principles. It is about having something called "consistent character," which means that you have the same principles, regardless of the circumstances.

You cannot change your principles just because circumstances change. Wear your integrity on your sleeve: always be yourself and always do the right thing. Always do what you know to be right and best.

~

You can't change your principles just because your circumstances change.

~

Do What Is Right, Because It Is Right

You do what is right, in spite of the fact that it may be hard; you do what is right, in spite of the fact that it may be unpleasant; you do what is right, in spite of the fact that it may be difficult to do and that you may not want to do, or keep doing it. You do what is right, for no other reason than *because it is right*.

~

"To know what is right and not do it is the worst cowardice."

~ The Philosopher, Confucius

Do The Right Thing In Your Relationships

Make a commitment in your relationships. Do right by your girlfriend, your fiancé, or your wife. Always be faithful to her. Always be there for her, always be honest with her, and always be true to her.

~

If you have a girlfriend, be faithful to her and do right by her.
If you have a fiancé, be faithful to her and do right by her.
If you have a wife, be faithful to her and do right by her.

~

Being a REAL Man is about being faithful in your relationships; it is about doing right by the one woman who fills the relational role in your life. Being a REAL Man is about doing right by that woman—whether she is your wife or merely your girlfriend. The title does not matter. What matters is that you act like a REAL man and be faithful to her at all times. What matters is that you be a REAL man and do right by her ... *always* ... and in *all ways*.

Always Do Right

Always do the right thing,
and always do right by people.

Being a REAL Man is about being loyal to ideals
and living by your principles. Every time. All the time.
Do right by your girlfriend. Do right by your fiancé. Do right by your wife.

Always be there for her, and always be faithful to her.
Always do right by her. Always.
No excuses. No exceptions.

~

"Always do right.
This will surprise some people
and astonish the rest."
~ *Mark Twain*

~

Make Good Decisions

Don't Make Decisions Based Solely on Emotion

Don't ever make a decision based on emotion. As much as you may want to (whether it's out of anger, excitement, or passion), always think things through logically. It's the only way to make good decisions and to avoid making bad ones.

Don't Make Decisions When You Are Angry or Upset

Don't ever make a decision or do something when you are highly emotional, especially if you are angry or upset. Wait until you calm down and have put the volatile feelings behind you to make the decision. Otherwise, you'll regret it.

~

"When anger arises, think of the consequences."
~ *Confucius*

Use Your Head and Your Heart... But Use Your Head First

When faced with options, try to take a step back and be objective about the situation. List out all the positive aspects of each choice, and then list all the negative ones of each. Add them up and figure out which one has more positives and less negatives, and which of those positive and negative aspects is more important to you.

Let your brain determine the most logical outcome, and then let your heart guide your decision, and in that order. Too much heart and not enough thought will lead to a rash and emotional decision. But too much thought and no heart will lead to an unimpassioned choice.

Use your head first, then your heart. But make sure that you indeed use both.

Think of the Consequences Before You Act

When faced with a tough decision (like whether you should do something or not, or whether a particular action is right or not), again, try to take a step back and look at the situation objectively. Think through both choices, and then think through the consequences of each.

~

Your actions have consequences.
When you choose an action, you are also choosing the potential consequences
that go along with that action. Stop and think things through; make good decisions.
When you choose an action, you also choose the consequences of that action.
So choose wisely.

Make Good Decisions, and Leave No Room For Regrets

There are two things that you should never have to say in life.
The first is: "Man, I wish I had done that! What was I thinking...?"
The second is: "Man, I wish I had *never* done that! What was I thinking...?"

~

The main message: Don't be afraid to take chances and experience life,
but never do anything that you (or your family) wouldn't be proud of.

Have Fun, But Be Responsible

One of the great pieces of advice that my father gave me before heading off to college was this: have fun, but learn to be responsible doing it.

Have fun, but be responsible: it sounds like a very simple notion, and really it is. Although, it doesn't always appear to be easy to adhere to. In truth, balancing fun and responsibility is not all that difficult to do, it merely requires a little bit of conscientious thought before making decisions and prior to taking actions.

Having fun while still carrying yourself respectfully—and while still behaving responsibly—really is a matter of thinking before you act. It does not mean that you can't have a good time; it simply means that you try to be rational and sensible in the process. You can enjoy yourself without being careless; you can have a good time without being irresponsible. In other words… You can put on your "fun hat" without taking off your "thinking cap."

Have fun, but be responsible. To put it simply: think before you act.

The people who get the most out of their experiences in life are the ones who are able to enjoy themselves responsibly; they are able to have fun while still acting sensibly. Understand the importance of acting responsibly. Make sure that you always think before you act; make sure you never do anything that you, or your family, might regret in the future. Don't be a prude who never enjoys himself, but also don't overdo it and push your limits. Have a good time, but be responsible about doing it. Enjoy yourself, but don't get carried away in the process.

You do not have to be a prude who never enjoys himself,
but you also do not need to push your limits either.

When it comes to enjoying yourself and having a good time: You don't have to be a perfect saint, but you also don't have to resort to debauchery either. **Have fun, but be responsible.** Have fun, enjoy yourself, and enjoy life… just learn to be responsible and reasonable about doing it.

~ Always remember to enjoy life, and always remember to do it responsibly.

~

"Have fun, but be responsible."
~ *Lou DiCocco*

Make Good Decisions ~ Three Questions to Consider

Deep down, I believe each of us wants to live a moral and honorable life. Regardless of who we are and what each of us believes in, we are all striving to live life the best way we know how. We all want to make the most of our opportunities and decisions, and every one of us wants to do what's best as often as we possibly can.

We all have hundreds of choices to make on a daily basis: everything from what to say or what not to say—and whether or not to actually say it—to choosing what one should or should not do—and whether or not to actually do it. It isn't always easy to determine which choices are the most moral and honorable ones to make. In this hectic and fast-paced world, figuring out what's best (and what isn't) can be a very challenging task. So, how exactly do we go about determining the best choices to make and the best courses of action to take?

In any given situation, when faced with a potential decision to make, there are three simple questions that you should ask yourself:

1. Is it *right*?
2. Is it *responsible*?
3. Is it *respectable*?

Keeping these considerations in mind will help you determine whether a decision is a good idea or not, and whether a particular course of action should be pursued or not. Hopefully, these questions—and your answers to them—will help you navigate your way through the murky waters of everyday morality.

That being said, let's take a brief closer look at each of the three:

1. Is it **right** – Is this the right thing to do? In other words, is what you are about to say or do truthful? Is it honest, is it just, and is it fair?

2. Is it **responsible** – Is this the responsible thing to do? In other words, will it have a positive impact on you, on your future, (on your chances for future success, on your character development and on the person that you ultimately will become,) and on the other people who will be affected by it? Is it keeping in-line with the obligations you have and the commitments you've made?

3. Is it **respectable** – Is this the respectable thing to do? Will other people respect you for doing it? Will it increase or decrease the amount of respect that others have for you? Will it increase or decrease the amount of respect that you have for yourself? Also, would you want your words, decisions, or actions to be broadcast to the entire world? If not, then it may be a sign that what you're thinking about saying or doing isn't the most respectable choice available.

~ Is it right?
~ Is it responsible?
~ Is it respectable?

If you can answer "yes" to each and all of these questions, then you can be sure that what you're thinking of saying is the appropriate and honorable thing to say. If not, then it probably isn't... and therefore, you probably shouldn't say it.

If you can answer "yes" to each and all of these questions, then you can be sure that what you're thinking of doing is the appropriate and honorable thing to do. If not, then it probably isn't... and therefore, you probably shouldn't do it.

If You Have to THINK ABOUT Whether or Not Something is Right... Then It Probably Isn't.

You usually know right away when something is the right thing to do. If you have to think about whether or not something is right, then it probably isn't. The fact that you have to think about it means that you're trying to rationalize it or justify it.

If you ask yourself whether a potential action is the right one to take, and the word 'yes' doesn't immediately jump out at you within the first two or three seconds, then it's probably not the right thing to do. Any longer than those first three seconds and you enter into the 'rationalization' phase, where you start trying to rationalize why something could be okay to do. After three seconds, you're at that point where you *want* to do something that your instincts are telling you is wrong, but you're trying to find a way to make it seem right—you're trying to fit a particular puzzle piece where it doesn't belong.

That's when you start telling yourself things like, "Well, I *guess* it would be alright..." Or, "It's *probably* okay..." Or "I'm *probably* going to get away with this..."

When you honestly ask yourself if something is right, and you don't have a clear and resounding answer within the first three seconds, then a flashing red light should go off in your head. It should alert you that something's up with what you're thinking about doing. Something isn't right. Trust your instincts...you usually know right away when something is the right thing to do. If your instincts don't tell you that it's right...then don't try to fit the square peg into the round hole. Don't try to talk yourself into doing something that you can't immediately say is right.

If you find yourself trying to rationalize something, that in and of itself should be a warning sign. If you have to talk yourself into thinking that something is right... then it probably isn't. If your gut doesn't tell you that something is okay... then it's probably the wrong thing to do. In a situation like that, it is best to leave the thing undone and move on. Otherwise, you'll only get yourself into trouble.

~

If you have to think about whether or not something is right...
then it probably isn't. Just don't do it.

A Simple, Yet Great Piece of Advice

"It's easier to *stay out* of trouble than to *get out* of trouble."
~ H. Jackson Browne

~

Integrity and the Tough Decisions

For the important decisions: let your head guide you.
For the meaningful decisions: let your heart guide you.
For the difficult decisions: let your integrity guide you.

~

Always Do The Right Thing … Always.

Being a good person is about always doing the right thing…even if it's unpopular, even if it's inconvenient, and even if it costs you. It's not always easy to do the right thing. In fact, a lot of times it's very difficult. But then again, if it were easy to always do what's right, then you simply would be expected to do it. Where's the distinction in that?

Anyone can do the right thing when it's not very hard to do. What separates people of character from everyone else is that they do the right thing when it's not very *easy* to do. They do what's right when it's challenging to do so; they do what's right when it is seemingly impossible or even impractical to do so as well…

When it's going to make you unpopular, when it's going to cost you, when it's going to make you stand out from the norm…that's when you have to stand up for what you believe in and show people what you really are all about.

Everyone has heard the phrase, *"If all your friends jumped off a bridge, would you do it too?"* As simple as it sounds, it also has a very important meaning. What the question really is asking is this: "Are you strong enough to do the right thing, regardless of what other people might think?"

Anyone can be a follower. It takes true strength and conviction to always do the right thing…not just when it's easy, not just when you get something out of it…but also when it costs you…*especially when it costs you.*

No matter what anyone else says or does, you always have to do what you believe is right. People with strong character don't care about the surrounding opinions or circumstances; all they care about is doing what's right.

~

"The ultimate measure of a man is not where he stands in moments of comfort and convenience, but where he stands at times of challenge and controversy."

~ Dr. Martin Luther King, Jr.

"Rule #1: Use your good judgment in all situations.
There will be no additional rules."
~ Nordstrom's Employee Handbook

~ Put Yourself in Good Situations ~

If you put yourself in good situations, it makes it a lot easier to do the
right thing, because you won't be exposing yourself to temptation.
Make Good Decisions, Put Yourself in Good Situations …
and Good Things Will Happen.

~

"Virtue is the truest nobility."
~ Miguel de Cervantes

"The 80 Rule" ~ A Little Something To Keep In Mind

The average life expectancy in America is about 80 years. (Actually, it's right around 78, but I'm optimistic.) In light of that, I have a little something I like to call "The 80 Rule." What The 80 Rule says, is that you take the number 80 and subtract from it however many years-old you are right now. Whatever number you get for an answer, that's how many years you'll have to live with the decisions you make today.

So, for example, if you're 18: then the equation is $80 - 18 = 62$. That means that whatever you say and do today, you'll have to live with for 62 years. <u>That's a long time.</u>

The 80 Rule is a great little idea to keep in mind whenever you're faced with a choice. It should help you realize the importance of thinking things through before you act, and that the decisions you make in the present are going to affect the course of your life for many years to come. The decisions you make will shape your life *forever*.

There is no "reset" button in life. You can't take anything back, and you can't undo anything. All of your actions have consequences, and the things you say and do today will have a lasting impact on the rest of your life. You have to understand that, and you have to be aware of it while making your decisions.

~

Life might be short, but it certainly is long enough for you to
have to live with the decisions that you make ... for a very long time.

~
~ **The decisions you make shape the path you take.** ~
~

What You Do In the Dark Will Eventually Come To The Light

What you do in the dark will eventually come to the light. The things you do in private somehow have a way of showing up in public. Ultimately, what you do in life will eventually be brought to the light of day.

Sooner or later, you are going to be exposed for who you really are and for what you've really done in life. If you have done the right things, if you have lived with integrity, and if you have treated others fairly and respectfully, then people are going to find out about it and they are going to respect you for it. If, on the other hand, you have done the wrong things and you have mistreated others, then people are going to find out about that too.

What you do in the dark will eventually come to the light. You may be able to get away with something for a little while, but you can't hide who you are forever. Some day, sooner or later, you are going to be exposed. Better to live a good life and have everyone find out about it in the end, than to take the wrong path and try to get away with it.

One way or the other, it will all catch up to you in the end ...
because ultimately, what you do in the dark will eventually come to the light.

~

The truth always rises to the top.
"Truth will rise above falsehood as oil above water."
~ *Miguel de Cervantes*

Surround Yourself With Good People

Surround yourself with good people: people of high character and high intellect, people with ambition and a strong sense of purpose. Spend time with people who have their priorities straight and who know where they're going in life. If you can't find any of those types of people, then learn to occupy your own time.

In all seriousness, if you can't surround yourself with good people, then surround yourself with representations of good people: read a book or a magazine article about someone you respect; watch a television show or movie about people you admire or that has respectable characters; or simply take some quiet time to reflect on yourself and the way your day is going or on the way you're living your life.

As the old proverb says: "Better to be alone than in bad company."

~

"Bad company corrupts good character."
~ 1 Corinthians 15:33 (from the Christian Faith Tradition)

Surround Yourself with the Right People
Surround yourself with the right people.
Surround yourself with people who bring out the best in you.
Surround yourself with people who bring out your best attitude.
Surround yourself with people who help you make good decisions.
Surround yourself with people who encourage you.
Surround yourself with people who support you.
Surround yourself with people who build you up.
Surround yourself with people who help you to be yourself.
Surround yourself with people who help you to be your *best* self.
Surround yourself with people who will help you make the most of
your talents, your opportunities, your influence, and your life.

It's About Being the Right Kind of Person
Who you are will determine the type of people you attract. The type of person you are will be reflected directly by the type of people who gravitate toward you.

Be the best friend that you can be. Strive to act your best, and you will bring out the best in others. Be as good a person and as good a friend to others as you can be, and you will attract good people and good friends more often than not. Try to be the right kind of person, and you will find that the right kind of people will gravitate toward you.

~

"Good values attract good people."
~ John Wooden

Be the Type of Person You Want to Attract

Be a kind person, and you will attract kind people into your life.

Be a good person, and you will attract good people into your life.

Be an honest person, and you will attract honest people into your life.

Be a genuine person, and you will attract genuine people into your life.

Be a positive person, and you will attract positive people into your life.

Be an authentic person, and you will attract authentic people into your life.

Be an ambitious person, and you will attract ambitious people into your life.

Be an enthusiastic person, and you will attract enthusiastic people into your life.

Be a responsible person, and you will attract responsible people into your life.

Be a respectable person, and you will attract respectable people into your life.

Be an honorable person, and you will attract honorable people into your life.

"Be honorable yourself if you wish to associate with honorable people."

~ Welsh Proverb

Some Things to Consider When Choosing Your Friends

Surround yourself with people who encourage you, not who discourage you.
Surround yourself with people who build you up, not who tear you down.

~

"Keep away from people who belittle your ambitions. Small people always do that, but the really great make you feel that you, too, can become great."
~ *Mark Twain*

Associate with the type of person that you would aspire to be:
surround yourself with people of high character and high intelligence,
people with great work ethic and even greater integrity.

~

"Don't choose friends because they are popular, or because they are good-looking, or because they are rich or athletic. Choose your friends because you enjoy being with them and because they are good people." ~ *Tony Dungy*

~

"Choose your friends based on their values, not their status in society."
~ *Tony Dungy*

Surround yourself with good people who bring out the best in you
and who are going to make you a better person.

~

"Who you will be five years from now will be determined largely by
the people you interact with and the books you read."
~ *Charlie "Tremendous" Jones*

You cannot choose your family, but you can choose your friends.
Choose wisely and choose carefully, because the people you decide
to surround yourself with will have a big impact on your life.

"A righteous man is cautious in friendship"
~ *Proverbs 12:26*

~ **The Integrity Rules** ~

1. Always do the right thing: Always do what is right, always do what is responsible, and always do what is respectable.

2. Always be genuine: Be who you say that you are. Be transparent. Be forthright. Make your words and your deeds match up.

3. Always be yourself: Respect yourself. Be true to yourself. Live by your principles. Be consistent in who you are and in what you believe in, live according to your priorities, and always be true to your values.

4. Always be responsible: Make good decisions, put yourself in good situations, and act appropriately at all times. Do what you're supposed to do; be where you're supposed to be; be on-time, and do what is expected of you when you get there.

5. Always be accountable: Take ownership of your decisions and your actions, and be answerable for their consequences at all times. Assume responsibility for your mistakes, do not blame others; do not make excuses or complain; know when to apologize; know when to grant forgiveness—both to yourself and to others.

6. Always be reliable and dependable: Do what you say you are going to do, and be where you say you are going to be.

7. Always be in control of yourself: Control your emotions, control your compulsions, control your desires, control your behaviors, control your habits, and control your life.

8. Always be honest: Tell the truth at all times, and in its entirety. Be honest with others and be honest with yourself. Be true with others, be true with yourself, and be true with the words you speak. Do not withhold the truth, and do not attempt to stretch it. The truth shall set you free, so long as you respect it.

9. Always be humble: Humility is the ability to see yourself in the correct perspective: to see yourself as you *really are*, not in the way you think you are. Put your personal bias aside, and examine yourself objectively—be able to see yourself for who you really are, both your strengths and weaknesses.

10. Always be respectful: Be respectful to others, be considerate of others, and be civil toward others. Do not make disparaging or hurtful remarks, refrain from gossiping about others; speak all the good you know of others, and speak none of the bad. Give credit where credit is due; praise when appropriate and deserved. Speak ill of no one.

11. Always keep your word: Be true to your word. Keep your promises. Do what you say you are going to do. Value your good name.

12. Always honor your commitments: Do right by others. Fulfill your obligations. Carry out your responsibilities. Follow through on all that you do. Finish what you start.

~

"You can take pride in being an individual of integrity...
People will gravitate to you, seek your counsel, and cherish your friendship."
~ *Lou Holtz*

Always Be True To Yourself ~ Always Be Genuine

No matter who you are or what you do, every night before you go sleep, you have to be able to face the man in the mirror and ask yourself one question: 'Am I genuine?'

What's more important than asking that question, however, is being able to answer it with an honest "yes." If you can respond without hesitation in that manner, then you can walk through this world with your head held high, confidently knowing that you have the respect of both yourself and others.

~

You cannot be perfect, but you *can* be authentic.
And, since you cannot be perfect, then you had *better* be authentic.

What Does It Mean To Be Genuine?

Genuineness can be defined simply as "consistency between one's words and deeds." To put it another way: being genuine means that you are who you appear to be. It means that what you *say* you are, what you *say* you do, and what you *say* you believe in… are the things that you actually *are*, actually *do*, and actually do *believe in*.

Being genuine means that you are sincere and authentic—that what you *say* is matched by what you *do*. To be genuine means to be *real*. It means that the image you put out there for others to see, is indeed who you truly are. There are no smoke signals. There are no efforts to deceive or mislead others, and there are no deliberate attempts to "throw people off your scent."

Being genuine means that you *are* who you *say* you are.
You are authentic: you are the real deal.
There is nothing fake about you.
You are 100 percent real.

Being genuine implies that you have no ulterior motives: you say what you mean, and you mean what you say. People don't have to try to "figure you out" or guess what you're really all about. They don't have to try to determine what, if anything, you are up to. They know who you are, and they know what you are about. They know it, because you have a quality referred to as "transparency." You don't put up a false front; you don't intentionally send mixed messages. To put it simply: **You *are* who you *say* you are**.

~

Being genuine means that *who you appear to be*, is indeed who you *actually are*. It means that the way you appear to be, is, in fact, the way that you really are. Being genuine means that there is nothing fake about you. It means that you are authentic, that you are 100 percent real. Make that: 100 percent *REAL*.

~ So, the question is… Are You Genuine?

~

"The shortest and surest way to live with honor in the world
is to be in reality what we would appear to be."

~ Socrates

Always Be Yourself, and Always Live By Your Principles

No person, event, or circumstance should cause you to change your principles.
If you let other people dictate how you think and act, then your life will never be stable and you will never be strong enough to stand on your own, especially during times of adversity and trial.

      If you set yourself firmly in your principles, however, then you will not be fazed by anything that happens to you, or by what anyone else does to you. You can never let the people around you define the kind of person you are, and you certainly can never allow others to decide what type of character you possess.

~

~ Always Be Yourself ~

Know who you are, and know who you are trying to become.
Know who you aren't, and know who you don't ever want to become.
Make your decisions in life according to your own expectations,
and live your life based on your own standards.

~

~ Be True to Yourself ~

Be true to who you are.
Be true to who you want to become.
Be true to the person you are today.
Be true to the person you wish to become tomorrow.
Keep to your ideals, and always live by your principles.
Know who you are, and always be who you are.
Know who you are working to become,
and always live up to your highest standards.
Be genuine at all times. Be true to yourself in all ways.
Be yourself, always. Be your *best self*, in *all ways*.

~

"With people of integrity, you know what you are going to get
because that person is the same way all the time; situations don't change them."

~ *Tony Dungy*

Know Who You Are, and Be Who You Are

Know who you are, and have the courage to be who you are. One of the most important things to understand in life is that… No matter where you go, no matter what you do, and no matter who you are around… **You should always be yourself.**

In a world where self-respect and self-esteem are greatly lacking, more and more people need to get a grip on who they really are and what they really want for their lives.

Too many people walk around this world pretending to be someone else. Sadly, we live in a world where not enough people know who they are. Even more unfortunate is the fact that very few people have the courage to actually be who they are.

Less people need to try to be like others, and more people need to stand up and be themselves. What each and every one of us needs to do is figure out who we are—and who we want to become—then have the strength and the courage to be that person.

~

~ Know Who You Are, and Be Who You Are ~

Don't go through life pretending to be someone else.
Have the courage to be yourself. Don't try to be who you aren't.
Know who you are, and Be who you are.

~

~ Be Strong Enough To Be Different ~

Be strong enough to be different.
Have the courage to be yourself.

~

The world doesn't want you to be like someone else.
The world needs you to stand up and be yourself.

~

Be strong enough to be different.
Have the courage to be yourself.

~

"Be who you are, and be that perfectly well."
~ *St. Francis de Sales*

Always Keep Your Word

Being a REAL man is about keeping your word. Whatever it is, if you say you are going to do something, then follow through and do it. That's part of what being responsible is about. A real man keeps his word; it's that simple.

Keep Your Word, and Keep Your Integrity

Whenever you give your word to someone, you have to follow through on it.
You have to keep your word, because that's the right thing to do; because that's the *respectable* thing to do.

Whenever you make a promise, you have to deliver on it. When you give your word that you are going to do something, you had better do it. Otherwise, don't make promises you don't intend to keep, and don't commit yourself to things that you aren't willing to follow through on, regardless of what might possibly happen in the future.

No one ever forces you to give your word. So, if you do indeed decide to give it—
and if you do decide to make a promise—then you had better follow through on it.
When you give your word, you have to keep it. Whether you want to or not is irrelevant.
You do what's right, simply because it's right. And keeping your word, no matter how difficult or unpleasant (or costly) it may turn out to be, is the right thing to do.

~

Always keep your word, in spite of the fact that it may be hard to do.
Always keep your word, in spite of the fact that it may cost you—either in terms of popularity, time, or in this case money… lots of money. Always keep your word, in spite of the fact that it may be difficult for you to do so, and regardless of whether or not you want to. Always keep your word, because it is the right thing to do…
because it is the honorable thing to do.

~

"Once you've given your word, stick to it."

~ John Wareham

It Takes A REAL Man To Keep His Word

Any man can give his word. It takes a REAL man to keep it.
If you give your word to another, then stay true to it.
If you give your promise to someone, then hold tightly to it.
If you say you are going to do something, then follow through and do it.
If you say that you are reliable, then go ahead and prove it.

"Breaking of your word is a folly, a dishonor, and a crime.
It is a folly, because no one will trust you afterwards; and it is both a dishonor
and a crime, truth being the first duty of religion and morality…
and whoever has not truth, cannot be supposed to have any one good quality."

~ Lord Philip Stanhope Chesterfield

Keep Your Word, Even If It Costs You ... *Especially* If It Costs You

There are times when keeping your word may cost you personally. Doing the right thing and staying true to your word may cost you in terms of your popularity. It may cost you in terms of your time or energy. It may cost you in terms of your convenience. It may even cost you in terms of your money. However, doing the right thing and keeping your word will save you something far more valuable than any of the above things. While it may cost you in terms of financial wealth or material possessions, keeping your word will save you perhaps the most valuable possession that you have: your *integrity*.

~

While you may be losing your popularity, status, time, or even money by keeping your word... you will be saving a few things of far greater value. Namely among them are: your *Integrity*, your *Dignity*, your *Trustworthiness*, your *Respectability*, the *Respect of Others*, and your own *Self-Respect* as well.

In addition to all of these "savings," you also will be able to hold onto your *Good Name*, your *Dependable Reputation* (also known as that priceless "You-Can-Count-On-Me" factor); and, perhaps most important of all, you will be able to maintain your *Honor*.

~

Sure keeping your word may cost you in some way. But, when you look at what you will be *saving* by following through on your commitment, it really adds up to a whole lot more than what mere money can buy. That is because, ultimately, when you get right to the heart of the matter, you realize that money is tied merely to your bank account. **Your word**, however, is tied to something much more important than just your "bottom line." It's tied to your **Integrity**.

~

"You have to live by your principles,
even if it costs you ... Especially if it costs you."
~ Bo Schembechler

Keep Your Word, & Don't Count The Cost

Guard your dignity and protect your integrity.
No matter what happens, and no matter what you may lose in the process:
Make sure that you always hold onto your integrity.
Keeping your word might cost you.
But, the one thing you can't put a price tag on, is integrity.
Preserve your integrity at all costs.

~

"If you give someone your word,
you have to realize what that means.
Your word is the most important possession you have.
If I tell someone I will do something or be somewhere,
I will do everything within my power to do it."
~ Fisher DeBerry

Always Honor Your Commitments

Always Honor Your Commitments

Being a REAL man is about honoring your commitments. Whatever it is, if you make a commitment to do something, then follow through on that commitment and do it. That's part of what being a responsible and accountable person is about. That's what being a real man is all about. A real man honors his commitments; it's that simple.

~

If you say you are going to do something, then follow through and do it.
If you say you are reliable, then go ahead and prove it.

Commitment ~ A Rare and Precious Thing In Today's Society

Commitment is a rarity these days, unfortunately. Everywhere you turn in our society, it seems as if people have forgotten, or simply ignored, the meaning of true commitment. Everywhere you look, the ill effects that stem from a lack of commitment can be found wreaking havoc on our culture.

You see it in marriages, with more than 50 percent of unions ending in divorce or separation. You see it in the working world, where employers hire and fire people at will, and where people change companies at the drop of a hat. You see it in coaching, where schools and teams will sign a head coach to a five-year contract and then turn around and fire him or her two years later. You see coaches sign a five-year contract and then break it two years in to leave for a better job.

~

The sad truth is that many people don't live up to their responsibilities and don't live out their commitments. The people who do—the ones who remain faithful and loyal to the people and purposes they commit to—are worthy of great respect and admiration. Such people are to be highly esteemed, as they are a rare and special breed. In an all-too-casual world where most people are satisfied with being common, it is the uncommon man—the man who stands by and carries out his commitments—who makes a lasting impact on the world. This honorable and dutiful man—this uniquely *uncommon* man— is both the backbone of our present society, and the hope of our future world.

~

The world does not need any more common souls who will settle for average mediocrity. The world needs uncommon men who will do something special with their lives and who will mold society into a better and greater place.

~

Do Something Special With Your Life.
Become Someone Special In Your Lifetime.

~

Commitment ~ An Uncommon and Special Attribute In Today's World

All-too-common is the man who will quit and relinquish his dream merely for the sake of convenience; average is the person who will give in when he has gotten tired from hard work and when he has grown selfishly annoyed with his sacrifices. **Uncommon** is the man who can stick to his purpose, no matter how difficult, trying, or unpleasant it may be to do so; **special** is the person who will give all that he has to give, in order to live *by*— and live *up*—to his commitments.

The first of these two types of people simply go through the motions in life. They never really accomplish anything because they never really work long enough to bring anything worthwhile to bear. The second type—*the uncommon and special type of person*—accomplishes a great multitude of significant achievements. Such people invest themselves wholeheartedly into their pursuits, and thus, they are able to bring many and great dreams to fruition.

~

It is not the common man who does anything worthwhile; nor is it the average person who leads the world onward. It is the **uncommon** man who carries society forward. It is the **special** person who illuminates the future or our world, by forging boldly ahead with unmatched courage and conviction.

It is the uncommon and special individual who lives his life with desire and determination, who lives by his words, who lives out his commitments, and who lives for some purpose greater than himself. It is the uncommon and special person who lays the foundation for an excellent and noble world.

~

Do not settle for what society expects of you. Exceed expectations and live extraordinarily. Do not be common. Do not be average. Strive for excellence. Work for greatness. **Be Uncommon. Be Special.**

~

"Success is uncommon, therefore not to be enjoyed by the common man.
*I'm looking for **Uncommon** people."*

~ Cal Stoll

Commitment Means… Finishing What You Start

Commitment means finishing what you start.
It means following through on what you say that you are going to do.
Commitment means valuing your words and keeping your promises.
It means honoring your responsibilities and fulfilling your obligations.
Commitment means starting something that is worth doing; but more importantly,
Commitment means finishing off everything that you start.

~

A promise is made with a start,
But a commitment is realized when you finish what you begin.

~

"Commitment is finishing what you begin."

~ Fisher DeBerry

The Commitment Hall of Fame

Eddie Robinson

~ Head Coach, Grambling State University ~

Coach Eddie Robinson retired from Grambling State University as the NCAA's all-time winningest Division 1 college football head coach. He had the same job for 57+ years, and he was married to the same wife for 65+ years.

John Gagliardi

~ Head Coach, St. John's College of Minnesota ~

Coach John Gagiardi has spent neary six decades at St. John's of Minnesota. He currently is the NCAA's all-time winningest college football head coach at any level. Gagliardi has had the same job for 57+ years, and he has bee married to the same wife for 54+ years.

Joe Paterno

~ Head Coach, Penn State University ~

Coach Joe Paterno has served the Penn State University football program for more than a half-century. He currently is the NCAA's all-time winningest Division 1-A (FBS) college football coach. Coach Paterno has been at the same school for 54+ years, and he has been married to the same wife for 48+ years.

John McKissick

~ Head Coach, Summerville High School; Summerville, South Carolina ~

Coach John McKissick has been the head coach at South Carolina's Summerville High School for nearly six decades. He currently ranks as the nation's all-time winningest high school football head coach. Coach McKissick has held the same job for 58+ years, and he has been married to the same wife for 55+ years.

Between them, these four men have dedicated themselves to nearly 450 years of family and football, remaining faithful to their professions and their wives for almost half a millennium. ~ Now that's commitment!

You Must Live Commitment

Each of the men in the Commitment Hall of Fame is at the top of his profession, and each is the all-time winningest coach at his respective level. In addition to the great deal of success that each man has had, every single one of these men has made a commitment to his school and to his wife. More importantly, every single one has *kept* his commitments.

In addition to their great degree of professional success, these men all have one very important thing in common: they all made commitment *a way of life*. All these men understood the true value of commitment. Each made a lasting commitment to his program and to his wife—and in truth, a *lasting commitment* is the only real type of commitment there is. When you realize the importance each of these men placed on making and keeping their commitments, the level of success that each enjoyed should come as no surprise. After all, commitment is a very powerful thing, and it shows itself in every aspect of a person's life. *~ Commitment will show itself in every aspect of a person's life. You cannot merely talk about commitment. You must live it.*

Always Be Humble

The Essence of Humility
Humility is about being able to see yourself in proper perspective, both in terms of you who really are and with regard to others. It requires that you first be able to understand the nature of your own life: that you are a human being, and that you therefore are worthy of all the respect and dignity that are due to any—and every—human being. Having humility also requires you to understand the nature of all life: that all people are people, and that all people therefore are worthy of all the respect and dignity due to any—and every—human being.

Humility is about being able to see yourself for everything that you are, everything that you are not, and everything that you are capable of becoming. It requires that you be aware of your strengths and weakness, and that you actively search for ways to improve upon each. Having humility means understanding that you are not perfect, and that for as long as you live, you will always be able to become better and more complete in some aspect of yourself or in some area of your life. It means knowing that you never have a reason to think that you are superior to anyone else, or that anyone else is inferior to you. Having humility means understanding that you are just as important—never more, and never less—than anyone and everyone else; that all people, yourself included, are equally important members of humanity.

Humility is about being able to see yourself in proper perspective to other people as well. It means understanding that you are part of something that is far bigger than your own self and your own life. It means realizing that you belong to a greater team; that you are a member of a greater family. Having humility means recognizing that you are an equal member—just as everyone else is—of the *human* team and the *human* family; that you are an important part of the whole of humanity. Having humility means recognizing that all people—regardless of race, creed, gender, or anything else—are all equally important members of that whole as well. Having humility means understanding that you are not superior to other people; but neither are you inferior either. Having humility means understanding that you are no better than anyone else; but that you are no worse than anyone else either.

~

"Humility is a true knowledge of oneself as one is."
~ M. Scott Peck

~

Being humble means not drawing attention to yourself, but giving attention to others who are equally—or even more so—deserving of attention themselves. Being humble means not trying to be the center of attention; it means not showing off or praising yourself, but instead being modest and gracious at all times. Acting humbly means deflecting any praise that you may receive onto others, and acknowledging the efforts and contributions of others before accepting any acclaim for your own accomplishments.

Being humble is not about basking in your own individual glory; nor is it about boasting of your own individual accolades. Being humble means realizing, recognizing, and acknowledging the contributions of others who have helped you succeed. It means expressing gratitude for any and all help that you may receive from others. It means showing appreciation for other people's efforts, and offering those people thanks by giving them encouragement and praise for their hard work.

On a team, it may mean pointing out the block of a teammate that allowed you to make a big play; it may mean pointing out a great pass that allowed you to score, or it may mean thanking your entire team and coaching staff for their hard work in helping you to have a great game.

In your daily life, being humble may mean showing your appreciation to loved ones for their continual support and encouragement. It may mean expressing your gratitude to co-workers or associates for their efforts to help succeed in your business endeavors or in your career. It may mean showing your thanks to a teacher or coach for their work in helping you to succeed in the classroom or on the playing field. It may mean showing your appreciation to friends and family for the things they have given to you, or for the things they have done for you.

Regardless of how you choose to show your gratitude and appreciation for others, the important thing is that you actually show it, some how and in some way.
Regardless of what your particular notion of humility might be, or what humility means to you… the important thing is that you have it: that you act with modesty and humility, that you recognize and acknowledge the efforts of others, that you do your best not to draw attention to yourself and to instead deflect any praise you may receive onto others, and that you carry yourself with class and dignity at all times.

Humility is one of the most honorable of all virtues. It is one of the highest ideals and qualities that a man can possess. Humility is one of the ultimate forms of respect, because it shows respect not only for oneself, but for other people as well, and also for all of life itself. People who have humility are respected and admired greatly. They are a joy to be around, because they always offer acknowledgement and encouragement to others. People who show humility and who act modestly are a pleasure to be with, because they make other people feel valued, appreciated, and important… at all times, and in all ways.

~

"Humility comes before honor"
~ Book of Proverbs: 15:33

~

Be Humble and Stay Humble

One of my old football coaches always used to talk about the importance of being humble. He would always impress upon us the idea that, no matter how good we may have been, that there were always other teams and other athletes out there that were better. At the very least, there was always the potential within ourselves to become even better than we already were. In either case, it was important not to get complacent with who we were, or with what we had done. Regardless of what we had already accomplished, there was always still more that could have been done, and there was always more that needed to be done in the future.

My former coach taught us the importance of staying humble, no matter how good we may have been, or how good we may have thought we were. It was important to understand that there was always more work to be done, always more progress to be made, and that we should never become overconfident or develop feelings of superiority.

~

No matter how good you are, and no matter how good you may think you are, there is always some team out there—and some athlete out there too—that is capable of doing more. At the very least, *you* are always capable of doing more. No matter how much you have accomplished, someone has done more; and ultimately, you are capable of doing more. *Good* can always be *great*. *Hard* work can always be *harder* work.

Never let yourself be satisfied with what you have done, and never allow yourself to think that you are above anyone else. Stay humble and stay hungry.

Keep your sense of perspective, keep your sense of humility, and above all, keep working to continue to get better. Never become complacent, and never become overconfident. If you do, someone, somewhere will eventually find you and prove you wrong; and when they do, it will not be pleasant. Be humble and stay humble.

~

"Accept that we're all pretty small potatoes.
Yet always know how great each of us can be."
~ Joe Paterno

Remain Humble, For Your Own Safety's Sake

It's nice to be in a position of power and success. Everyone enjoys such roles, and conversely, everyone strongly dislikes losing and the lower status that comes with it. Yet life is cyclical. There are ups and downs, spread through life in an unending landscape of peaks and valleys. When we find ourselves at the bottom of the ladder, it is important to remain humble.

Success is not a birth right, it is a privilege. No one is entitled to achievement simply because they bare a certain name or have a particular title. Anything of value in life has to be earned through hard work and persistence. Each of us is bound to experience the low points just as much as the high ones, if not more. If we approach those high points with humility, we can learn a valuable lesson about ourselves. For if we are not on top, there is a reason for it.

Often times, we are not ready to handle success at a particular time in our lives. Trial and tribulation prepare us both to face challenges and accept achievement. When you find yourself at the bottom of a valley, always remain humble. Keep your head up, keep thinking positively, and keep your feet moving forward. You may be in a valley, but that means that you are still standing in front of a mountain.

Your humility and graciousness in defeat will determine the extent to which you will succeed in the future. And when you do succeed, remember where you came from and that mountains are always surrounded by valleys. When you are on top, everyone will try to bring you back down to the bottom. That is when it is most important to remain humble. After all, people are determined enough to knock you off the mountain top, there is no need to provide them with any further motivation.

Wherever you are in your life's journey, always be humble. Wherever you find yourself—whether on top of a grand mountain or in the depths of a deep valley—always remain humble. If you can stay patient and modest, then you will find the footing much more solid. (Plus, people won't be throwing as many rocks at you on your climb as well. That always makes for an easier climb.)

~

"Be very, very humble."

~ The Talmud (Ethics of the Fathers 4:4)

~

Be Humble … Or Somebody is Going To Make You Humble

"Be humble, or somebody is going to make you humble."

That warning is simple and accurate enough. Regardless of whatever it is that you are doing, and regardless of whoever it is that you are, one things always remains true: if you get overconfident and full of yourself, then someone else or something else is going to come along and knock you off your high horse.

The universe always has a way of balancing itself out. The Law of Gravity tells us that "what goes up must come down." Along similar lines, is what I like to refer to as The Law of Humility, which says that "**At the end of the day, you are going to be humble**. One way or another—either by your own choosing, or by someone else's doing—you are going to be humble."

You can either learn to be humble on your own, or you can have someone or some set of circumstances come along and make you humble. To put it simply… be humble, or get humbled.

It is a lot easier to do things the first way.

~

"Be humble, or somebody is going to make you humble."

~ P. J. Kavanagh

Always Tell The Truth

Always Be Honest

Being honest means always telling the truth… the whole truth… and nothing but the truth. It means being truthful at all times, and in all ways. Being honest means telling the truth, in its accurate entirety: not distorting it in any way, not adding to it or leaving anything out of it, and not embellishing or diminishing by any means.

Being honest means always telling the truth… always. It means speaking the truth, even if it is inconvenient… *especially* if it is inconvenient. It means telling the truth, even when it costs you… *especially* when it costs you.

You can never be wrong if you always do what is right. Likewise, you can never be in the wrong if you always *say* what is right.

~

"If it is not right do not do it; if it is not true do not say it."
~ Marcus Aurelius

Honor and Honesty

There are certain virtues that a man must possess in order to have honor. One of the very first of these virtues is honesty. Without honesty, a man can never be truly responsible or trustworthy. He cannot be responsible, either to himself or to others, because he can never be fully honest with himself in terms of what he is obligated to do, and with regard to holding himself accountable for doing it. He cannot be trustworthy in the eyes of others, because they will never be able to believe what he says. Therefore, honesty is a precursor to trust.

A man must possess the virtue of honesty before he can ever hope to develop the virtue of being trustworthy. He must maintain both honesty and trustworthiness, before he can ever hope to lay claim to the highest of all virtues: honor.

~

"Nothing is more essential than always to speak the truth."
~ Lord Philip Stanhope Chesterfield

Always Tell the Truth, Because Ultimately…The Truth Always Rises to the Top

The truth always has a way of making itself known. If you proclaim it, then others will hear it in your voice. If you do not, then rest assured that someone else will proclaim in your place. One way or another, the truth will make itself heard.

The truth always rises to the top. Whether you bring it to the surface or not, the fact of the matter is that someone—or something—ultimately will. One way or another, the truth always has a way of making itself known. Like the cream that rises to the top of the glass, and like the sun that rises in the morning sky, the truth always rises to the top.

~ Be honest at all times.
    ~ Be honest in all things.

100% Truth, 100% of the Time
A man who is not honest at all times, is not an honest man.
A man who is not honest all the time, is not honest, period.

~

A person who tells the truth 99% of the time cannot be counted on 100% of the time.
A person who cannot be trusted all the time, cannot be trusted at any time.
When it comes to the percentage of time that a man must tell the truth, it has got to be one hundred. Because, as the legendary James Brown sang it, *99½ just won't do.*

~

A man who tells the truth 99% of the time can never really be trusted.
After all, you never know when that one percent of the time will be.

~

~

The Time for Truth Is Always At Hand

The moment of truth may come but rarely,
But the moment *for* the truth is always at hand.
The time for honesty is always upon us,
The time for truth is always at hand.

When it comes to telling the truth:
Now is as good a time as any,
And any is as good a time as now.

~ Honesty has no office hours.
~ There time is always right for speaking the truth.

~

~

Dare to be honest.
Have the courage to tell the truth.
~
An honest man is respected by everyone,
even if what he has to say is not agreed upon by anyone.
~
*"I hope I shall possess firmness and virtue enough
to maintain what I consider the most enviable of all titles…*
the character of an honest man."

~ *George Washington*

~

Be Responsible and Be Accountable

Always Be Responsible

Being responsible is about keeping your word, following through on your promises, fulfilling obligations, and honoring your commitments. Being responsible means making good choices, thinking things through before making important decisions, considering the consequences of your actions, and considering who might be affected by the decisions you make and by the actions you take.

Being responsible for yourself means being where you're supposed to be, when you're supposed to be there; and doing what you're supposed to do when you get there. It means being on-time and prepared. Being responsible for yourself means being ready to perform what is expected of you. It means being willing to go the extra mile to exceed the minimum requirements and basic expectations.

Being responsible to others means understanding the long-term consequences of your choices, taking ownership of your decisions and actions—both good and bad—and being accountable for those decisions and actions to others. It means putting the concerns and considerations of others before your own wants and desires.

Being responsible for your decisions means making good decisions and putting yourself in good situations. It involves thinking through to what the possible outcomes of your actions may be, and choosing to act accordingly based on what's appropriate.

Being responsible for your actions means first making good decisions, and then following through on those good decisions. Being responsible for your actions also means being accountable to others for the consequences of your actions. It means taking ownership of your choices and actions, and also the results that those choices and actions produce.

~

"The ultimate sign of maturity is taking responsibility for your own actions."
~ *Daniel Harkavy*

~

"The price of greatness is responsibility."
~ *Sir Winston Churchill*

Always Be Accountable

Accountability is about nothing more than taking ownership of your choices and your actions, and the results that those choices and actions produce. Being accountable means taking ownership of your actions. More importantly, being accountable means taking ownership for the consequences of those actions.

Being accountable also means assuming ownership of your *inactions* as well—of what you do *not* do, but should do: of what you did *not* do, but should have done. It means taking responsibility for the consequences of your failure to act.

Being accountable means not blaming others, and not making excuses for yourself. Blaming and making excuses are both ways of transferring responsibility to other sources—taking it off you and putting it on others or on circumstances.

Being accountable means taking ownership for both your actions and your inactions; it means assuming responsibility for what you do and do not do, and for the consequences of either your actions or inactions.

Ultimately, being accountable means being answerable to others, to yourself, to the ideals of truth and honor, and to your Creator.

~

Being accountable means not complaining, not making excuses for yourself, and not blaming others. It means taking responsibility for your actions, and more importantly, for the consequences of your actions.

Don't Complain, and Don't Make Excuses.

You cannot allow yourself to make excuses.
Take what life gives you and make the most of it.

Three Maxims
1. Don't complain about your problems: find a solution to them.
2. Don't blame other people: take responsibility for yourself.
3. Don't make excuses: find a way to get the job done.

"Excuses build bridges to nowhere." ~ Lee Huguley

Take Responsibility for Your Actions

Don't whine. Don't complain. Don't make excuses. Don't blame others.
Assume responsibility for your situation, and accept responsibility for your life. Take responsibility for your actions at all times, and be accountable for them in all ways.

~

Make good decisions, and put yourself in good situations.
Think through to what the possible outcomes of your choices might be,
and understand that whenever you choose an action, you also indirectly choose the consequence that goes with that action. Be responsible for your decisions and for your actions, and always be accountable for their consequences.

~

**The more responsible you are with your actions,
the easier it is to be accountable for them.**

A Question of Responsibility and Accountability ~ "How Do You Handle It?"

At some point in your life, no matter how perfect you try to be and no matter how good a person you try to be, you are going to make a mistake…maybe even a really big one. It doesn't matter if you've been a model citizen for 50 years, or a great friend or father or mother…at some point you're going to make a mistake. When that happens, the most important thing is not the mistake itself; it's about how you handle it. It's not what you did, but what you do from that moment on that will matter most.

When the time comes, you will have a choice to make. You can take the easy way out and handle things the wrong way (i.e. - you can try to cover up your mistake, blame others for it, you can get discouraged and let the mistake bring you down and maybe even ruin you). OR, you can choose to handle it with **class**—you can take responsibility for your mistake, swallow your pride and own up to it, and do all you can to move forward in a positive direction.

When you make a mistake, you have to accept responsibility for it and do the right thing. Don't try to run from something, because it will always catch up to you. Own up to your mistakes and face the consequences…in short: always handle things with class.

~

Do not show me a man's mistakes. Show me how he responds to them,
so that I may see what he truly is made of.

~

Own Up to Mistakes; Be Responsible and Accountable for Your Decisions

If you make a mistake, own up to it.
Admit your mistake, learn from it, and move on.
Don't try to run from something, because it will always catch up to you.
If you make a bad decision, then own up to it.

We all make mistakes from time to time.
The important thing to understand is that when you do make a mistake, you have to take ownership of it and face the consequences. That's what being mature is all about.
That's what having character is all about.
That's what being a REAL man is all about.

~

"Take responsibility for your actions.
If you make a mistake, admit it. If you hurt someone's feelings or say
something that you shouldn't, then apologize. Learning to be responsible and accountable
means learning to be a person of honor and integrity—it means being a person of character,
and being a person of character is a goal we should all set for ourselves."

~ Unknown Author

<u>Be Reliable and Be Dependable</u>

The Nature of Reliability and Dependability

Being reliable and dependable means doing what other people expect you to do, when they expect you to do it, and doing it the way they expect you to do it… if not even better. Being reliable and dependable means doing what other people count on you to do; it means doing what other people *need* you to do.

After all, life is a team sport, and each of us relies on other people in order to become successful, and in order to effectively make it through the day. Life is a team sport, and therefore, other people rely on each of us in order to become successful, and in order to effectively make it through their day as well.

~

~

The Essence of Reliable and Dependable People

Someone who is reliable, first and foremost, does not let himself down. He realizes the expectations both he and others place upon him, and therefore, knows the importance of being reliable.

A reliable person arrives when he is expected to arrive, works as he is expected to work, and often exceeds the demands which others have of him. He sets an example through his deeds, and is not afraid of a difficult task. A reliable person does not need to ask for responsibility, or tell people that he is responsible—others will see it in that which he has done and that which he continues to do.

~

~

Someone Who Is Reliable and Dependable

Someone who is reliable and dependable always comes through and does what he says he is going to do. If he makes an obligation, you can be sure that he will fulfill it. If he takes on a responsibility, you can be sure that he will live up to it. Whatever it is that a reliable and dependable person says that he is going to do, you can always be sure of one thing: no matter what, no matter where, and no matter what he has to deal with in order to do what he said he would do… he is going to come through.

To put it simply: if a reliable and dependable person says he is going to do something or be somewhere… You can carve it in stone.

~

~

"There are three principles of dependability: taking full responsibility for the task; following the task through to fulfillment; and standing by the result."

~ Travis Lamb

Finish the Job; Bring the Ship In

Being reliable and dependable means that people can count on you to do what you're supposed to do. It means that they can count on you to finish what you start. Being reliable and dependable means that people can count on you to DO YOUR JOB, and more importantly, to FINISH THE JOB.

~

Doing what you say you are going to do.
Walk your talk. Deliver the goods.
Take care of business. Take care of what needs to be taken care of.
Do what needs to be done, and do it when it needs to be done.
Do what must be done, and do it the best it can be done.
Get it done. No excuses, no explanations… no exceptions.
Don't make excuses, just get the job done.

"Don't tell me how rough the sea is, just bring the ship in."
~ Vince Lombardi

Be Reliable and Be Dependable

~ Keep your word. Honor your commitments.
~ Fulfill your responsibilities. Follow through on your obligations.
~ Do what you say you are going to do. Deliver on your promises.
~ Be on-time. Be early.
~ Get the job done. Finish what you start.

~

"No excuses; get it done."
~ Dan Hawkins

You Have To Earn Your Reputation As A Reliable Person

Many people seek to burden themselves with responsibility, yet not many are willing to earn it. In order to be seen as responsible, and thus be given responsibilities, you must first prove yourself to be a capable and reliable person.

~

Be reliable and be dependable.
Be responsible for yourself and for your actions, and be accountable to others.
If you say you're going to do something, then do it.
If you say you're going to be somewhere at a certain time, then be there.

Be responsible. Be accountable. Be reliable. Be dependable.

Be Trustworthy: Earn People's Trust

Make Deposits in the Bank of Trust

You earn people's future trust by what you do in the present. By demonstrating responsibility, accountability, reliability, and dependability, you prove to others that you are worthy of their faith and trust. By acting humbly, speaking honestly, always carrying yourself respectably, you build up your amount of "trust credit." In other words, every time you do and say the right things, you make deposits into the Bank of Trust.

~

You earn people's future trust by being trustworthy in the present. Each and every time you do what you say you are going to do, be where you say you are going to be, do what you are supposed to do, and be where you are supposed to be… you give people yet another reason to put their trust in you.

You also earn people's trust by keeping your word. Each and every time you give your word to someone and keep it, you prove yourself worthy of being trusted to follow through on your word in the future. Each and every time you honor your commitments, you establish yourself as someone who can be counted on. When you give your word and keep it, it shows people that you are reliable and dependable. When you say you are going to do something and do it, it shows others that you are responsible and accountable.

In addition, you also can earn people's trust by telling the truth… at all times, and in all ways. Each and every time you tell the truth, you make deposits into the Bank of Trust. Every time you are honest about the past, and every time that you tell the truth in the present, you assure people's trust in the future. You give people a reason to believe in what you say, and that what you will say in the future will be both accurate and true. Each time that you speak honestly and humbly, you add one more deposit into the Bank of Trust. The more deposits you make—the more times you are truthful in the present and about what happened in the past—the more trustworthy and credible you become in other people's eyes.

~

You gain people's trust when you show them that you are reliable, dependable, responsible, and accountable. You earn people's future trust by being truthful in the present, and by being honest about what happened in the past. If you say you will do something, do it. If you say you will be somewhere at a certain time, be there. If you make a commitment, follow through on it. If you say something, make sure it is true. If you make a mistake, be humble enough to own up to it and try to set things right.

The Building Blocks of Trust

Responsibility, accountability, reliability, and dependability are the building blocks of trustworthiness. Responsibility translates into reliability; accountability translates into dependability; and reliability and dependability ultimately work together to create the foundation for TRUST.

Be responsible. Be accountable. Be reliable. Be dependable.
Be honest. Be truthful. Be respect-worthy. Be Trustworthy.

Trust Creates the Foundation for Success

Trust creates the foundation for success in sports, business, relationships, and life.
A team cannot be successful without trust. A business cannot be successful without trust.
A family cannot be successful without trust.

~

In sports, you cannot have a successful team without first having trust.
In business, you cannot have successful partnerships without first having trust.
In life, you cannot have successful relationships without first having trust.

~

In sports, your teammates must be able to trust you.
They have to be able to count on you being where you are expected to be, when you are
expected to be there, and doing what you are expected to do when you get there.

~

In business, your co-workers must be able to trust you.
They have to be able to count on you to do your job, when you are supposed to do
your job, and the best way that you possibly can do it.

~

In life, your friends and family members must be able to trust you.
They have to be able to count on you to do what you need to do, when you need to do it,
and to do it the best way that you possibly can do it… in order to be there for your
family, support your family, and take care of your family.

~ Reliable and Dependable ~

In every walk of life, people have to be able to trust you.
In anything and in everything that you do, people have to be able to count on you.
In order to be trusted, and in order to be counted on, you have to be
Reliable and Dependable.

"There are only two types of ability that you need in this world:
Reliability and Dependability."

~ Sylvester Croom

Always Keep Your Composure

Always Keep Your Composure
Part of being responsible means acting with self-control at all times, and handling yourself in a mature and rationale way in all situations. This means being able to conduct yourself with poise and composure, as well as respect for those around you.

Being responsible for yourself involves carrying yourself the right way, and with class, at all times. Part of this is being able to conduct yourself with poise and composure, as well as respect for those around you. It means taking the High Road when tempted to retaliate against someone; it means knowing when to stand up for what you believe in, and when to step away from a potentially dangerous situation; it means knowing when to let cooler heads prevail, and when something simply is not worth losing your composure over.

Always Be In Control of Yourself:
Never let other people or outside circumstances cause you to lose your composure. Keep your poise, remain calm, and always think before you speak or act. Understand the importance of carrying yourself with class at all times, and realize that any and every decision you make has the potential to impact your own life, as well as the lives of others. Do not allow one moment of anger or passion to cause you to lose control of yourself or your life. Control your emotions, control your compulsions, control your desires, control your behaviors, control your habits, control your tongue, and control your temper. Control yourself, and control your life.

Always Think Before You Act
Whenever you find yourself getting angry, always take a moment to stop and think for a second. Take a minute to gather yourself. Take a deep breath if you need to, but always stop and collect yourself before speaking or acting.

Whenever you do something or say something out of anger, nothing good ever happens. Relationships are hurt, friendships are ruined, property is damaged, and fingers are broken (usually on a wall or some other target of aggression.) Be aware of your emotional state, and always be careful. If you find yourself getting angry, take a moment to stop and think. Make sure you don't say something or do something that you will regret in the future.

Take a chill-pill: It is always better to not do something and not say something out of anger. Anything you do, you cannot undo. Anything you say, you cannot take back. Always keep this in mind, and always stop and think before you act.

~

Always stop and think before you speak.
Always stop and think before you act.

<u>Always Think Before You Act</u>

Always think things through.
Always think before you speak or act.
Always think of the consequences before you act.

~

"Whatever is begun in anger ends in shame."
~ Benjamin Franklin

~

"How much more grievous are the consequences
of anger than the causes of it."
~ Marcus Aurelius

~

"A man of quick temper acts foolishly,
and a man of evil devices is hated."
~ Proverbs 14:17

~

"The surest way to lose is to lose your composure."

~ George Allen

~ Before you act, think of the consequences. ~

Keep Your Poise: Stay Calm In the Face of Chaos

Staying calm allows you to think clearly. Being able to think clearly allows you to be able to act logically. Keeping your composure and remaining poised allows you to accurately assess the situation, think clearly about how you will address the situation, and then act logically to begin to resolve the situation.

Keeping your poise allows you to think clearly and act logically, giving you the best chance of being able to successfully resolve the situation and overcome the challenges you face. When adversity arises, when chaos begins to surface, and when crisis rears it ugly head, one of the best things that you can do is to remain calm. *The best thing* you can do is actually to become even calmer in the face of your circumstances.

~

The more chaotic the situation, the calmer you must become.
The more tumultuous the circumstances in which you find yourself,
the more you must learn to keep your poise.

~

Poise requires composure. In order to think clearly and act accordingly, you first have to be composed. You have to have your full faculties available: you have to have "your wits about you" in order to take-in and process what is happening around you. You must be able to see the situation fully and clearly, and then be able to think quickly and act appropriately in response.

Be alert and be aware. By being alert and aware of the situation—of what it is that you are doing, what your possible choices are in any given situation, what the potential outcomes of those decisions might be, who is around, and who also might be affected by the choices you make—you increase the chances that you will put yourself in good situations and make good decisions.

~

"Nothing gives one person so much advantage over another
as to remain cool and unruffled under all circumstances."

~ Thomas Jefferson

Becoming calm and remaining calm is the best way to keep your composure and to maintain your poise. Keeping your poise, above all, is the best way to respond to a difficult and trying situation. Keeping your poise allows you to accurately and objectively assess your circumstances, to think about what can be done and to determine what needs to be done, identifying what you should do, and then carrying out those actions in an effective and intelligent way.

~

"If you can keep your head when all about you are losing theirs…
Then … You'll be a man, my son." ~ Rudyard Kipling

One Play Can Change a Game; One Choice Can Change Your Life

In the sport of football, there may be 80-100 plays in a game. Any single one of those plays has the potential to change the game, or even to decide the final outcome. Over the course of an entire football game, there may only be a handful of plays that ultimately determine who wins and who loses. The important thing to understand is that those plays could happen at any moment. You never know which play might turn the momentum or change the game. It could be this play, it could be the next play. And so, you must always be alert, aware, and ready to meet the moment at hand.

You never know which play is going to decide the outcome of a game, and so you must approach each play—every single snap—as if it were the most important play of the game. You have to be fully poised, fully present in the moment, and ready to think clearly and act decisively. You cannot be over-emotional, otherwise your vision and your judgment will be clouded. You cannot be distracted or disinterested, otherwise your focus and motivation will be lost.

In the game of life, a person may make thousands of choices—some small and some big. And, just like in a football game, where any one play can make the difference; any one decision can make the difference in a person's life. Each choice has the potential to make or break a person's future. And, just like in the game of football, so too in life, you never know when one of those "key moments" is going to happen.

Therefore, you have to approach every decision, and every situation, as if it could be one of the most important choices you will ever make. You never know which decision will impact your life forever, and so you must always be ready—always alert, aware, and prepared to handle each situation with poise.

In order to make the right choices when it counts… when the "game is on the line" … you have to have your wits about you. You have to be poised and be able to stop and think before you do anything or say anything. Just like with each play in a football game, so too in life must you always be fully poised, fully present in the moment, and ready to think clearly and act intelligently. You can't be overly emotional, otherwise you might make a poor decision out of anger, or put yourself in a poor situation out of frustration. You cannot get distracted, otherwise you might make a bad choice that could cost you in the long-run. Keep your poise, keep your composure, and keep your wits about you. Be alert and be aware; be ready to think clearly and act intelligently. Always stop to think about what it is you are about to say or do… before you do something that you might regret for a very long time.

In a game of 100 plays, only a handful may ultimately determine the outcome. In a person's lifetime, a lifetime which may involve thousands of choices, only a few of those choices may ultimately decide the way that person's life unfolds. In football and in life, you never know when the "big plays" or the "big decisions" are going to happen. Only one or two of them might end up making the big difference in the grand scheme of things; and you never know which play—or which decision—will end up being one of them. Therefore, you always have to be alert and ready. You always have to be poised and focused, prepared for each play and each decision that you face. You have to approach every single play, and every single decision, as if it were going to be the most important one of your life… because eventually, one of them will be.

~ Always keep your poise, and always be steady. ~
~ Always be prepared, and always be ready. ~

Always Take the High Road

Timing Is Everything ~ It's Important To Know When To...

It has been said that timing is everything in life. And so, it would seem important then to always know when to do certain things. An interesting thought. Let's explore it further:

~

In life, it's important not only to know *how* to do the following, but also *when* to do them as well:

Know when to honest.
Know when to be patient.
Know when to be understanding.
Know when to be forgiving.

Know when to be open to new ideas.
Know when to be open to new people.
Know when to be open to new opportunities.
Know when to be open to new experiences.

Know when to do your best.
Know when to give your all.
Know when to seek perfection.
Know when to strive for excellence.

Know when to believe in yourself.
Know when to have high expectations.
Know when to be optimistic.
Know when to be realistic.

Know when to be resilient.
Know when to keep persevering.
Know when to keep your composure.
Know when to continue achieving.

Know when to be kind.
Know when to be compassionate.
Know when to be fair.
Know when to be considerate.

Know when to be there for others.
Know when to *reach out* to others.
Know when to help out a friend in need.
Know when to help out a stranger in need.

Know when to be respectful to others.
Know when to be tactful in word.
Know when to be hopeful in your thought.
Know when to be helpful in deed.

Know when to keep your head up.
Know when to keep your guard up.
Know when to defend your dignity.
Know when to protect your integrity.

Know when to be true to yourself.
Know when to live by your principles.
Know when to stand up for what you believe in.
Know when to evaluate what you believe in.

Know when to uphold your honor.
Know when to oppose what is wrong.
Know when to stand your ground.
Know when to never back down.

Know when to keep your commitments.
Know when to be responsible.
Know when to keep your word.
Know when to be accountable.

Know when to appreciate all that you have.
Know when to be grateful for all that you've been given.
Know when to make the *most* of everything that you have.
Know when to make the *best* of everything that you have.

Know when to be humble.
Know when to be polite.
Know when to be courteous.
Know when to be unselfish.

Know when to tell the truth.
Know when to *seek* the truth.
Know when to be passionate about life... and …
Know when to do what is right.

~ So, how do you know *when* to do each of these things… ?
Good question. The answer is simple
The answer is … **ALWAYS**.

~ *You can never be wrong, if you always do what is right.* ~

Always Take The High Road, and Always Show Class

Sometimes people say things that get under our skin. Sometimes people say things that *really* get under our skin. And when that happens, most of us want to immediately retaliate; we want to respond with hurtful words of our own; we want to lash out and get back at that person or at those people. We want to get straight-up defensive, or down right offensive.

At moments like these, it is best to remember the following words: **Always take the High Road, and always show class.** Whether it's saying something hurtful, making a point or sending a message, or running up the score in an athletic contest… when it comes to wanting to retaliate, the best thing to do is to take the High Road.

No matter how upset or aggravated you may feel, it is always wisest to do your best to shake off the situation. Regardless of how insulted or disrespected you may feel, the best thing you can do is shrug off the comments and not let the other person anger you.

Always take the High Road, and always show class. Keep in mind that, just because someone else is being mean, doesn't mean that you have to be mean also. Just because someone else may be acting like a jerk, doesn't mean that you have to act like one also.

If someone is being rude, do your best to shake it off; don't compound the situation by adding even more hostility to it. Simply smile and go about your business. Don't make the situation worse by trying to retaliate. Doing so will only make you even more emotional, and it likely will incite the other person even further, which will cause them to act even more disrespectfully toward you than they already are… and the whole cycle will only keep escalating.

"The person who angers you, controls you."
~ Anonymous

Always take the High Road, and always show class.
Just smile and go about your business. As the saying goes, *wave goodbye to the haters.*

~

Let the quarrel die out, let the flames of rudeness or gossip die down. Walk away…
and when you do, make sure you take the High Road. You may not gain a victory in the argument—(*although really, when both people leave the situation angry and upset, neither person truly wins*)—but you will however, gain something more important as a result: *peace of mind.*

~

So, along those lines… it is always important to know when to do the following in life:

Know when to take the High Road.
Know when to show class instead.
Know when to let a quarrel die out.
Know when to leave something unsaid.

~ Always take the High Road, and always Show Class. ~

How Do You Treat Those Who Mistreat You?
The True Test of Your Character

How do you treat people who mistreat you? How do you respond to people who are mean to you? How do you act when people are cruel to you? What do you say when people are rude to you? … How do you treat those who mistreat you?

The way you respond to people who mistreat you is the true test of your character.

After all, anyone can be kind when other people are kind to them. Anyone can be polite when others are polite to begin with. However, it is how you respond to people who aren't kind to you that shows your true character

Anyone can do good things for people who do good things for them. Anyone can say nice things about people who speak nice words about them. However, it is how you react to people who try to hurt you, and it is what you say about those who try to slander you, that truly speaks to the quality of your character.

Anyone can show respect to people who show respect to them. However, it is how you respond to people who are mean and hurtful that shows your true character. It is how you treat people who are disrespectful to you, that shows your true level of class.

Anyone can treat people well who first treat them well. However, it is how you treat those who mistreat you, that really shows your true character.

~ How do you treat those who mistreat you?

~

"If you love those who love you, what credit is that to you? Even sinners love those who love them. And if you do good to those who are good to you, what credit is that to you? Even sinners do that. And if you lend to those from whom you expect repayment, what credit is that to you? Even sinners lend to sinners, expecting to be repaid in full. But love your enemies, do good to them."
~ *Luke 6:32-35 (from the Christian Faith Tradition)*

~

"Love your enemies, do good to those who hate you,
bless those who curse you, pray for those who mistreat you."
~ *Luke 6:27-28 (from the Christian Faith Tradition)*

~ **Be About Respect** ~

Be respectful to all people, no matter who they are or how they treat you.
Be respectful to others… not necessarily because they are respectful;
But because you are.

~

"It's easy to hate, it's harder to love…"
~ Maino, from the song 'All the Above'

~ Treat all people with respect, regardless of how they treat you. ~

Always Do The Right Thing

Do The Right Thing: Be True to What is Right
Uphold your highest loyalties: your loyalties to what is right and what is good.
Do what is right, because it is right… and for no other reason than this. Do not worry
about when to do the right thing, for the time to do the right thing is always. Do not
worry about how much good to do, for the amount of good to perform is always
as much as you possibly can. Always do the right thing; always be true to what is right.

~

"Always do what is right.
This will gratify some of the people and astonish the rest."
~ Mark Twain

~

Do the Right Thing Because…
You do the right thing … not because it's going to benefit you in some way, not because
it's the popular thing to do, and not because other people will like you for it … but you do
the right thing *simply because it's the right thing to do.*
There may be times when doing the right thing will benefit you in some way.
However, there may also be a lot of times when doing the right thing may cost you.
So what? **Do the right thing anyway!**

~

Always, always, always do the right thing. Do the right thing… even if it costs you…
especially if it costs you. Do the right thing, and don't worry about what you are going to
get out of it, or if it might cost you in some way. **Just do the right thing.**

You do the right thing… not because it is going to benefit you in some way—because in
fact, it usually is going to cost you in some way…

You do the right thing… not because it is going to make you more popular—in fact, it
probably is going to make you less popular…

You do the right thing… not because it is going to win you approval from others—in
fact, it probably is going to cost you in terms of some people's approval…

You do the right thing… simply because it is the right thing to do.
You do the right thing, for no other reason than because it is the right thing to do.
You do the right thing because… *it's the right thing to do.*
And truthfully, that is the only reason you need.

~

"You don't do the right thing because you have to do it.
You do it because it is the right thing to do."
~ Mark Sanborn

Just Do the Right Thing

Just do the right thing: Don't over-think things and make the situation more complicated than it needs to be. Focus on doing what is right and what is best, and then don't worry about the rest. If you do what is right and what is best... the rest will take care of itself.

Just do the right thing: because, if you do what is right and if you do what is best, then you won't have to worry about any of the rest. It will all take care of itself.

Just do the right thing: Don't make it harder than it needs to be. Just do the right thing, and forget about all the other stuff... like what it might cost you, or what you might be sacrificing, or what other people might think or say.

Just do the right thing.

~

Always do what's right and always do what's best...
And you'll never have to worry about the rest.

~

Do the right thing, no matter what the situation.
Make the right choices, no matter what the circumstances.

Do the right thing... the first time and every time.
Do the right thing... every time and all the time.

Are You Strong Enough to Do the Right Thing?

Are you strong enough to do the right thing even when no one else knows about it?
Are you strong enough to do the right thing even when it's difficult to do it?
Are you strong enough do the right thing even when it is unpopular?
Are you strong enough to do the right thing at all times, every time, all the time?

"There comes a time when one must take the position that is neither safe nor political nor popular, but he must do it because his conscience tells him it is right."
~ Dr. Martin Luther King, Jr.

~

"You don't do things right once in a while. You do them right all the time." ~ Vince Lombardi
~ You don't do the **right things** once in a while. You do the right things **all the time**." ~

~

"I love the man that can smile in trouble, that can gather strength from distress,
and grow brave by reflection. 'Tis the business of little minds to shrink;
but he whose heart is firm, and whose conscience approves his conduct,
will pursue his principles unto death."

~ Thomas Paine

The Reward For A Life Of Principle

It's not always easy to live by your principles. As a matter of fact, a lot of the time it's pretty hard to do. But, the sacrifices you make in doing so is more than worth it, because the reward you receive for living by your principles is not so much about what you get for it, but who you become as a result of it.

What you become is a person of character: a person who is respectable, reliable, and trustworthy—a person of conviction, who others look upon with admiration. You become someone who lives with honor, who has a positive effect on others, and who makes a worthwhile contribution in this world. And long after you leave, if you have lived by your principles and done your best to conduct yourself with integrity and class, you will have left your mark on the world. And in so doing, you will leave behind an enormously positive legacy.

~

There is no greater praise that can be given, no greater compliment that may be paid, than simply to be called *an honorable man.*

~

A Clear Conscience Is the Key To A Good Night's Sleep

Aside from his mattress and pillow, nothing has a greater effect on the quality of a man's sleep than his conscience. The conscience is a pillow for the soul, and nothing is softer to lay one's head upon than a clear and honest conscience. The conscience is the soul's pillow, and nothing is more rough and uncomfortable than a guilty one.

"There is no pillow as soft as a clear conscience."
~ *French Proverb*

Clean Thinking and Clean Living

The best rap sheet is a blank one, and the best conscience is a clear one.
Do the right things, and do them the right way, and you don't have to worry about getting in trouble. After all, there will be nothing to hold you culpable for, because there will be nothing that you will be guilty of.

~ Nothing creates a sound peace of mind
Like doing the right thing, each and every time.
Nothing creates a clear and healthy conscience
Like doing the noble and decent thing, every single time.

"Have impeccable integrity. It brings peace of mind and a reputation of honor."
~ *Hal Urban*

~ A Great Motto To Live By ~

~ If you always do what is right, you will always be able to sleep at night. ~

The List of *Never's*

If *doing the right thing* and *taking the High Road* are things that you should *always* do…
then what are some things in life that you should *never* do? An interesting thought…
Let's explore it further:

1. **Never be afraid of hard work.** It is the only road that leads to progress.
2. **Never make excuses**, and never allow others to make excuses for themselves.
3. **Never accept losing.** Never accept defeat. You may have to deal with defeat at certain points during your life, but always learn from those instances, use them as opportunities to improve yourself, and use them as fuel to motivate you to succeed the next time.
4. **Never accept anything less than your best**.
5. **Never be satisfied** with "good" when "better" is possible.

"Don't measure yourself by what you have accomplished,
but by what you should have accomplished with your ability." ~ John Wooden

6. **Never do something just to take part in it.** Work hard and enjoy your experiences, but never do anything that isn't worthwhile. Never run in a race just to run in it.
Run in it to win.
7. **Never give up.** In anything you do in life, never quit. Keep working hard. Too often, people give up right before their hard work and sacrifice is about to pay off. Keep persevering, keep hoping, and stay positive. Good things will happen.
8. **Never give in.** Do the right thing, at all times. Never compromise with what you know to be right. Even if it costs you… *especially* if it costs you.
9. **Never ask yourself if you've done enough**. Ask yourself *what more* can you do. Whether it's in your career, your training or athletic career, or you friendships and relationships: there is no such thing as ever doing enough or too much. You can always do more. Never be satisfied with what you've already done. Keep adding to it.
10. **Never compare yourself to someone else's potential**. Focus on your own potential, and do everything you can to work toward achieving it.
11. **Never let someone else or something else dictate your attitude.** Attitude is a choice, and it is entirely your choice. Ultimately, your life is determined by the way you react to each situation that you face. You may not get to choose your circumstances, but you do get to choose how you respond to them.
12. **Never let other people dictate your character.** Be yourself, and dictate your own character. Don't let someone else determine the choices you make and the actions you take. Be yourself, and be confident in yourself.

"Be who you are, and be that well." ~ St. Francis de Sales

13. **Never forget who you are. Never lose sight of who you want to become.**
Never forget where you came from; never lose sight of where you want to go.

~

~ Why should you have to settle, when you have the chance to be something special? ~

~

Be Respectful and Be Respectable

Be Respectful and Be Respectable ~ The Most Important Lesson In Life

At one point in my life, I found myself thinking about all the valuable lessons I had learned up until that time. I began wondering about which of those lessons might be the most vital of all to living a right and honorable life. And so, I challenged myself to determine what the most important lesson in life was.

I asked myself, if I could pass along just one piece of advice to others—one simple lesson to live by—what would it be? In other words, what would I consider the most important life lesson?

After a great deal of thought, I came up with the answer to my question. I did my best to make it as compact and comprehensive as possible. After much contemplation, here is what I have decided upon:

Be respectful to everyone you meet; **be respectable** in everything you do.

~

~ If I could leave only one thought in the hearts and minds of others,
that is what I would want it to be.

~

"Respect for ourselves guides our morals; respect for others guides our manners."

~ *Laurence Sterne*

~

Two Important Rules In Life

Rule #1: Always do the right thing.
Rule #2: When in doubt... refer to Rule #1.

No matter what happens to you in life...
Always do the right thing, and you will always be alright.

"There is but one test of everything, and that is, is it right?
If it is not right, turn away from it."

~ *Henry A. Wise*

~

Travel the path of integrity without looking back...
for there is never a wrong time to do the right thing."

~ *Ray Wilkerson*

L

Live a Life
That Matters

Live A Life That Matters

Live a life that matters

Being a REAL man is about striving for excellence in every aspect of life.
It is about always doing your very best to reach your full potential in this world.
Living a life that matters means striving to maximize your life, by making the most
of your talents, opportunities, and potential to impact others in a positive way.

Being a REAL man is about investing yourself in your own success, and more
importantly, in the success of others. Being a *real* man is about maximizing your life, as
well as the lives of those around you. It is about making a constant and consistent effort
to give the world your best, and it is about doing all that you can to help bring out the
best in others as well.

Being a REAL man means understanding that life is all about relationships. It's
no accident that we were put on this Earth with one another. If we were meant to live
selfishly and on our own, then we would have been put here by ourselves.

A REAL man knows that the two greatest things in life are to love and to be
loved. Therefore, he works hard to cultivate and maintain meaningful relationships.
A REAL man strives to be a leader of both himself and others, to be a role model for
others, and to be a positive presence in other people's lives. A REAL man tries to set an
example worth following and strives to live a life worth emulating.

~

Living a life that matters means living respectfully, responsibly, and honorably.
It means dedicating yourself to a life of personal excellence and social significance.
Living a life that matters is about going above and beyond the individual confines of your
own life, in order to reach out and help enhance the lives of those around you. It is about
positively affecting other people's lives and leaving your mark on the world in which you
live. Simply put, living a life that matters means doing your best, and giving your best,
to live well and to live right.

~

Live well and live right.
You only live once.
But, if you live well and if you live right…
Then once is exactly enough.

~

We are all part of something that is bigger than ourselves.
Live a life that matters.

~

"The greatest legacy we can leave behind is a memory of a life lived fully
and honorably, a life dedicated to being the best we can."

~ Lou Holtz

The Meaning of Life

The Reason for Living

The reason for living is *self-actualization for the purpose of serving others.*
The entire reason for living—the ultimate meaning of life—is to make the absolute most of your talents and opportunities, and to do it in service to some community that is greater than yourself. The meaning of life is to maximize your talents and opportunities, in order to maximize your influence in this world.

~

Make the most of your talents, opportunities, and potential impact on this world. Do all you can to become everything you are capable of becoming. Strive to live your best life, and endeavor to help others live their best lives as well.

Do your best to be your best.
Do your best to give your best to others.

The meaning of existence is to do everything you can to maximize your life, while helping others to maximize their lives as well; it is to do all that you can to work toward and reach your full potential, while assisting others as they continually work toward reaching their own full potential as well.

Make the most of yourself, so that you can do the most for others.

~ It's Amazing ~

It's amazing how much you can accomplish in life…
if you simply focus on doing everything you can to reach your full potential.

Always give your most; always give your best,
Always give your all… never anything less.

~

"Give all thou canst;
High Heaven rejects the lore
of nicely-calculated less or more."
~ William Wordsworth

~

Maximize yourself.
~ *Maximize your talents. Maximize your opportunities. Maximize your impact.* ~
Maximize your life.

~

~ **Make the Most of Your Talents** ~

Maximize Your Ability ~ The Parable of the Talents
(A Passage from the Christian tradition: the Gospel of Matthew 25:14-30)

"Again, it will be like a man going on a journey, who called his servants and entrusted his property to them. To one he gave five talents of money, [A talent is a coin—a monetary amount] to another two talents, and to another one talent, each according to his ability. Then he went on his journey. The man who had received the five talents went at once and put his money to work and gained five more. So also, the one with the two talents gained two more. But the man who had received the one talent went off, dug a hole in the ground and hid his master's money.

"After a long time the master of those servants returned and settled accounts with them. The man who had received the five talents brought the other five. 'Master,' he said, 'you entrusted me with five talents. See, I have gained five more.'

"His master replied, 'Well done, good and faithful servant! You have been faithful with a few things; I will put you in charge of many things. Come and share your master's happiness!'

"The man with the two talents also came. 'Master,' he said, 'you entrusted me with two talents; see, I have gained two more.'

"His master replied, 'Well done, good and faithful servant! You have been faithful with a few things; I will put you in charge of many things. Come and share your master's happiness!'

"Then the man who had received the one talent came. 'Master,' he said, 'I knew that you are a hard man, harvesting where you have not sown and gathering where you have not scattered seed. So I was afraid and went out and hid your talent in the ground. See, here is what belongs to you.'

"His master replied, 'You wicked, lazy servant! So you knew that I harvest where I have not sown and gather where I have not scattered seed? Well then, you should have put my money on deposit with the bankers, so that when I returned I would have received it back with interest.

"'Take the talent from him and give it to the one who has the ten talents. For everyone who has will be given more, and he will have an abundance. Whoever does not have, even what he has will be taken from him. And throw that worthless servant outside, into the darkness, where there will be weeping and gnashing of teeth.'"

~

The Main Message
Make the most of your talents and abilities.
If you are capable of greatness, then don't settle for anything less.
~

"From everyone to whom much has been given, much will be required; and from the one to whom much has been entrusted, even more will be demanded."

~ Luke 12:48 (From the Christian Faith Tradition)

Always Strive For More ~ Never Be Satisfied

Always Keep Trying To Improve, & Always Keep Chasing Perfection

We have all been there. You dedicated yourself to a worthy cause and achieved your goal. What a feeling it is to succeed at something in which you poured you heart. Emotional peaks are many times followed by letdowns. This is only natural.

It is easy to become complacent, especially after having accomplished a great feat. One of my football coaches always used to say to us after victories, "I'm happy, but I'm not satisfied." We had a very successful team and won a lot of football games. After hearing this statement the first couple of times, we thought our coach was crazy.

We may have just beaten an opponent very easily and had functioned to what we thought was the best of our potential. However, upon hearing this over and over again, the team began to adopt our coach's point of view. We began focusing not on how well we had performed, but on how well we could have performed. We began to scrutinize ourselves heavily.

What our coach knew, and was trying to teach us, was that it is often okay to be contented with what you have achieved. However, there is always more of which you are capable, and your potential is rarely realized. It is thus important to never allow yourself to be satisfied with your performance. There are always aspects which need improvement. Perfection is an unattainable dream. To this extent, we can always be one step faster, one ounce lighter or heavier, a bit stronger, more mentally tough, etcetera.

We must realize that we can never reach true perfection. Yet, we must also realize that by pursuing this illusive goal, we make ourselves far better than we could have been if we had allowed ourselves to be satisfied with our initial achievement.

When you succeed at a meaningful pursuit, enjoy it. You have persevered and dedicated yourself. But never let yourself be satisfied, because deep down, you know in your heart that you can always reach just a little beyond your current grasp. The continual stretch for this out-of-reach goal is what keeps men moving forward.

~

"For me, life is continuously being hungry.
The meaning of life is not simply to exist and to survive:
but to move ahead, to go up, to achieve, to conquer."
~ *Arnold Schwarzenegger*

~

It is Not Enough: Keep Giving More

Whatever you do, it is not enough. There is always more to be done, and you are always capable of doing more. There may be times when you do not want to give anymore of yourself, but give you must. For when you give, you create. When you give your time and energy, you create meaning and value, and you create pursuits worthy of your effort and memories that will last a lifetime.

~

"Improvement: that's the meaning of life."
~ *Robert Ladouceur*

The Road To Success Is Always Under Construction

Similarly to the world of sports—and truly any pursuit that you undertake in life, whether it be a job, hobby, relationships, or anything else—the process of improvement is never complete. No matter what the circumstance, you can always get better at something, or you can always do something a little bit better.

The only way to get the absolute most out of yourself is to realize that "the road to success is always under construction." Truthfully, in everything you do, you have to constantly revise and refine yourself. You have to search for that little improvement that is still lurking out there somewhere, and you have to stalk it like a tiger stalks its prey.

Improvement is a process. If you truly want to improve as much as you possibly can, then you have to focus on the process. That is the only way that you can maximize your potential.

~

Improvement is a <u>process</u>, not an outcome.

~

In order to be successful and to reach your absolute full potential, you have to understand the value of improvement, realize that improvement is a process, and then buy into the importance of focusing on the process.

~

There is no such thing as a final draft.
The story of life is meant to be written, refined, and re-written anew, each and every day.

"The only thing I have ever tried to do was to get better. All I have ever tried to do was to improve. I have always tried to be the best I can be." ~ Dan Hawkins

~

"Ever to Ascend"

~

_____

Life should be a never-ending climb up the ladder of improvement.
Life should be an ever-ascending hike up the mountain of achievement.

_____

~

Always keep ascending.

~

*If you're still thinking about what you did yesterday…
It means you haven't done anything yet today.*

Get to work…

And Keep Working!

Work To Reach Your Potential

Potential means nothing, unless you take it upon yourself to work toward making the most of your ability. In order to reach your full potential, you first must have the vision to see what you are capable of doing and becoming. Then, you must make a commitment to do everything in your power to make sure that you grab hold of that vision and work as hard as you can to turn it into a reality.

~

You must realize what your potential is, recognize where you are *right now*, in relation to that potential, and then determine how you are going to close the gap between who you are now and who you could become.

~

Life is about closing the gap between who you are and who you are capable of becoming. It is about making the reality of your life equal the potential of your life. All the potential in the world doesn't mean a thing, unless that potential is realized. Until *production* equals potential—until reality equals fantasy—then that potential is nothing more than a hope or a dream.

Unused potential is like unused talent. And, just like talent, all the potential in the world doesn't mean a thing if it doesn't become realized. Unused potential is like unused opportunity: it doesn't mean anything if you let it go to waste. Much like talent and opportunity, potential only matters to the extent that you make it matter. It only means something if you act on it and make the most of it.

~

"Potential means you haven't done anything yet."
~ Bill Parcells

~

You cannot rest on the laurels of 'having potential,' otherwise you will never reach yours. Don't get complacent or develop a false sense of confidence based on your potential. Figure out what your potential is, and then set out to begin working toward it. The two saddest things in life are wasted talent and wasted opportunity. It's great to have a lot of potential, but it doesn't mean anything unless you turn that potential into reality. The only way to make that happen is to go out and consistently work at improving yourself, day-in and day-out.

A Commitment to Excellence

To be continually striving for something better,
To be constantly reaching for something greater,
To be perpetually in search of perfection:
This is the essence of excellence.

"Lead me to the rock that is higher than I." ~ Psalm 61:7

"The rung of the ladder was never meant to rest upon, but only to hold a man's foot long enough to enable him to put the other somewhat higher." ~ Aldous Huxley

Who Are You Comparing Yourself To?
Make Sure You Chase *Your Own* Potential.

No one else was born with your exact talents and in your exact situation in life. So why would you compare yourself to someone else? Why would you compare what you accomplish with what someone else accomplishes, when each person is working with a different set of abilities and opportunities? It's like comparing apples and oranges.

When you fall short of achieving as much as you are capable of achieving, then it does not matter what you did in relation to other people—even if you still achieved more than someone else—because ultimately, it still is not good enough. After all, if you are capable of doing *better*, then *good* is not *good enough*.

Conversely, if you accomplish as much as you are capable of accomplishing, then it does not matter what other people accomplished in comparison—even if they accomplished more than you—because ultimately, you did the absolute best that you were capable of doing. When that happens, it does no good to compare your results with other people's, because there was nothing more that you could have done.

In that instance, you cannot get down on yourself. Instead, you simply have to continue to keep working and keep striving to reach your potential. If you indeed do fall short of what other people have done, then you can take that experience and use it as motivation to keep improving *yourself* as best you can.

The Ideal You

Somewhere down the proverbial road of life, there is a person with your same exact name, who is the perfect version of you. That person is everything that you're capable of developing into… he is the "ideal you."

Now, it may be difficult to see that person, or at least his face. Because he is running away from you. Or, more appropriately, he is running *beyond* you. You see, the "ideal you" represents your potential. He represents everything that you are capable of doing and becoming. Understand that your "ideal you" will not turn around and start running toward you. That would be too easy. And where is the challenge in what is easy?

Your whole objective in life is to chase down that ideal version of yourself, to catch him, and to grab hold of him. Your mission in life is to do everything that you can do to catch that person. And in order to do that, you are going to have to work and run as hard and as fast as you possibly can. In other words: you are going to have to do all that you can to make the most of your talents, your opportunities, and your life… if you want to catch the "ideal you." And through it all, you always have to remember how important it is to put forth maximum effort in pursuit of your ideal self… because when you catch that person, you become that person.

~

Be constantly comparing yourself to that "ideal version" of you. Do not get caught up in comparisons with other people and with what other people do. After all, each person has his own unique talents and abilities, and therefore, each person has his own "ideal self" whom he is chasing. Make sure to keep your mind focused on your own potential; make sure you keep your eyes focused on making the most of your own talents and opportunities, and make sure you do everything that you possibly can to not only *catch* that "ideal you," but to *become* him.

Focus On What YOU Can Do, Not On What Other People Can Do

You can't make the most of your abilities and opportunities,
if you continually focus on the abilities and opportunities of others.
Do the best that *you* can do, and do the best with what *you* have to work with.

Like the artist Young Jeezy says, *just do you*. Don't worry about what other people are trying to do, and don't try to be anyone else. Just do *you*… and just do *your best*.

Focus On the Hand You Were Dealt; Make the Most of the Cards You've Been Given

Focus on living your life the best way you are capable of living it. Stay focused on becoming who you are trying to be. Focus on the hand you were dealt. Make the most of the cards you've been given. You can't play anyone else's cards, so do the best you can to make the most of the cards you've been given. You can't live anyone else's life, so do all you can to make the most of the one that *you've* been given.

Make the Equation Balance Out: Make Potential Equal Reality

The two saddest things in life are wasted talent and wasted opportunity. Make the most of everything you have and every chance you get. Make the most of yourself and make the most of your life. Make the most of your talent and your opportunities. At the end of it all, the question isn't going to be 'How much did you do?' … it's going to be 'How much did you do in relation to how much you *should* have done?'

Make sure the equation balances out. Make sure that your reality equals your potential. Turn your potential into your reality. Make sure you accomplish everything that you are capable of accomplishing. Make sure you carry your dreams to fruition. Make sure you do all that you set out to do, and make sure that you do it all to the very best of your ability—the finest way you know how.

One Day, When You Are 80 Years Old…

One day when you are 80 years old, you are going to have to look back on your life and honestly reflect on the way that you have lived. You had better be happy with what you see when you look back on the path you've chosen to travel. You had better be proud of every step you have decided to take along the way, and you had better be pleased with who you have become during your way through this world.

~

Ultimately, everyone has an obligation to work toward closing the gap between the person he or she is at the present moment, and the person who he or she is capable of becoming. Regardless of whether it is as a student, as an athlete, or as a human being in general, it is each person's responsibility to make reality equal potential.

~

"Become your potential."
~ Myles Munroe

You Are Not In This World for Free: You Are Here On Scholarship

You are not in this world for free; you don't get to just live here without paying rent or earning your stay. You aren't just here to take care of yourself and have as much fun as you possibly can and that's it. Quite the contrary: you are basically here on a *scholarship*: you get to live and experience all this world has to offer, but in exchange, you have to put in the work. That is the bargain of being alive.

Just like when you are on an athletic scholarship—where you have to go to practices, you have to go to meetings, you have to participate in early-morning workouts, you have to be responsible and accountable, you have to have class, you have to represent your "program" and your "family" well, you have to be a leader, and you have to be a builder and an encourager of others—so too in life, must you learn to do all the things that are expected of you... and to do them all to the best of your ability, at all times, and in all ways. You must honor your scholarship. You must uphold your end of the bargain.

Whether you are on a scholarship in school, or on a 'scholarship' in life, the same fact remains true... You have a great opportunity, but it doesn't come without a price. In exchange for all you get to experience, you owe it to the rest of the world to give your best, to do your best, to help others do their best, and to be a blessing to the lives of others in the process... and you are expected to uphold your end of the bargain. Otherwise, you are practically stealing.

"Any person who does not fully believe in himself and fully utilize his ability
is literally stealing from himself, his loved ones, and in the process –
because of reduced productivity – is also stealing from society."

~ D. W. Rutledge

Any person who does not work to develop his talents and take advantage of his opportunities, robs himself of the wonderful experience of realizing what he is fully capable of becoming. What is even worse, he robs the lives of those around him and the world in which he lives, of all the wonderful and meaningful contributions he is capable of making. Such a man is stealing from everyone, everywhere.

In another sense, the person who neglects his talents and opportunities is like a gift-giver who wraps presents for others, but then never actually gives them. A gift to the world which forever remains unopened, is not a gift at all, but a travesty. A man's potential which forever remains untapped, is not a blessing at all, but a tragedy.

~

"If you don't use your talent, then you're stealing.
You're stealing from yourself, you're stealing from this world,
and you're stealing from your Creator."

~ Herman Edwards

"To give anything less than your best is to sacrifice the gift."

~ Steve Prefontaine

~ **Make the Most of Your Opportunities** ~

Be Grateful For Everything You Have;
Make the Most of Everything You Have Been Given

Nothing in life is promised, and nothing in this world is guaranteed.
Be grateful for everything you have, and make the most of everything that you have been given. Life is short. Be grateful for the one life you have, and make the most of the one chance that you have to live it.

There is nothing in this world more precious than life itself. Make the most of your opportunity to be alive; make the most of your opportunity to live each day to the fullest; make the most of your opportunity to live excellently and to do all you can to reach your absolute full potential.

Make the most of your opportunities for growth, experience, and impact. Realize what you have been blessed with, be thankful for and appreciative of all that you have, and strive to do the best and most with everything that you have been given.

~

> **"Each person is obligated to develop himself to the best of his ability."**
> ~ *Rabbi Yosef Leib Bloc*

Make the Most of Where You Are Right Now

Wherever you are, and whatever you are doing, you have to make the most of your present situation. Life has brought you to a specific set of circumstances for a reason … It may be a great situation or it may be a difficult one; it may be a great place or it may be a less-than-stellar one; but regardless, you have to do everything you can to get the most out of your time while you're there.

If you are meant to contribute something, then invest yourself fully and give everything you have to give. If you are meant to learn something or to develop yourself in some way, then try to grow as much as you can from the experience. Learn from it, so that you not only won't have to go through it again in the future, but that it will also prepare you for bigger and better things down the road.

Don't get caught up in "what if's" and hypothetical's. Don't start wishing you were someplace else or in some other situation. That's all fantasy, and none of us lives in fantasy; we live in reality.

We've all heard the saying, "the grass is always greener on the other side." Well, sometimes it is, and sometimes it isn't. The point is not to worry about someone else's grass, but to focus on your own grass. Keep your eyes on your own backyard … If you need to cut your grass, then cut it. If you need to water your grass, then water it. Don't mess up what's in front of you right now because you're preoccupied with something that you can't control. Stay focused on the here and now.

You never fully can understand why life has brought you to a particular set of circumstances until you are beyond those circumstances. It's not until you are able to look back and see everything in hindsight that you are able to make sense of it all. It does no good to try and figure all that out right now, while you're still going through it. Just trust that everything happens for a reason, and believe that every situation in your life is an opportunity to improve yourself.

Nothing will ever be 'perfect,' and nothing will ever be just as you want it to be. So don't wait for the future to take advantage of opportunities: live in the present moment. Make the most of where you are right here and right now.

~

"The greatest opportunity is found in *today*."
~ *Ray Lewis*

We All End Up Exactly Where We're Supposed To Be, Exactly When We're Supposed To Be There

Wherever you are, that is where you are meant to be. It's not about how long you are there, but the reason why you're there. What's important isn't the quantity of days that you're there; it's about the quality of purpose…the purpose for your being there.

Wherever you are, embrace it for the time being, and give it your all. Do your best to make the best of your current situation, and do all you can to take full advantage of the opportunities at your disposal. Don't neglect your current circumstances in the hopes that better ones will one day arise; don't waste your present opportunities or your chance to make a valuable contribution in your present situation.

Whatever your set of circumstances: make the most of it, and don't assume that everything is set for life. Don't take for granted that you'll always be somewhere or in some situation. We live in a temporary world, and nothing lasts forever. Where you are is where you are meant to be, but don't take it for granted. Maximize your opportunity. Focus on the quality of your purpose there, and not necessarily on the quantity of how long you'll be there.

~

Make the most of where you are right now.
Don't worry about how long you will be there, or about where you will go next.
Live in the present moment, and make the most of your current situation. Do your best, and give your best, to make the absolute most of where you are right now.

~

Focus On Quality, Not Quantity

Focus on the quality of your contribution, not on the quantity of how long you will be there to contribute. Concentrate on doing your best and on doing the most that you can do, to have as big of an influence as you can on those around you *right now*. Don't get caught up in the hypothetical's or tomorrow; don't get tangled up in the dreams of the future… instead, make your contribution in the right-here and right-now. Give your best effort to do your best work in the present. Don't wait for tomorrow, and don't assume anything about the future. Focus on today, and concentrate on the quality of what it is you do today. Focus on quality, not quantity.

Make the Most of Each Moment

Make the most of each moment; savor it, and then prepare to move on
so that you may make the most of the next moment that follows.

Time Marches On, and We Must Learn To March With It

One of the blessings and curses of football is that there is always another game on the horizon to prepare for. The bad thing about that fact is that whenever you win, you don't always get to enjoy the victory as much as you would like to, because inevitably, you have to get right back to work and start preparing for the next game.

To the same extent, the good thing about that fact is that whenever you lose, you don't have much time to dwell on the defeat or to feel sorry for yourself, because you also have to get right back to work and start preparing for the next game.

The same is very true for life. Whenever good things happen to us in our everyday lives, we have to enjoy them and take the opportunity to savor them (if we don't, then we will get burned out from all the work we put into making them happen) yet, we must also be prepared to move on from those moments so that we can experience newer and oftentimes even greater opportunities.

Likewise, whenever bad things happen to us, we have to allow ourselves to fully experience those negative moments and properly grieve them; but once again, we must learn from those experiences and then be prepared to move on to meet whatever opportunities will come our way next.

The key lesson is that we always have to keep moving forward: we have to take the memories of the past with us, but we can never allow those memories to prevent us from being ready and willing to experience whatever new adventures life has in store for us.

Every day, no matter what happened the day before, you have got to learn from your experiences and then move on. Ultimately, nothing lasts forever. And, whether you like it or not, time always marches on. No matter what life brings your way, there is always something else waiting for you—there is always that proverbial "next game" on the horizon to prepare for. Regardless of what happens in life, you must learn from your experiences and then begin to move on. If you dwell on the past, you will surely miss out on the present. Time marches on… and so too, you must learn to march on with it. This is the only way that you can ever hope to fully experience the life that has been given to you.

~

Time marches on…
and we either learn to march with it,
or else we get left behind.

~

Make the Most of Each Day

Make the most of each day; embrace it, take hold of it,
and make the most of it, Make your life a masterpiece, one day at a time.

Let Go of the Past, and Grab Hold of the Present

You have to let go of what is behind you in order to fully embrace what is right in front of you. You cannot move forward in life if you are too busy looking backward. You cannot grasp new experiences if you are unable to let go of past events.

~

Don't let the past rob you of the present.

~

In order to fully embrace each day, you have to learn to let go of the past, so that you grab hold of the present. Don't let thoughts of yesterday rob you of today's experiences. Don't allow the past to prevent you from experiencing all that the present has to offer.

~

"You can live in the past ... or you can flourish in the present."
~ Jeff Fisher

Live Life Now

There is a saying: Ten minutes ago is the same as 10,000 years ago. In other words: once something happens, it's over. You can't do anything about it, so don't dwell on it. Learn from it and then move on. Live your life right now. Live in the present moment.

~

Focus on the present. Focus on now.
Concentrate on what you are doing right now.
Ten minutes ago might as well be 10,000 years ago.
The only time that life is fully alive… is RIGHT NOW.
The past is dead, and the future hasn't been born yet.
The only time life is fully alive is right now.
Embrace it. Seize it. Live it.
~ Live life now. ~

~

"You must live in the present, launch yourself on every wave, find your eternity in each moment. Fools stand on their island of opportunities and look toward another land. There is no other land; there is no other life but this." *~ Henry David Thoreau*

~

Focus on right now. Live in the moment.
"I have learned to live my life one step, one breath, and one moment at a time."
~ Muhammad Ali

Life Is Short ~ So Live It Right, and Live It Well

At the high school level, you only get a certain amount of time—48 minutes—to go out and try to win a football game. At the college and professional levels, it is 60 minutes. Either way, it is not a whole lot of time. Therefore, there is no sense waiting around for things to happen *to* you. You have to get yourself going and get after it from the opening kickoff. You have to be proactive and purposeful in your approach, and you have to get out there and start making things happen *for* you.

In life, the nature of the "game" is very similar. As is the case with the duration of a football game, life as well is very short, and therefore, there is no sense waiting around for things to happen to you. Just as in football, you have to set out at the very beginning of each day, each week, each month, and each year with a purpose. You have to be proactive and intentional about living. You cannot sit around and wait for circumstances to align in your favor, and you cannot wait around for events to start going your way on their own. **You have to live life with purpose**. You have to get after it from the very beginning, each day and every day.

It is important to understand that you are only in this world for a short amount of time, and during that time you are given a specific and wonderful task—a great purpose. In whatever length of time you receive in this world, you are expected to carry out your task to its fullest extent and to the best of your ability.

You are not here entirely for yourself; you are not here just to go through the motions in life; and you are not here simply to have fun and nothing more. You are in this world for a very specific and powerful purpose, and that purpose is one that goes far beyond yourself.

~

Nothing in life is promised, and nothing in life is guaranteed.
Life is short. Be grateful for everything you have, and make the most of everything that you have been given. Most importantly of all, be grateful for the one life you have, and make the most of the one chance that you have to live it.

~

In the game of football, you only get a short amount of time to go out and try to win a game. Whether it is 48 minutes or 60 minutes, the fact of the matter remains that there is much work to be done, and not very much time to do it in. Therefore, whatever you do, you must do with a sense of purpose and urgency. There is no point in waiting around for the ball to start bouncing in your favor, or for things to just start suddenly going your way. You have to take it upon yourself to seek out victory. You have to be proactive in your approach and you have to play the game with a purpose. In other words, you have to get after it from the very beginning and do your best to play the game right, and to play the game well.

In the grand game of life, you only get a short amount of time to do what you are entrusted to do. Whatever your unique purpose may be in this world, you will be expected to carry it out and make as big a difference as you can, with however much time it is that you've got in this life of yours.

Much like the duration of a football game, life itself is also very short. There is no sense waiting around for things to start going your way or to start falling perfectly into place on their own. Ultimately, you have to take it upon yourself to seek out a meaningful existence. You have to be proactive in your approach to living your life and to fulfilling your life's mission. You have to go out and do your best to live each and every day of your life with a purpose. In other words, you have to get after it from the very beginning and do your best to live life right, and to live life well.

~ You only get one life, and that life is short. So live it right, and live it well. ~

Be Grateful for Every Opportunity That You Have, & Make the Most of Every Chance That You Get

There are a lot of opportunities that you will never get in life. Not everything you want, you will get in life; and not every opportunity you hope for will end up coming your way. So whatever opportunities that you do get, you have to take full advantage of. You have to do everything you can within your power to make the absolute most of them.

~

"Never forget that life is precious and fleeting.
Don't take it—or your opportunities—for granted."

~ *Jim Calhoun*

~

Be Appreciative of Everything that You Have, & Make the Most of Every Opportunity You Get

It's not how much you have, but how much you appreciate what you have. It's not what you have been given, but how much you do with what it is that you have been given. *Make the most of what you have; make the most of every opportunity that you get.*

~

"Be very careful, then, how you live—
not as unwise but as wise, making the most of every opportunity"

~ *Ephesians 5:15-16 (from the Christian Faith Tradition)*

~

~ **Make the Most of Your Impact On This World** ~

The Purpose of Living

The purpose of living is to do all that you can to reach your full potential in every regard, and to find a way to do it in service to some community that is larger than yourself. It is to do the absolute very best that you can do—at all times—to help enhance the world in which you live and the lives of those around you.

    We are each called to a specific role and a specific purpose in this world, and in order for us to fulfill that purpose, we must make the absolute most of every ounce of talent and every single opportunity that we are given. What is equally as important is that we help others to make the absolute most of their talents and opportunities as well, so that they may be able to reach their full potential also.

    Essentially, each of us must continuously work toward becoming who we are fully-capable of being, so that we may do all that we are capable of doing: for ourselves, for others, and for the world in which we live.

~ **Live With A Purpose** ~

You have to live life with a purpose.
It is important to understand that you are only in this world
for a short amount of time, and during that time you are given
a specific and wonderful task—a great purpose.
In whatever length of time you receive in this world,
you are expected to carry out your task
to its fullest extent and to the best of your ability.

~

You are not here entirely for yourself;
you are not here just to go through the motions in life;
and you are not here simply to have fun and nothing more.
You are in this world for a very specific and powerful purpose,
and that purpose is one that goes far beyond yourself.

~

"The meaning of existence
is to pass on to something far greater
than our own immediate selves."
~ Pierre Teilhard de Chardin

"What Did You Do With Your Life?
What Did You Do For The Lives Of Others?"

I once had a conversation with a colleague of mine about the importance of impacting lives. In the midst of our discussion, this colleague made an interesting statement. He said that if he could change one person's life—that if he could make a difference in just one person's life—then he would have been satisfied with his life.

I thought about that remark for a moment, and then decided that I disagreed with it. It was not the part about changing a life or making a difference that I had an issue with. It was the part about changing only *one* life, and making only *one* difference.

To me, that did not seem to be enough. It seemed to be pretty good… but 'pretty good' is not great. And so, why should anyone settle, when they are capable of being and doing something special? Why be satisfied with changing only *one* life? Why be contented with making a difference in only *one person's* life? After all, if you invest your entire life to help make a difference in one other life… doesn't that mean you are only breaking even? One life for one life… does not seem to me to be a contribution. It merely seems to be an even exchange. Rather than trying to change just one person's life, shouldn't we do all we can to change *as many lives as we possibly can?* Rather than attempting to make a difference in just one other person's life, shouldn't we try to make a difference in *as many people's lives as we possibly can?* Rather than trying to have a little bit of an impact, shouldn't we do as much as we can to have *as much of an impact as we possibly can?* Shouldn't we strive to **maximize** our impact in this lifetime?

~

Never be satisfied, and never be contented. Always work to keep doing more with your life and for the lives of others. You should start by giving your all to make a difference in one person's life, but then you should continue further by trying to make a difference in as many people's lives as possible. You should do all you can to make the most of your talents and your opportunities, in order to help do the most you can do for others. You should strive to maximize your impact in this lifetime, you should strive to do absolutely everything you are capable of doing in this world, and you should strive to do as much for the lives of others as you possibly can.

~

We should always be striving to do more, to make more of a difference: to make a difference in one person's life, to make more of a difference in that one person's life, to make a difference in more people's lives beyond that, and to keep striving to make even more of a difference in even more people's lives beyond that.

We should not be satisfied with trying to change just one life… we should do all we can to change and impact as many lives as we possibly can. We should approach this, not as a burden, but as an exciting challenge and a worthwhile opportunity: an opportunity to try to answer the questions… *How much good can one man do? How much of an impact can one man have? How much of a difference can one man make?*

Furthermore, we should approach this task as a wonderful opportunity to prepare ourselves for the day when we will be asked two even greater questions…
What did you do with your life? What did you do for the lives of others?

Maximize Your Impact In This Lifetime:
Strive to Do Absolutely Everything You Are Capable of Doing In This World
"What did you do with your life? What did you do for the lives of others? Those are two of the important questions that you'll be asked when you leave this world.

~ Make the most of your abilities and opportunities. Become everything you were meant to become. Accomplish everything you were meant to accomplish.

~ Make the most of your abilities and opportunities to impact the lives of others. Do everything you can to positively affect other peoples' lives. Do everything you can to improve other peoples' lives. Do everything you can to help raise other peoples' quality of life. Make the most of every chance you have to give hope and encouragement to others. Do your best to set a good example for others, and do your best to be a positive role model for others.

~ Do your best to reach your full potential, and do your best to help others reach their full potential as well. Strive to make the most of your life, and strive to help others to make the most of their lives as well.

~

Do all you can do, and do all that you can do for others.
Do the best that you can do, and do the most that you can do for others.

~

You only get one life, you only get one opportunity to live it, and you only get one chance to do the absolute most that you can in it. You have to do everything you can to get the most bang for your buck. Don't just be satisfied with doing a little, or even with doing a lot. Strive to **do absolutely everything you are capable of doing in this world**. Don't just try to make a difference in your own life or in just one other person's life; try to make a difference in as many people's lives as you can.

~

~ Paid In Full ~
Your life is not *your* life: it's merely on loan to you.
And, at the end of it—when you go to settle your debts—you are going to be expected to pay it back with interest. In other words: you had better have something to show for your time in this world. You had better be able to point to the contributions you made during your lifetime. You had better be able to speak of more than just what you did for yourself and in your own life. You had better be able to say that you took all the talents and opportunities that you were originally given, and that you maximized them and developed them as best as you could. You had better be able to say that, whatever you were loaned in the beginning, you have paid back with interest.
When you sign your name on the final page of your life,
you had better be able to follow it up with the words:
"Paid In Full."

~ **Maximize Your Life** ~

Opportunities and Choices

The more I live, the more I realize that life is a series of opportunities: some big, some small, and some in-between sizes. The fact of the matter, though, is that opportunities abound. When you look at the human existence from a basic perspective, you will find that life is all about opportunities and choices. It is a continual series of opportunities and choices—choices about how you will use those opportunities, and choices about what you will do with those opportunities.

~

Will you take advantage of your opportunities and make the most of them,
or will you neglect them and allow them to you pass by?
… And …
If you choose to take advantage of them, then to what extent will you use them?
Will you use them only to some degree, or will you make the absolute most of them?

~

"The little choices along the way are what makes a character.
People frequently make the mistake of believing that it is the big decisions in life
that are important, but the truth is that life is made up of the little choices more than
anything else. All the little choices are important."

~ Andrew Cromwell

You Are Responsible For Your Own Life

You are responsible for your own life: for everything that you make of it or don't make of it. You are responsible for the choices that you make, for the actions that you take, and for the destination that you eventually arrive at when all is said and done. You are responsible for whether you neglect your various blessings and chances, or whether you take full advantage of them and make the most of every opportunity you get. Ultimately, you are responsible for whether you squander your talent, or whether you reach your absolute full potential.

~

"One of the great undiscovered joys of life comes from doing everything one attempts
to the best of one's ability. There is a special sense of satisfaction, a pride in surveying
such a work, a work which is rounded, full, exact, complete in its parts, which the
superficial person who leaves his or her work in a slovenly, slipshod, half-finished
condition, can never know. It is this conscientious completeness which turns any work
into art. The smallest task, well done, becomes a miracle of achievement."

~ Og Mandino

Take Responsibility For Your Ability

You have to learn to take responsibility for your own ability. You have to assume the role of recognizing your talents, working to hone and sharpen them, and then putting them to use for the betterment of others. You have to learn to recognize what ability you have, develop it to its fullest, and then ultimately, find a way to use it in ways that serve others. You have to look for a way to use what you have been given to help create value, and then to deliver that value into the lives of other people.

~

"You must take responsibility for your ability—no one else can do it for you."
~ Myles Munroe

Take Responsibility For Your Opportunity

You have to learn to take responsibility for your opportunity. You have to learn to recognize what opportunities you have been given, and to recognize when those opportunities are presented to you; you have to learn to prepare yourself in advance for when those opportunities do arise, and you have to learn to work hard and work smart in order to take full advantage of them. Finally, you have to learn when and how to create your own opportunities, when the ones you want do not make themselves readily available. You have to learn to take responsibility for your opportunities in life. You have to learn to make the most of any and every opportunity that comes your way… after all, no one else can do it for you.

Take Responsibility For Your Impact

You have to take responsibility for your impact. You have to take ownership of your purpose in this world: for seeking to determine what it is that you have been put on this Earth to do, for finding the best ways to go about cultivating your talents in the direction of your purpose, for utilizing opportunities to make your abilities work toward fulfilling your life's purpose, for finding the most effective way to bring that purpose into being, for living your purpose out each and every day, and ultimately for carrying out your purpose to the fullest. You have to take responsibility for fulfilling your mission in this world. You have to take responsibility for doing all that you are capable of doing, for doing all that you are meant to do, intended to do, and destined to do… and you have to take responsibility for doing it all the very best way that you can do it.

~ Take responsibility for your ability.
Take responsibility for your opportunity.
Take responsibility for your impact.
Do these, and you will take responsibility
for your destiny.

~

~ Maximize your talents. Maximize your opportunities. Maximize your impact. ~

~

Life and Oranges

Attack your opportunities with purpose. Make the best of them, and make the most of them. Take full advantage of your opportunities; do not allow them to pass you by without making the absolute most of them. Do not just acknowledge the opportunities for success and significance that come your way. Embrace them, grab them, seize them, and squeeze them as tightly as you can. Get the most out of them. Squeeze them for every drop.

Opportunities are like oranges: the more you squeeze them, the more juice you'll get out of them. And when it comes to life… I hope you came thirsty. In other words: don't just settle for a few drops of orange juice; squeeze that orange and get every drop out of it that you can.

~ Three Things To Do ~

Work hard, & keep working hard.
Make the most of your talent.
Get the most out of your life.

~

"Make the most of yourself,
for that is all there is of you."
~ Mark Twain

The Entire Aim of Life Is Simple

The entire aim of life is simple: Make the most of your talent, make the most of your opportunities, and make the most of your ability to positively impact others.

~ Maximize your talent.
~ Maximize your opportunities.
~ Maximize your impact.

You have to measure your life by what you have done in relation to what you could have done based on your own talent level. You have to make the most of your talents, your opportunities, and your ability to contribute to something greater than yourself.

You have to live your life with a burning to desire to love and serve as much as you possibly can. You have to do your best to appreciate your time in this world, and you have to do all that you can do to leave this world a better place for your having been here.

~

~ Maximize your life. ~

~

Live With Honor

Live with Honor

To live with honor means to strive to do your best in all aspects of your life. It means living with courage, integrity, purpose, and dignity. Above all, to live with honor means to pursue excellence in all that you do, and ultimately, to make the most of your life and time in this world.

~

*Honor is about always doing the right thing, always saying the right thing,
and always standing for the right thing; it is about always doing the right things,
the right ways, and for the right reasons.*

Live Honorably & Maximize Your Life

To make the most of your life, to make the most of your opportunities in this life, and to make the most of your impact in this world… this is what it means to live honorably. Maximize your life … Do all the good you can, and do it all the very best that you can do it. Always give your all, and always do your best. If you strive to do these things with all your heart and soul, then you will make the most of your talents, opportunities, and influence in this world. As a result, you ultimately will end up maximizing your life.

Live Honorably and Make Your Life a Masterpiece

To live honorably means to do all you can to make your life—
every day and every moment of it—a perfect masterpiece of excellence and virtue.

~

Make your life a masterpiece; sign your name to everything you do.
To strive to make your life a masterpiece in every way…
this is what it means to live honorably.

~

"Make your life a masterpiece."

~ John Wooden

~

Make each moment a masterpiece.
Make each day a masterpiece.
Make each week a masterpiece, and…
Above all… make your life a masterpiece.

~

Honor: The Supreme Virtue

The word *honor* is one of the greatest, most reverent words in all of human language. *Honor* is a word with much depth. In a sense, it is the "mother of all virtues." Honor is the supreme virtue. It embodies all other virtues, and it comprises the ultimate ideal to which any human being can hope to aspire. In much the way that a rainbow is made up of all the colors in the color spectrum, *honor* is a collection of all the positive character traits that a person can possess. It is a composite of every respectable, admirable, and noble virtue that exists. If you were to make a single-column list of all the virtues and positive character traits, that list would be entitled "***Honor.***"

~

To Live With Honor, Is To Live In Such A Way…

~ To live with honor is to live in such a way that no one has a reason to say anything disrespectful about you.

~ To live with honor is to live in such a way that you earn the respect and admiration of everyone you meet.

~ To live with honor is to live in such a way that no one has any reason to think poorly of you, speak disrespectfully of you, or treat you in an unjust or unfair manner.

~ To live with honor is to engender love, to earn respect, to give the best of yourself, to bring out the best in others, to give of yourself to those in need, to bring hope to the lives of others, and bless the lives of all you meet.

~

"Take care that no one hates you justly." *~ Publilius Syrus*

~

A Definition of Honor

Honor is defined as "the quality of uncommon respect and esteemed reputation; the possession high-character, the continuous display of excellence, and the constant exhibition of noble and humble virtue.

Always…

Honor is about always doing the right things, always saying the right things, and always standing for the right things, and always standing up for the right things.

Always do what's right.
     Always say what's right.
          Always stand for what's right.
          And always stand up for what's right.

~

"To be ambitious of true honor …
is the very principle and incentive of virtue."

~ Walter Scott

~ 12 Steps To An Honorable and Successful Life ~

Be Positive.
Start each day with a positive outlook, stay positive,
and prepare to enter tomorrow with a positive mindset as well.

Develop Good Habits.
Your habits form you, so form good habits.

Develop Good Relationships.
Work hard to cultivate and maintain meaningful relationships with quality people.

Learn from Good Sources and Utilize Good Resources.
Seek out wisdom from good books and intelligent people.

Make the Most of Every Day.
Appreciate each moment, and invest in excellence on a daily basis.

Live With Passion and Purpose.
Make the most of everything the world has to offer,
and give to the world everything that you have to offer.

Have A Vision.
Know what you want to do in life, and know who you want to become in life.

Have A Plan.
Create a logical plan to help you achieve what you want, and to help
you become the person that you desire to be. Then get down to business
and execute that plan to the best of your ability.

Be Flexible.
Always be prepared to adjust, adapt, and improvise in order to
overcome challenges along the way.

Be Eternally Grateful.
Don't take anything for granted, and don't take any*one* for granted.

Treat All People With Respect.
By showing respect to other people, you will be making
the world a better place in which to live.

Live Well and Live Honorably.
Try to live each day as if it were the only day
you were going to be judged on when your life is over.

~

Be Honorable and Live Honorably.

~

"An Honorable Man"

On all the shores and in all the ports,
You'll find men, young and old, and of all sorts.
But none of them finer than he
Whose dream it is to be
The one whom people trust,
And the one they see as just.
His are deeds that all admire,
And his is a life that all desire.

Yet, fate is fickle, and this he knows.
Though with ease he walks, and never slows,
Nor ever shows on any day
The slightest contempt in any way.
And on every day,
And in every way,
He answers the call and gives his all,
Whether fortune should assign his rise or fall.

Upon Honor's mantle he sets his aim—
His thoughts and his words, one in the same.
From the throne of high-Heaven he seeks his applause,
And strives onward always, toward a worthy cause.
Putting lives of others before himself:
On this he counts his truest wealth.
On all that he does he signs his name,
And plays his part in the eternal game.

~

~ Be An Honorable Man. Live An Honorable Life. ~

~

Wherever it is that you go in life:
Do your best and do your part.
Autograph your work with excellence.
Craft your life into a beautiful work of art.

Live Accordingly

If you want to be known, then live with Passion.
If you want to be liked, live then with Enthusiasm.
If you want to be respected, then live with Integrity.
If you want to be admired, then live with Class.

If you want to be thought well of, then live with Sincerity.
If you want to be spoken well of, then live with Kindness.
If you want to be trusted, then live with Honesty.
If you want to be loved, then live with Humility.

If you want to be influential, then live with Strength.
If you want to be inspiring, then live with Courage
If you want to be significant, then live with Intention.
If you want to be successful, then live with Purpose.

If you want to be happy, then live with Gratitude.
If you want to be fulfilled, then live with Excellence.
If you want to be revered, then live with Grace.
If you want to be remembered, then live with Honor.

~

We are each given the blessing of a life to be lived.
The question is not whether or not we will live, but rather, *how* we will live.
What truly matters is not that we seek simply to exist—to merely live—but that
we seek to live well. We should strive not merely to spend our time in this world,
with little to no consideration; but rather, we should seek to live-out the highest ideals
to which the human spirit is capable of aspiring. Above all else,
we should strive to live with honor and excellence.

~

~ **The Building Blocks of a Worthwhile Day** ~

In my best opinion, there are 6 great and meaningful feelings a person
can experience in a given day. These sentiments are as follows:

1. To wake up with an excitement about,
and a strong sense of purpose for the day ahead

————————

2. To be able to put your arms around someone and say
"I love you," and to hear those words in return.
Do not be afraid to say it first.
Chances are, if you say it, someone else will too.

————————

3. To be forgiven, or to forgive someone else…
even if it is just for something minor.
Forgiveness is a powerful thing.

————————

4. To be able to look yourself in the mirror and ask
"Am I genuine?"
… and to be able to say "yes" without hesitation.

————————

5. To make someone else's day:
Whether it's doing a kind deed or speaking a kind word—
or just doing something nice without expecting anything in return,
simply to experience the joy that comes with seeing another person's
happiness or just to see them smile… Now that is a very rewarding thing.

————————

6. To lay your head down on your pillow at night and be able to
sleep well because you have a conscience that approves your conduct.
The best sleep remedy is to go to bed happy with the job that
you've done as a human being over the past 24 hours.

~ **Build A Life Of Excellence, One Day At A Time** ~

A life of excellence must continually be crafted.
It must be built daily—one brick at a time—
And added to continuously each and every day hence forth.

~

~ ***There is no greater masterpiece than a life of honor.*** ~

~

Live With Purpose

Live Your Life With Purpose

Each of us has a specific purpose in this world—a unique and powerful mission given to us individually, to carry out to the absolute best of our ability. Every one of us has been given a unique set of talents and a special set of opportunities. We re charged with the responsibility of making the most of both, in order to help improve the lives of those around us.

Whether it is to enhance the world around us on a grand scale, to improve the community in which we live and to shape our own little corner of the world, or simply to impact the life of just one other person… each of us has the powerful opportunity and obligation to help improve the quality of the world in which we live.

The Two Most Important Days of Your Life

The two most important days of your life are…

1. The day you were born, and
2. The day you understand *why* you were born.

~ You have been given the power of a life.
~ Now, it is up to you to decide what you will do with that power.

Start Thinking About Your Purpose In Life

Everyone has a specific purpose in this world. Once you start thinking about what that purpose might be, you are on your way to finding your role in the grand scheme of life. You don't have to figure it out right now. But it's always good to start thinking about it early on and to simply be aware of the concept.

"Strong lives are motivated by dynamic purposes." ~ Kenneth Hildebrand

Determining Your Purpose In Life

So, how do you figure out what your purpose in life is? Well, there are a couple of key questions that you should keep in mind throughout the next several years:

What things do I really have a passion for and enjoy doing?
What things am I really good at?
What does the world, or what do other people, need me to do?

~ When you find something that you have a passion for, that you are really good at, and that there is some need for in the world or in your community, then you will have found your purpose.

~

"Discover something in life that is worth doing, not simply something that you're good at or something from which you make a large profit. But find something that is worth doing, a true and genuine vocation, which is where your great joy meets the world's great need."

~ *Reverend Peter J. Gomes*

Give Your Life A Purpose
Give Your Life a Meaning

The Secret of Your Life's Meaning
Come close, my friend,
And a wonderful secret I will tell to you:
One that is known by only a few,
And by only too few not to be true.
When the final day is finally cast,
And the breath last breathed is finely the last,
People will ask at the close of a life—
By then too late when time's surpassed—
"For what did all this serve to be—
What meaning did all this hold for me?"

So listen close and hear my words, and
With all that I say, you'll one day agree.
For what I say you may not believe,
But believe it or not, I have come to see,
That my life and your life, his life and hers,
Has no meaning—of this I am sure—
You see, it has no purpose, entirely none,
Until, my friend, you give it one!

———————————

"Your life has no meaning, until you decide to give it one."

~ Peter Rice ~

———————————

Which Type of Person Are You?

There are two types of people in this world: there are those who live day-to-day and who are just trying to get by—the ones whose only goal is simply to make it to tomorrow. Then, there are those who have some great hope for their lives—something grand and worthwhile that they want to accomplish... some unique and special thing that they want to do with their lives—the ones who realize that there is something special the world needs them to do.

~

"Great hopes make great men."
~ Thomas Fuller

~

The world calls each of us to greatness. Unfortunately, not everyone is able to hear that call, and not everyone who hears it is actually willing to answer it. Those people who have great hopes and high expectations create an overwhelming purpose in their lives. They wake up each and every day, ready and willing to battle through any adversity that comes their way, flexible enough to adjust to any situation that may arise, open to change and prepared to embrace new opportunities for growth, and ready to enjoy the many blessings that life has to offer.

Those **strong souls are motivated by something greater than mediocrity**; they live for something far beyond what the average person would be satisfied with. Such people strive to reach onward and upward toward some great and worthy purpose. These inspiring individuals are made great by their lofty aspirations and their unyielding determination. Their lives are made special by the pursuit of, and ultimately, the bringing to fruition of the most extraordinary of hopes.

~

There are two types of people in this world: there are those who are content to live day-to-day, and those who are spurred on by something of greater significance. There are those who are satisfied merely with trying to get by, and there are those who have a burning desire to do something special—something *extraordinary*—with their lives.

~ **So... Which type of person are *you*?**
~ **And, more importantly, which type of person will you *choose to become*?**

~

~ Honor, Excellence, and Purpose ~

~ Live with honor, and live according to the highest ideals. ~
~ Live with excellence, and live according to the highest forms of achievement. ~
~ Live with purpose, and live according to a higher calling. ~

~

"Once a person realizes that he is capable of excellence,
he is never quite satisfied with less."
~ Ron Berger

Live With Determination

In order to make the most of yourself, in order to make the most of your life, in order to make the most of your time in this world, and in order to make the most of your impact in it… you are going to have to develop the determination to do so.

In order to make the absolute most of your life, you have to learn to live it the right way. In order to make the absolute most of your one-and-only life, you have to live with excellence, you have to live with honor, you have to live with purpose, and—equally as important—you have to *live with determination*.

What It Takes To Succeed In Life

It takes determination to excel in anything you do. It takes determination to excel at *everything* you do. It takes determination to reach your full potential: to achieve all that you are capable of achieving, and to accomplish everything that you are capable of accomplishing. It takes determination to be successful, and it takes determination—*and a few other things*—to ultimately succeed in life.

~

"It is the nature of man
to rise to greatness if greatness is expected of him."
~ *John Steinbeck*

~

It Takes Hard Work To Succeed In Life

No One Owes You A Thing
No one owes you a thing. If you want to become successful, no one is going to show up at your doorstep and just give you the right to be so. If you are going to be successful, it will be because of the hard work you invest into making your own success.

The World Does Not Owe You A Thing
The world does not owe you a thing. If you want to become successful, no one and no thing will suddenly shake the universe until it gives you what you want. If you are going to be successful, it will not be because the world will just give you success: it will be because you go out and work hard to achieve it.

~

"There's no success, without the work required to be successful."
~ Clark Kellogg

~

The Nature of Success
Success is not something that just happens to you. It is not something that happens to come your way while you're sitting around doing nothing. You do not find success; and success does not find you. You don't stumble upon success; you don't bump into success; and you don't catch success. You EARN success.

In this world, you don't become successful by sitting around and doing nothing. Success will not all of a sudden just come to you. If you want to achieve success, you have to go out and look for it. More importantly, you have to go out and work for it.

In anything you do in life—whether it is in sports, in the classroom, or in your job—if you want to achieve success, then you have to roll up your sleeves and make it happen.

~

No one has success coming to him. If a man wants success, he must go out and look for it. What is more important: he must go out and *work* for it.

~

"There's a lot of blood, sweat, and guts between dreams and success."
~ Paul "Bear" Bryant

~

The Nature of Continued Success:
If You Want to Enjoy MORE Success, You Have to EARN MORE Success

You are not born with success. You are not given success. You do not inherit success. Success is not something that you can talk your way into, nor is it something that you can back your way into. Rather, success is something that you must earn.

Whenever you experience success to any degree, you have to remember what got you there in the first place. You have to keep in mind the same thing as before you achieved anything: that in order to achieve success, you must work for it. Then, you must realize that you will have to continue to work in order to continue to be successful.

You have to earn the right to be successful. What is more…
You have to earn the right to *continue* to be successful.

Any achievements that you experienced in the past were a direct result of what your hard work earned you. Any accomplishments that you will have in the future, again, will be a result of what your labor will earn. If you have had success in the past, great; enjoy it. But, understand that if you want to continue to have success in the future, then you will have to continue to work for it in the present.

~

If you want success—no matter when, no matter where, no matter how much, and no matter how often—you must constantly be working to earn it. Every bit of success that you want to experience, you must work for, you must labor for, you must pay the price for. There is no escaping it. If you want to enjoy success, you have to *earn* success. If you want to enjoy *more* success, then you have to *earn more* success.

~

"Success is like anything worthwhile. It has a price.
You have to pay the price to win and you have to pay the price
to get to the point where success is possible. Most important,
you must pay the price to stay there."

~ *Vince Lombardi*

~ Pay The Price ~

"All life is based on the fact that anything worth getting is hard to get.
There is a price to be paid for anything. Scholarship can only be bought at the price of study,
skill in any craft or technique can only be bought at the price of practice,
preeminence in any sport can only be bought at the price of training and discipline.
The world is full of people who have missed their destiny because they would not pay the price.
No one can take the easy way and enter into any kind of glory or greatness."

~ *William Barclay*

For Everything In Life, There Is A Price To Pay

**Everything In Life Has A Price,
And You Always Get What You Pay For**
Everything in life has a price, and you always get what you pay for.
Everything in life is a trade-off, and you always get what you bargain for.
Whether you give a lot or a little, you will always receive your just reward in return.
No matter who you are or what you do, you can be certain of one thing in life…
That everything has a price, and you will always get what you pay for.

In life, everything has a price…
And you always get what you pay for.

"The price of victory is high, but so are the rewards."
~ Paul "Bear" Bryant

How Much Are You Willing?
Great success requires great sacrifice. How much you accomplish in life will be
determined by how you answer the following two questions:

> **~ How much are you willing to *give*?** … and…
> **~ How much are you willing to *give up*?**

"He who would achieve much must sacrifice much."
~ *James Allen*

~ Expect Only What You Are Willing To Earn ~

Expect only what you are willing to earn… nothing more, and nothing less.
After all, you will only accomplish as much as you are willing to work for…
Nothing more, and nothing less.

~

"There are no real secrets to success.
Success in anything has one fundamental aspect: effort."

~ *Sam Parker*

Aim for success. Expect success…
And then do everything you can to make sure that you **deserve** success.

~

*You'll accomplish as much as **YOU** are willing to work for.*

~

"There are plenty of rules for attaining success, but none of them work unless you do."

~ *Mark Twain*

Nothing Worth Having Comes Without A Price
In order to accomplish anything meaningful, you will have to pay your dues. There simply is no way around it. You cannot get to where you want to go without putting in the time and effort. And if you want some quick fix, then that is all you are going to get, something that works for a short time, and then it's time for another quick fix, and none of them really work anyway.

If you want improvement, you have to earn it. There is no substitute for hard work and dedication. If you put in the time and effort, and do so on a consistent basis, and if you do all you honestly can to get the most out of yourself, then you will get to where you want to be.

If you decide to take the easy way, then you are going to get exactly what you paid for. And if you decide to take the right way, and to put in the effort and pay the price for excellence, then you are also going to get what you pay for.

~

~ Everything in life has a price, and you will always get what you pay for. ~

~

Hard Work Is the Difference Between Good and Great
The difference between mediocre and good is not that much at all. Yet, the distance from good to great spans miles. If you want to move from mediocre to good, all you need to do is put in a little extra time and effort. However, if you want to make that difficult journey from goodness to greatness, you have to do every single little extra thing in every single little opportunity. **The better you want to become, the harder you have to work.** It is that simple.

The Nature of Commitment: It's All or Nothing
You get out what you put in. Often, it is quite that simple. In anything you pursue, the level of your dedication will play an important part in the level of excellence which you achieve. What you repeatedly do, whether on the smallest or largest of scales, will have a direct correlation to your results.

The difference between achieving excellence and falling short of your goals lies not in a lack of effort, but in a lack of commitment. Improving yourself is a basic building block of success, as is the will to win. Everyone wants to win, but not everyone wants to work. There are those who choose not to give fully of themselves and still expect excellence to give itself to them, as if they were entitled to it for simply showing up. Champions, however, realize the importance of hard work. They know that nothing worthwhile or valuable comes without effort. Many people who want to win are willing to work, but only when it is convenient for them. However, *true champions* are forged through preparation. They understand that the will to prepare, the desire to work, and the willingness to pay the high price of winning are what ultimately produce victory.

~

"Wanting to win and being willing to pay the price to win—
that's what separates winners from losers."

~ Sylvester Croom

~

Champions know that ultimately, victory is not decided on the field of battle, on the day of the war. Instead, it is won in the secret places of the heart and mind, far before the battles are even fought. It is decided in the preparation of the combatants, on the humble practice fields and in the damp weight room. Victory is to be found in the daily habits of its captors and in their will to work for results.

~

"There are only two options regarding commitment.
You're either IN or you're OUT. There's no such thing in life as in-between."

~ Pat Reilly

~

Making a commitment to excellence is not an occasional occurrence. Like winning, it must be a full-time pursuit. It cannot be a half-speed attempt at something you feel like doing; it must be a whole-hearted effort toward something worth doing.

Commitment is a 24-hour-a-day job. It is not a hobby. It is a lifestyle, and it is a way of life. Commitment begins when you take that first breath at the start of each day, and doesn't end until you close the chapter on another night of your life. Commitment continues when you first step onto the field of play, and it carries on still further, when you take that first step off.

~

Commitment is in the little things. You cannot excel at great things if at first you do not conquer the smallest and most significant of obstacles. Like anything in life, you have to ascend the ladder of accomplishment gradually. If you look too far ahead, you will not focus on the task at hand. If you continually seek to win the war, yet neglect the outcomes of the various battles, you will ultimately be defeated. You cannot win the war if you do not first fight the little battles.

Commitment is in the details. It is in the seemingly insignificant issues that many people often neglect. It is found in the mundane little moment that most people overlook. Each instance in life offers an opportunity to become better in some way. Every moment provides a chance to improve as an individual: mentally, physically, and spiritually. All of those little opportunities to get better eventually add up, and when they do, they create much larger opportunities to become great. Understanding commitment means understanding that, ultimately, there is no such thing as an unimportant moment. In life, every minute counts; every moment matters.

~

Commitment Is a Way of Life
Commitment is not simply an approach, nor is it merely a philosophy. It is not something you can talk about having, and it certainly is not something you can pretend to have either. **Commitment is a way of life**. You must live it through your beliefs and through your actions. You must walk the walk of commitment, even though it is not often a pleasant one. It is, however, an effective one, and your level of commitment will play a big role in determining the level of excellence—and the level of success—that you ultimately achieve in life.

~ The measure of a man's success is determined by the measure of a man's commitment.

It Takes Hard Work To Get To The Top

Winners do not succeed during the moment of truth because of some sudden inspiration they receive or some ability they quickly find. Winners succeed because long ago, when the competition was sleeping, or preoccupied with hobbies and entertainment, they were hustling, planning, and working hard to improve themselves.

There are no shortcuts to success. The truth of the matter is that, if you want to be successful in what you do and in who you become, you will need to fully invest yourself in the journey. If you want to reach the top of the mountain, you have to climb each and every step along the way. There are no easy paths to anyplace worth going in life. There are no elevators to success. There are no ski lifts to the summit. To put it simply…
If you want to see the view from the top, you have to climb the mountain.

"The heights by great men reached and kept,
  Were not attained by sudden flight,
  But they, while their companions slept,
  Were toiling upward in the night."

> ~ Henry Wadsworth Longfellow

It Takes Harder Work Than The Competition

It's a really simple equation: if you want to be better than everyone else,
all you have to do is <u>outwork</u> everyone else.

"No champion has ever achieved his goal without showing more dedication than the next person; making more sacrifices than the next person; working harder than the next person; training and conditioning himself more than the next person; studying more than the next person; enjoying his final goal more than the next person." ~ Doak Walker

"The only thing that separates successful people from the ones who aren't is the willingness to work very, very hard." ~ Helen Gurley Brown

"Today I will do what others won't, so tomorrow
I can accomplish what others can't."
~ Jerry Rice

All It Takes

~ All it takes to be successful… is everything you've got. ~

~

Hard Work Pays Off

"Achievement is the crown of effort."

~ *James Allen*

Four Steps To Achieving Success

Step One:
VISUALIZE

You must first determine your definition of success: What does success mean to you? What you are trying to achieve, what mission are you going to set for yourself? What does the final outcome or the finished product look like in your eyes?

~ **Have a Vision**: See what is possible for you to do. See what is possible for you to become. Figure out exactly what you want. Determine your intended destination.

Step Two:
CONCEPTUALIZE

Once you have established your objective, you must then determine what it will take to achieve success: How will you work toward accomplishing your objective? What steps will you take? How long will you need to do it? What is your plan of attack going to be?

~ **Create a Plan of Attack:** Put together the plan, determine what steps you will need to take in order to achieve the end-goal of that plan, understand what you will have to go through in order to effectively navigate your pursuit of success. Create a plan of attack to reach your goals, then prepare to attack every step of that plan with a strong and determined sense of purpose. Get ready to work toward accomplishing your goals.

Step Three:
ACTUALIZE

Once you have established a plan of attack, you must begin to actively attack the plan. You must roll up your sleeves, get to work and get down to business, and make success happen. After all, success won't just come to you; you must go to it.

~ **Implement the Plan**: Put the plan into action. Breathe life into your mission by beginning to walk the walk of success. Begin living out your mission by taking each and every step—one focused and determined step at a time—along your pathway to success. You have already created the plan of attack, now it is time to attack the plan. *Actualizing* means taking what you *plan* to do… and ***actually doing it***.

Step Four:
REALIZE

Once you have worked and labored in the direction of achieving your goals, you must follow through and persevere to the very end of the course you set for yourself. You must finish the job. You must do everything in your power to take your original dream—that initial vision—and turn it from a fantasy into a reality. You must do everything you possibly can to bring your ultimate mission to fruition.

~ **Finish**: Finish the plan. See it through. Bring the mission to fruition. No matter how long it takes, no matter how hard it gets, and no matter difficult it becomes… Finish the job. Take the final steps toward your ultimate destination. Bring the dream to life. Focus on the task at hand, and finish what you began. Transform your original dream into reality. Make it happen, and make it real.

Visualize. Conceptualize. Actualize.
REALIZE.

Aspire and Persevere

Each year, all across America, football teams of every level set out with high expectations for the season ahead. No matter who they are or where they are from, one thing is for certain… for everyone, everywhere, expectations are high.

Every team in the country will set out with the same goals in mind: to win games, to win the conference, to go to playoffs, and to win a championship. What will separate the teams that go on to achieve their goals from the ones that don't, will not be the level of expectations, but the level of work ethic and commitment that go along with those expectations.

Aspire and Persevere. Those words are the motto of my high school alma mater. It's a very simple slogan, and one that is highly effective. The idea is very straightforward: set a high goal, and then work as hard as you can to accomplish it.

In a lot of ways, that motto is more like an equation than anything else: in order for it to work properly, you have to balance both aspects of it. What I mean, is that the degree of perseverance has to match the degree of aspiration. In other words, **you have to make the level of your work ethic match the level of your expectations.**

On the playing field, we used to say "aspire and *perspire*." That was our way of stressing the importance of hard work. It reminded us that wishing was not doing, and that ultimately, **goals don't reach themselves, objectives don't achieve themselves, and potential doesn't fulfill itself.**

~

High expectations are great. But the truth is that championship expectations don't mean a thing, unless you have championship work ethic to go along with them. Anyone can talk about achieving success; any team can talk about winning games, going to playoffs, and winning championships. But the people and the teams that actually go out and succeed in this world, are the ones whose work ethic and commitment match their expectations.

No one is ever going to show up at your front door and simply give you what you want … the world doesn't work that way. Life is never going to just give you something without you having to earn it. What life *will* give you, however, is an opportunity to work your butt off in order to go after what you want. Whether you make the most of that opportunity or not, is up to you.

What's for certain, is that talk is cheap, and dreams don't put points on the scoreboard. It is not the wishing, but the *doing*, that turns expectations into reality. The day-in and day-out commitment, the continuous sacrifice, and the persistent effort … ultimately, those are the things that make the difference.

In the end, it's not about what you *want* to achieve. It's about what you are willing to go out and *earn*. All the aspiration in the world means nothing without an equal or greater amount of perspiration. When it comes to the game of football— and the game of life—one thing holds true: **you will always get what you earn.**

~

"I can't promise you that we'll get what we want. But I can promise you one thing:
We will get what our works deserve."

~ Dennis Green

Aspire and Perspire

Accomplishments don't just happen on their own; they are the result of intentional design, deliberate action, and sustained effort. Great achievements are the byproduct of setting lofty goals, and then working as hard as you can to turn those goals into reality.

The greatest dreams in the world don't mean a thing, unless your level of effort equals or exceeds the heights of those dreams. If you don't make the work ethic match the expectations, then all you end up with is a fantasy.

Dream big... but don't forget the most important ingredient of success: hard work. Make sure you aspire to accomplish great things, but then, make sure more than anything that you *perspire*, and that you ultimately accomplish the things you set out to do. You must make your efforts equal or exceed your expectations.

~

The expectations create the vision,
but the work ethic is what turns that vision into reality.

~

"Your success in life will be due to your earnest efforts."

~ Message within a fortune cookie

~

"It's not going to happen just because you *want* it to happen.
It's going to happen because of your *persistent effort to make it happen.*"

~ Robert Zimmerman

~ Successful People ~

Successful people set goals for themselves.
Then they establish a clear and logical plan to achieve those goals;
Then they work hard and persist, until they accomplish their objective.
They persevere until they bring their mission to full fruition.

~

~ Accomplish Your Mission ~

You have to work hard and keep working hard;
You have to persevere and keep believing;
You have to resist the temptation to quit and to give in;
You have to continue to press on until finally,
At long last, you have accomplished your mission.

~

**Ambitious people set goals. Passionate people work toward those goals.
Committed people—*successful people*—finish the job and accomplish those goals.**

~ Start Strong, Stay Strong, and Finish Strong. ~

It Takes Persistence and Perseverance…
And A 'See It Through' Attitude

Thomas Edison, the famous American inventor, scientist, and businessman, was known for his many creations and contributions to the world. Among his many noteworthy accomplishments over the years, was the invention of the electric light bulb for commercial use.

In addition to his scientific genius, Edison was also known for his incredible determination and persistence. He often attributed his so-called "genius" to nothing more than shear hard work and tireless resolve. Regardless of what it was, if Edison thought something needed to be done, or that it *could* be done, he set out to do it. More importantly, he continued to work hard at it until he had finally done it. It was Edison's ability to see his work through to completion, and to never quit until he had done what he had wished to do, that paved the way for his many successes in life.

Years after his most famous invention, and well into a comfortable life of leisure in south Florida, a retired Edison was once asked by a reporter: "Sir, where do you think you would be in life right now, had you not found the answer to the electric light bulb?"

To this, Edison replied: "Young man, rest assured… had I not found the answer by now, I would still be in my lab searching."

~

"None of my inventions came by accident.
I see a worthwhile need to be met and I make trial after trial until it comes.
What it boils down to is… one percent inspiration and *ninety-nine percent* **perspiration**."
~ Thomas Edison

~

"Perseverance is the hard work you do after you get tired of
doing the hard work you have already done."
~ Anonymous

~

"The people who succeed in life are not the most talented, but the most determined."
~ Joel Osteen

~

"People of mediocre ability sometimes achieve outstanding success because they don't know when to quit. Most men succeed because they are determined to."
~ George Allen

Attitude, Effort, and Persistence

Attitude is what puts the key in the door.
Effort is what turns the key and unlocks the door.
Persistence is what eventually pushes the door open.

"Continuous effort is the key to unlocking your potential."
~ Winston Churchill

The Power of Persistence

"Nothing in this world can take the place of persistence.

> **Talent will not**; nothing is more common than unsuccessful people with talent.
> **Genius will not**; unrewarded genius is almost a proverb.
> **Education will not**; the world is full of educated derelicts.

Persistence and determination alone are omnipotent. The slogan 'press on' has solved and always will solve the problems of the human race."

~ Calvin Coolidge

It Pays To Be Persistent
It is often said that, *to the victor go the spoils.*
It may also be said that, *to the persistent goes the victory.*
"Effort only fully releases its reward after a person refuses to quit." ~ Napolean Hill
"It is to the one who endures that the final victory comes." ~ Buddha
"The habit of persistence is the habit of victory." ~ Herbert Kaufman
"You just can't beat the person who never gives up." ~ Babe Ruth
"If I persist, if I continue to try, if I continue to charge forward…
I will succeed."*~ Og Mandino*

Two Simple Rules of Persistence

"Rule #1: Take one more step.
  Rule #2: When you can't take one more step, refer to Rule # 1."

~ H. Jackson Browne

Persist, Persist, Forever Persist!

"The best way to handle anything in life
Is to give it your very best.
Push at it until you get what you desire.
Give it as many attempts as possible.
Perseverance pays at the end."
~ Alaba Oluwaseun

~

"Victory belongs to the most persevering."
~ Napoleon Bonaparte

"See It Through and Never Quit"

Whether you wish to win just a little bit,
Or you hope to conquer life and be a great hit,
If you wish to do whatever it is that you see fit,
Then see it through and never quit!

Some call it determination, and some call it grit.
Although it means the same, howe'er it be writ.
If you wish to do whatever it is that you see fit,
Then see it through and never quit!

If you've found something to be done, then go out today and do it.
If you know that it can be done, then go ahead and prove it.
But don't you stop and don't you sit; and don't you rest—not for just one bit.
See it through… and never quit!

~

"It is the surmounting of difficulties that make heroes."
~ Louis Kossuth

~

~

Success In Life Depends On Determination

Success in life depends much less on a person's outer circumstances than it does on his inner determination. Very often, we look for what we believe is the "ideal" situation to propel us toward success. We grow discouraged when that situation doesn't present itself right away, and we tend to get frustrated when our accomplishments don't show up as quickly as we'd like them to. Often times, we fail to realize that success is not something to be granted us, but rather, something that must be consistently and persistently worked for. **The key ingredient for success is not having the perfect situation, but instead, having a perfectly-determined attitude with which to face the current situation.** No set of circumstances, no matter how difficult, is any match for a determined attitude and a relentless effort.

~

"There is no chance, no destiny, no fate,
that can hinder or control the firm resolve of a determined soul."
~ Ella Wheeler Wilcox

~

It Takes Toughness To Succeed In Life

The Importance of Toughness

It takes toughness to accomplish anything worthwhile in life. If you want to be successful at anything, and at everything, then you have to have the toughness that is required to persevere through anything and everything. You have to have the will and the determination to do everything you know that you are capable of doing—to do everything that you know you are meant to do.

In order to succeed in life, and in anything that you do in life, you have got to have toughness. You have to have the mental toughness—and in some cases, the physical toughness and the spiritual toughness—to be able to persevere through your circumstances and to accomplish your goals. You have to have the toughness to persist in the face of hardship, to work through your adversity and to rise above your obstacles, and to follow through on what it is that you set out to do.

You have to have the dedication, commitment, drive, and determination to carry your dreams to fruition; to work at whatever it is you are doing—and to continue to work at it until, at long last, you have done it.

~

Great lives begin with a dream; they are fueled daily with desire;
and they are sustained and furthered through sheer determination.

~

The Mighty Bond of Toughness

Toughness is as strong and as sturdy as it gets. It is unshakable and it is unbreakable. Toughness is not simply one quality. Rather, it is a precise combination of many indestructible characteristics. It is a formidable bond, an inseparable chain.

Toughness is an unyielding alloy, forged of a steel determination and an iron will, strengthened by the striking blows of adversity, and of the unyielding resolve which strikes back. It is a mighty bond, molded by the roaring fires of desire; tempered over the burning coals of courage and conviction; and fortified by the unbreakable determination of a warrior spirit.

~

Toughness is grit and determination.
It is the heart and soul of a man on full display.

~

~ You Simply Have To Have Toughness ~
In any game you play, and in the game of life, toughness is *indispensable*.
If you want to win, if you want to be successful, if you want to reach your full potential…
You simply have to have toughness!

~

Toughness Is The Common Denominator of Champions

Toughness is one of the most important characteristics of both successful teams and successful people. Having watched a professional playoff game between two outstanding teams, I couldn't help but realize what made the eventual winner the superior squad of the two. Both teams were talented; both teams were on a roll and playing extremely well, and both teams looked by all accounts, at least on paper, to be championship contenders.

However, the entirety of the game—and its outcome—illustrated one very important point. When it comes down to *crunch time*—both in the world of sports and in the game of life—there is one thing, more than any other trait or quality, that separates championship teams from everyone else. There is one thing that separates championship *people* from everybody else. When it comes right to the matter, what separates the contenders from the pretenders is not talent or ability, not paychecks or payrolls, and not experience or expertise. **It's *Toughness*.**

~

The great teams and the great athletes all have a superior toughness about them. Look at some of the all-time great dynasties in sports history: Vince Lombardi's Green Bay Packers of the 1960's—perhaps the absolute epitome of toughness—the Pittsburgh Stealers and the famed "Steel Curtain" defense of the 1970's; look at Bill Russell and the Boston Celtics teams that won more than a dozen championships; the hard-nosed Detroit Pistons of Chuck Daley, who won back-to-back titles in the early 1990's; and the Alabama Crimson Tide teams that won six national championships under the legendary Paul "Bear" Bryant.

Think about some of the most successful individuals in recent sports history as well: people like Lance Armstrong, Michael Jordan, Martina Navratilova, Walter Payton, Jackie Joyner-Kersey, Emmitt Smith, and Tiger Woods. What is the one thing that they all have in common? Aside from greatness, the one word that characterizes all these people is *toughness*.

~

Toughness is the common denominator of champions. In order to be your best, and in order to be *the* best, you've got to be tough. Day-in and day-out, you've got to be willing to *grind it out*, *stick it out*, and *tough it out*.

Toughness is the main ingredient of success. When the challenges come, you've got to be willing to *work* a lot, *struggle* a lot, and *overcome* a lot… if you want to *succeed* a lot. That is the nature of a winner. That is the essence of a champion.

~

Whether in sports or in life, when it comes to success…
There is no substitute for toughness.

True Toughness

Toughness is the calling card of champions. The one thing that separates the best from the rest, more than anything else, is toughness. When push comes to shove, the tough not only stand their ground: they climb to even greater heights. Like cream rising to the top, the tough always find a way to rise above the rest. In order to be successful in any sport or endeavor, you've got to have toughness. Similarly, in order to be successful in life—and in everything you do in life—you have to possess a great deal of toughness.

So, What Exactly *Is* Toughness?

Toughness is about having grit and determination; it's about possessing a strong mind and a determined will. Toughness is having the discipline, the fortitude, and the courage to battle through both the good times and the bad: through all of life's ups and its downs.

Toughness is about gritting your way through, and doing what you need to do. It is about showing up for the fight, each and every day, and battling your way through whatever obstacles life may throw at you. True toughness is about having courage, and—more importantly—about exercising that courage and putting it to productive and disciplined use. It is a firmness of will: a laser-like resolve. At its core, true toughness is a burning desire to do what it takes to excel, and an unrelenting drive to succeed. It is the will to work, the will to overcome, and ultimately, the will to win.

In another sense, toughness also is about doing what has to be done. It means bypassing and forgetting about what you *want* to do, and doing whatever it is that you *need* to do. It is about making the sacrifices necessary to achieve something special; it is about doing what it takes to reach your absolute full potential.

Ultimately, toughness is a matter of mind, will, and spirit. It is giving your all in all things. It is battling on in the face of both adversity and success. It is about courage; it is about persistence. True toughness is about finding a way to do what needs to be done… and, when you can't find a way…true toughness means making one.

~

Where does toughness come from? Now that we know what toughness is, the question that remains is... Where does it come from?

True Toughness Comes From Within

When we speak of toughness, it is not muscles and power that we speak of. It is a toughness of mind; it is a toughness of spirit. True toughness doesn't necessarily mean *physical* toughness. As a matter of fact, it is more about having a *mental* brand of toughness than it is about possessing any kind of physical prowess.

Real, genuine toughness is about something much deeper than physical appearance and outward strength. More than anything else, and more than any *place* else, true toughness starts on the inside. It comes from the center—the core of who a person really is. Toughness springs forth from an inner strength—an internal will— rooted deep down in the soul of a man. True toughness ultimately starts on the inside of a person and works its way out. Physical toughness, then, merely is a manifestation of a person's strong mind and determined will. It is not so much about being strong in body, as it is about being strong in spirit.

~

True toughness comes from within.
What shows through on the outside truly is a projection of what one possesses on the inside. Genuine toughness, therefore, isn't as much about being physically strong, as it is about being mentally and spiritually strong. When you get to the heart of the matter, you find that real toughness is a matter of the heart.

~

"Toughness is in the soul and spirit, not the muscles."
~ Alex Karras (former Chicago Bear, and star of the movie Blazing Saddles)

Toughness Is In the Details

Toughness is in the details. It is about not only having the will to win, but also the will to prepare, that is the mark of toughness. Toughness is about doing the difficult and seemingly mundane things—the tedious, day-in and day-out chores that most people don't want to do. It is about doing the painful, tiresome, and even boring things that most people would rather not do.

It is doing what has to be done, when it has to be done, as well as it can be done… regardless of anything and everything else. It is doing what needs to be done, when it needs to be done, as well as it can get done… regardless of your feelings, regardless of whether or not you want to do it, regardless of whether or not you feel like doing it.

Toughness is about having the courage and conviction to do the challenging tasks that success demands. It is about having the desire to do all the "behind the scenes" things that go into making a champion. Toughness is not only about **giving your all** in the *big* things, but in all things: especially the little ones. It is about taking care of the business at hand, and always doing the absolute best that you can.

Toughness Endures

Toughness doesn't quit, and it doesn't give up.
Toughness battles its way through, and it does what it needs to do.
Toughness doesn't stop when the going gets tough, and it certainly doesn't back down.
Toughness keeps working.
Toughness may be tired, but it never admits it.
Toughness may be bloodied, but it never shows it.
Toughness keeps battling. Toughness keeps grinding.
Toughness keeps fighting.
Toughness endures.

The Will To Endure

For the person with an unstoppable determination and a will to endure, life's hardships are merely temporary obstacles that lie along the road to greatness and achievement. Through perseverance, hard work, courage, and strength, no obstacle will ever be too great, no task will ever be too difficult, and no challenge will ever be too daunting that it cannot—*and will not*—be overcome.

It is not a man's circumstances that determine his path through life; it is his will and determination. Through a man's will to endure, he dictates the steps of his journey through this world, and in the process, carves out in stone his own fate and legacy.

It takes strength and determination, and the will to endure;
It takes toughness and effort, and the courage to make it through;
Because in this world of ours, one thing holds true:
Tough times don't last… but tough people do.

"The beauty of the soul shines out when a man bears with composure one heavy mischance after another, not because he does not feel them, but because he is a man of high and heroic temper." ~ Aristotle

Come What May, The Tough Are Always Ready

Come what may, the tough are always ready.
Through trial and ease, through test and breeze, the tough are always steady.
They are always ready to give their all, always willing to answer the call;
The tough are prepared to do what it takes: to stand up, stand high, and stand tall.
They never shrink from any challenge, but instead raise up, to meet one and all,
Never content to settle, ready to rise after any and every fall.
They work and they labor,
Piling the odds of victory in their favor.
They go above and beyond what is expected,
Leaving nothing to chance or neglected.

~

The tough do what they need to do—and not necessarily what they *want* to do,
The tough do what they know that they *have* to do—not what they may *prefer* to do.
The tough always do what they must, in order to become the very best.
The tough prepare for the struggle, and the struggle prepares them for success.
No matter the challenge, no matter the test,
No matter the odds, no matter the rest,
No matter the pounds, no matter the weight,
No matter the burden hurled at them by Fate—
Though it may be hurtful and heavy…
Come what may… The tough will be ready.

~

No matter what happens, not in them or to them,
No matter what strikes them, not at them or through them—
Determined to become the ones victory chooses—
The tough never complain, and they don't give excuses.
They give of themselves, and that proves to be plenty.
Because, come what may… the tough always are ready.
They never back down and they never pack up.
They never give in, and they never give up.
No matter what life may have left for them in store,
The only thing that the tough ever have left to give… is *more*.

~

~ *Come what may, the tough are always ready.* ~

~

"The true champions in life possess the toughness
to handle all that comes their way."
~ *Jim Tressel*

Seize the Moment; Define the Moment

Sometimes, moments define people. Sometimes, people define moments.

Moments do not define champions. Rather, champions define moments. The kind of people who excel in life do so because they realize several things. First, they see each obstacle in their path for what it really is: an opportunity to prove and improve one's self. Second, they do not allow themselves to be overcome by the fearfulness and difficult nature of the situation. Instead, they seek to resolve the challenge in a proactive manner. They choose to act, rather than to react. Thirdly, such individuals are aware that others are facing similar circumstances, and that the person or organization that most likely will succeed in the given situation is the one that ultimately chooses to face the task at hand and approach it with resolve and determination.

Every moment in time has offered victory, and similarly, defeat, to only one party. The difference between the opposing sides of history is often the minutest of details. Chiefly among such disparities between conquerors and conquered, however, are often the immediate reactions of each party. Many times, the preparations and total attention paid to the situation is similar in amount. With all things being virtually equal, victory very often comes down to one simple aspect: who decides to *seize the moment*.

In almost anything you do in life, there will be opportunities to sit back and allow the moment and the opposition to dictate the outcome. Conversely, there will also be chances to step up and dictate to each. It has been said that a person is either a hammer or a nail: he either does the hammering, or he is the one who gets hammered. In the animal world, the equivalent adage would be that a man is either the hunter or the hunted. He is either the one who stalks his prey, or he is the one who becomes lunch for the day.

Whatever the terminology you choose to use, there will ultimately remain but one simple decision for you to make. Will you be the hammer, or will you be the nail? Will you hunt and survive, or will you be hunted and be eaten? The choice is yours to make.

Moments often define people. But champions rise to occasions and define moments. That is their legacy.

~ Seize the moment. Define the moment.

Seize the Moment, and Make It Your Finest Hour

Whether it's a football game, a marathon race, or some other type of competition or performance…when the moment of truth finally arrives, you have to remind yourself that this is the moment you've been waiting for. This is the moment you've been working toward, and looking forward too. All the preparation and work leading up to it, all those sprints and heavy weights, all those long runs, all that hard work, all that time and energy you invested: it's all for that one moment. When that moment finally comes, you have to take a deep breath, force yourself to smile, and remind yourself that this moment is what you've been looking forward to. When the lights come up, it's time to step on stage and deliver. You have a great opportunity in front of you; you have a tremendous chance to show yourself, and to show everyone else what you are made of, and what you have got inside you.

"There comes a special moment in everyone's life, a moment for which that person was born. That special opportunity, when he seizes it, will fulfill his mission—a mission for which he is uniquely qualified. In that moment, he finds greatness. It is his finest hour."
~ Winston Churchill

~ Rise to the occasion. Lay claim to your finest hour.

Adversity and Character

Some people say that adversity builds character. Others point out that adversity simply reveals the character that someone already possesses. Personally, I don't agree with either of those notions. Rather, I believe that what adversity does is provides people with the opportunity to create their own character.

It is during the difficult moments in life that you are forced to make important decisions—decisions regarding who you are and who you are going to become. The questions that adversity forces you to answer are: How are you going to react and respond to this situation? Are you going to quit? Will you respond to setbacks with resolve and determination, even if the odds are against you? Are you going to persevere through the tough times and attack the challenges that stand in your way? Will you lay down, or will you fight your way through the obstacles and find a way to rise above your circumstances? Are you going to make excuses and blame others, or will you take responsibility for your own attitude, your own actions, and the outcomes of those actions? … and, most importantly, Are you going to grow from your trials, and are you going to use this experience to somehow become a stronger and better person?

Ultimately, there is little correlation between adversity and character. Some people go through a lot of adversity but do not develop strong character traits as a result. Others, however, develop a great deal of character as a consequence of their trials. What distinguishes the two outcomes is not the amount or degree of adversity that people face, but the decisions that those individuals make about how they are going to deal with the adversity that they encounter.

Adversity, in and of itself, does not build a person's character…nor does it reveal it. Adversity, as life would have it, merely provides an opportunity for an individual to create his own character. A person can either use a difficult situation as an opportunity to develop his character—and to further build upon any character traits that he already possesses—or, he can simply let that opportunity pass him by. Whether or not he makes the most of his exposure to adversity … is entirely up to him.

~

Tough times do not reveal who you are;
they provide you with the opportunity to decide who you will become.

~

Sharpen Yourself On Your Struggles

Question: Why do we have to face adversity?
Answer: Because we are not yet what we are meant to be, and we are not yet prepared to accomplish what we want to accomplish.

Adversity is an opportunity for us to learn and grow, to continue to improve ourselves as we work incessantly toward our mission, and to help make us what we are capable of becoming. Every great person and great team first went through a very difficult time in their lives or careers that helped make them who or what they are.

Instead of bemoaning your problems or feeling sorry for yourself, learn to focus on what you can do to improve yourself and your current situation. Don't use today's adversity as merely a crutch to rest your excuses on; use it as a springboard to launch you toward future success.

Turn today's pain into tomorrow's gain. Use your struggles to sharpen you, just like the way a sword is sharpened by fire and metal. Take advantage of the things that are happening to you, by using them to make better things develop within you. Use the adversity you will face today, to help create the success you will enjoy tomorrow.

~ Turn today's adversity into tomorrow's successes. ~

During the times when you are going through adversity, the moments when you are struggling your way through life, the instances when you are bearing heavy burdens: do not be dismayed, do not lose heart. You are not being broken or battered, for no apparent cause; but instead, you are being sharpened–like a sword–for a great and worthy purpose.

What Will You Make of Your Adversity

Your adversity will either be the excuse for your failure, or the reason for your success. The choice is up to you… because ultimately… you will determine your future by the way you respond to your present.

"If you should achieve any kind of success and develop superior qualities as a man, chances are it will be because of the manner in which you met the defeats that will come to you just as they come to all men." *~ An Anonymous Stanford Professor*

~

Oak trees are made stronger by severe winds.
Swords are made sharper by severe tests of fire.
Men are made braver by severe trials.

~

"Your struggles develop your strength."
~ Arnold Schwarzenegger

Use Your Adversity to Gain Confidence for the Future

Each experience of adversity gives us the opportunity to grow stronger, better, more complete, and more certain of ourselves. Each experience of meeting and overcoming adversity gives us greater confidence in our ability to successfully meet and overcome whatever adversity we may face in the future.

Making Sense of Your Adversity: Why Do Bad Things Happen To Good People?
We've all asked or thought about the question "Why do bad things happen to good people?" After all, shouldn't good people deserve to have good things happen to them?

~

There are a few reasons why good people—sometimes more than anyone else—experience bad times in life. Perhaps first and foremost, I believe that bad things happen to good people, because good people are the ones who are most capable of dealing with adversity. People of character, determination, and integrity are better equipped to handle life's difficult moments. They are better able to take the adverse events that happen to them and use them for good. Good people are able to turn negatives into positives.

Maybe someone else wouldn't be able to keep it together in the face of challenging times, but good people are able to not only survive the difficult times: they are able to learn from them and to grow from them as well.

~

Another reason that good people go through difficult moments in life, is so that they can help show others how to handle such challenging times, and how to overcome the obstacles that life has laid before them. The courage and strength that good people exhibit in dealing with their adversity, can provide a valuable example for others. These courageous and noble actions can serve as an inspiration to other people who are struggling with the difficulties of life. Good people, by virtue of their overcoming adversity, can become an unwavering source of strength and encouragement for others.

~

~ When you are going through adversity, always remember that you can be an example to others, that your courage and strength can strengthen and encourage others, and that your determination to meet and conquer any obstacle you may be dealing with can inspire others who are facing similarly difficult situations in their own lives.

~ When you are going through adversity, always be assured that you have been put in a particular situation because you are capable of handling it—and overcoming it. Always remember that you have been given the responsibility of adversity in order to help show other people how to deal with the difficult situations in their own lives.

~ When you are going through adversity, always keep your head up, always keep your courage up, and always keep your hopes up. Take heart and be strong, and do your best to get through and get past your circumstances. If you can stay strong and find meaning in the midst of your adversity, then you will be able to get yourself through every one of life's challenges. Equally as important, you will be able to help others get through their own unique challenges as well.

Why do bad things sometimes happen to good people?
Because good people are strong enough to get through it,
and they are resourceful enough to figure out what to do with it.

~

Why does adversity strike good people?
Because good people can get through it,
and they know what to do with it.

Life Is A Battle:
It Takes Having to Battle To Succeed In Life

Life Is Hard. Life Is a Battle.

Life is hard. And it's supposed to be hard. Life is a battle, and it is supposed to be one as well. Once you are able to acknowledge and come to grips with that fact, then you are able to begin preparing for that battle. You have to take that first step, so that you can then move onto the next step, which is preparing to address the situation, so that you ultimately can successfully overcome it.

 Adversity is an inevitable part of life. Daily challenges are all part of the package that comes along with being alive. If you expect life to be easy, then it never will be. If you think that things will always go your way, and that things will always go easy… then when the first sign of adversity appears, you are going to end up getting discouraged and frustrated. However, if you expect life to be a challenge, if you expect life to be hard work, and if you expect life to be a battle… then you will begin to prepare yourself to face the challenges, to do the hard work, and to battle through anything and everything life brings your way.

~

"It's not going to be easy. But then again… no one ever said it would be."

~ Peter Rice

~

 Life is hard. Life is a battle. Don't expect it to be easy; because it won't be. Don't expect it to be convenient; because it never will be. Expect life to be a grind; expect it to be a struggle. More importantly, though, expect to grind it out; expect to battle through it. Expect to face and meet your challenges head-on, and expect to rise to the occasion and overcome your adversity.

~

"Once we accept the fact that life is hard, we begin to grow.
We begin to understand that every problem is also an opportunity. It is then that
we dig down and discover what we're made of. We begin to accept the challenges of
life. Instead of letting our hardships defeat us, we welcome them as a test of character.
We use them as a means of rising to the occasion."

~ Hall Urban

Life Is Hard. Life Is a Battle.

Life is hard. And it's okay to say it. It's perfectly alright to admit that life is tough. There is a difference, though, between acknowledging something and using it as an excuse. It is alright to acknowledge that life is a battle at times: that's a statement of fact. It's okay to say that, as long as you then begin thinking about and acting out your plan of attack to make it through the battle. It's not okay to use "life is hard" as an excuse, it's not okay to use it as a crutch to lean on.

 Acknowledge your situation and the obstacles that lay before you. But don't use them as excuses. Don't feel sorry for yourself, don't blame your circumstances or other people for your situation, and don't get discouraged. It's not okay to use it as an excuse not to give your all. Life is a battle. True statement. Now what are you going to do about it? Are you going to shy away from life, or are you going to prepare for the struggle and show up ready to do battle? Are you going to shrink away from who you could be, or are you going to give this life every single thing that you've got?

~

"Our success in life will be largely determined by how we deal with adversity: whether we run from it or face up to it, whether we shrink or grow from it, whether we surrender to it or triumph over it." ~ *Hal Urban*

Life Is Hard.
Life Is a Battle.

Life is hard,
      Get used to it.
Life is a battle,
      Get ready for it.
Life is hard,
      And life takes hard work.
Life is a battle,
      And life takes having to battle hard in order to win that fight.

~

Life is hard. Life is a battle. Get used to it, but more importantly: **Get ready for it**.

~

Every day is a battle, and you've got to show up and fight
if you're going to be successful.

Begin Each Day With A Battle Cry

Every morning, you must prepare yourself for the struggle ahead. You must not lie in bed and think to yourself, "I don't want to have to do this today." Instead, you must jump out of bed—ready to embrace the moment, and ready to seize the day. You must loudly declare, for all to hear, your battle cry for the fight ahead. Stand up tall, reach down in your gut, and proudly proclaim: **"Let's Battle Today!"**

Stand up to the challenge. Face up to the test.
Every day is a battle, and to win, you must give it your best.

    "Let's battle today!"

        ~ *Cleon McFarlane*

If I were asked to give what I consider the single most useful bit of advice for all humanity it would be this: Expect trouble as an inevitable part of life and when it comes, hold your head high, look it squarely in the eye, and say, **I will be bigger than you.** **You cannot defeat me.**

~ *Anne Landers*

~ Play to Dominate ~
Mediocre teams play to play.
Good teams play to win.
Great teams play to dominate.

Dominate the Game of Life

In sports, do not just play for the sake of playing.
Play to win, and, what's more, play to dominate.
In life, do not just show up and go through the motions.
Instead, live to win, and more importantly, live to dominate.
Live your life with purpose. Live your life with determination.
Live with strength and live with honor. Dominate the game of life.
Do not settle for mediocrity. Do not just go through the motions.
Live for something better. Live to be great. Live to dominate.

Live to Dominate
Good teams play to win.
Great teams play to dominate.
Dominate the game of life.
~ Dominate Life ~

Take Responsibility For Your Life

Take Responsibility for Your Life and Everything You Do With It

Take responsibility for your attitude, take responsibility for your actions, take responsibility for your behaviors and for your habits, take responsibility for yourself, and take responsibility for your life.

Take responsibility for your thoughts…

> Before a man can take responsibility for what his life becomes,
> he first must take responsibility for who *he* becomes.

Before a man can take responsibility for what becomes of his life, he first must learn to take responsibility of his actions, his behaviors, and the habits that he forms over the course of his life. It will be these actions, these behaviors, and these habits that will ultimately steer him down the path of life. Before a man can take responsibility for his actions, behaviors, and habits however, he first must learn the importance of attitude, learn to harness its enormous and influential power—a power which contains the ability to influence his life. Before a man can take responsibility for his life, he first must take responsibility of his attitude. Before he can take responsibility for his own self, he first must take responsibility for his own thoughts.

~

> *Thoughts lead to choices, and choices lead to actions.*
> *Actions lead to behaviors, and behaviors lead to habits.*
> *Habits lead to character, and character leads to consequences.*

~

The choices a man makes, the actions a man takes, and the habits a man takes to making, will determine the course of his entire life. A man may not be in complete control of his environment. However, he is always in complete control of his own internal environment: he can always determine his thoughts, his decisions, his actions, and his behaviors. A man may not always be able to dictate his outer circumstances. But, he will always be able to dictate his inner forces. Those internal components of a man give him the tools to shape the world which he sees around him; more importantly, they provide him with the machinery to create that which he does not yet see—that which has to come into existence, because it has yet to be brought into existence. What a man thinks, what a man says, what a man does, and what a man continues to do... creates the foundation for the person who that man is; and, what is more, it paves the road along which that man will travel each day henceforth in his life.

~

> A man is the architect of his own life; he is the builder of his own destiny.

~

A man is constantly creating himself, one thought after another. He is constantly building himself, one brick after another. A man is constantly shaping himself, one choice after another. He is constantly shaping his life, one action after another. A man is constantly creating the portrait of his ways, one brushstroke after another. He is constantly painting the picture of not only his present, but also that of his future, one paint-stroke after another. Thoughts, choices, actions, and habits: these are the blocks with which a man constructs his future. These are the materials with which a man shapes his own fate. Thought by thought, choice by choice, action by action, and habit by habit…one brick upon another … a man builds, brick by brick, the house in which he must live the rest of the days of his life.

"Attitude is the key to life." ~ Sheddrick "Buck" Gurley

The Importance of Attitude

Your Attitude Determines Your Success

Your attitude affects every aspect of your life. It affects the way you perceive yourself, the way that you perceive and approach your circumstances. Your attitude affects the way you view your past, the way you live your present, and the way you will meet and shape your future. Your attitude—more than anything else—will determine your overall level of success in life, because it is your attitude—more than anything else—that determines what you do with yourself, what you do with your circumstances, and ultimately, what you do with your life.

~

"As a man thinks, so he is."
~ James Allen

Your Attitude *Toward* Life Will Determine Your Success *In* Life

Your attitude toward life will determine the amount of success you experience in life, because your attitude shapes the way you perceive and approach every situation in your life; and it dictates the way you act and respond in all of those situations as well.

What you think, what you say, what you do, and what you continue to do… about anything, will ultimately have the greatest impact on deciding what you do… about everything. Even more importantly, what you think about yourself, what you say about yourself, and what you do and continue to do with yourself, will ultimately have the greatest influence on determining who you become as a person. How you think about yourself today, what you say to and about yourself in the here-and-now, and how you carry yourself in the present will all dictate who you become in the future.

~

"What a man thinks, he becomes."
~ Aristotle

Your Attitude Determines…

Events alone cannot determine the course of your life and how it unfolds.
It is your attitude toward the events that happen to you in your life—not what happens *to* you, but what happens *in* you—that ultimately will determine how your life proceeds. Events alone cannot determine your thoughts and your feelings. It is your attitude toward those events that determines how you think and how you feel—about yourself and about your life. **More than the events of this world, it is your attitude that dictates the course of your life and how it will unfold.**

~

"The saying, 'As a man thinks, so he is,' not only embraces the whole of a man's being, but is so comprehensive as to reach out to every condition and circumstance of his life. A man is literally what he thinks, his character being the complete sum of all his thoughts."
~ James Allen

You Have A Choice: You Always Have A Choice

We often have little to no control over the events that occur in our lives. But what we can control is the manner in which we approach those events: how we react and respond to them, how we deal with them, what we learn from them, and what we make of them. When it comes to your attitude, and when it comes to your life, the fact of that matter is that you always have a choice.

You have a choice. You can choose to get upset when the breaks don't go your way, or you can choose to stay positive and continue to give your best. You can choose to get frustrated when things don't fall in your favor, or you can choose to stay hopeful and keep working at what you are doing.

You can choose to be discouraged by setbacks, or you can choose to stay focused and determined. You can choose to get disappointed in the face of challenges, or you can choose to view adversity as an opportunity to grow. You can choose to be overwhelmed by obstacles and difficulties, or you can choose to be calm in the face of chaos and respond to the moment with poise.

You can choose to get angry when people mistreat you, or you can choose to give the world—and others—your best, regardless of the rest. You can choose to quit and give up when the times get tough, or you can choose to be resilient and keep persevering. You can choose to buckle under the weight of your burdens, or you can choose to stand up and carry the load without complaining.

You can choose to feel sorry for yourself when things don't work out perfectly, or you can choose to take it upon yourself to make the best of things in every way that you can. You can choose to blame and condemn others for what happens to you in your life, or you can choose to take responsibility for yourself and your life and do the best you can to improve both.

You can choose to focus on fruitless words when you don't feel like working, or you can choose to turn your attention to actions, and give up all the talking. You can choose to make excuses and complain when things do not go well, or you can choose to keep striving to make progress instead. You can choose to complain and make excuses when things do not go right, or you can choose to turn your focus from words to works, and continue to plug away. You can choose to grow tired and weary after working and toiling away, or you can choose to keep working and laboring anyway, until you've finished the job.

You can choose to be overcome by the many things that may happen to you in the world, or you can choose to rise up and rise above your circumstances. You can choose to shrink away from your challenges and your challengers, or you can choose to get up and meet them face-to-face. You can choose to scurry away from your tests and your trials, or you can choose to stand up to them both and stare them each down. You can choose to back down from your adversities and your adversaries, or you can choose to stand your ground and meet them head-on.

You can choose to back away from anything and everything that may seem difficult, or you can choose to walk right up to those things and face them with courage and strength. You can choose to let your moments determine your life, or you can choose to take hold of yourself and be the one who does the determining. You can choose to be defined by the circumstances of life, or you can choose to take it upon yourself and do the defining.

You Can Choose How You Want To Respond

You can choose how you want to respond. You can't always control what happens to you, but you can always control how you respond. And how you respond in the present often determines what will happen to you in the future.

You can choose how you want to act. You can choose how you want to respond. You may not always be able to choose what happens to you in your life, but you will always be able to choose what you do about what happens to you in your life. And what you do about it—and *with* it—will determine what you make of your life.

~

"The big thing is not what happens to us in life,
but what we do about what happens to us."

~ George Allen

You Always Have A Choice

In anything you do in life, you always have a choice.
You can choose what you think. You can choose what you say.
You can choose what you do, and you can choose what you continue to do.
You can choose how you act. You can choose how you react.
You can choose how you respond. You can choose how you move forward.
You can choose your character, and you can choose who you become;
And therefore, you can choose what will become of you,
And ultimately, what will become of your life.

"There is a choice you have to make,
  In everything you do.
  So keep in mind that in the end,
  The choice you make, makes you."

  ~ John Wooden

Choose Your Character & Choose Who You Want To Become

You Can Choose Your Character;
You Can Choose Who You Want To Become

Aristotle once said that "We are what we repeatedly do." And while there is no doubt that our individual actions have a direct bearing on who we become as people, I think there is much more to the process of determining character. Contrary to the Greek philosopher—who I will acknowledge is much, much wiser than myself and simply stated an opinion that happens to differ from my position on the matter—I believe character has less to do with *what we do* as it does with *who we wish to become.*

Prior to action, is conscious thought and decision-making. It is in this process of making choices—choices about who we want to become and how we are going to arrive at that destination—that ultimately determines an individual's character.

From an athletics standpoint, it is important to understand the idea that one loss does not make a person a loser, and that one win does not make a person a winner. What makes each man who he is—and who he will be—is the decision that each makes in regard to who he wants to become in life.

If a person wants to be a winner, then he is going to find out what traits are commonly possessed by winners, and strive to emulate them. Therefore, he is going to work hard, maintain his focus, make sacrifices, stay committed, and persevere through adversity. In short, he is going to keep fighting for constant improvement—because that is what "winners" do.

Once that person has made up his mind that he wants to be a winner—and not all people do: not everyone is willing to make all the sacrifices and pay the high price of excellence—and once he has figured out what it takes to become a winner, then he has to go about actually putting those traits into practice.

That may mean that when the first day of off-season conditioning begins, that he is going to wake up early and show up, on time, to run with his teammates. It also means that he is going to run hard and complete the workout to the absolute best of his ability. Why? … because that is what winners do, and this person recognizes this fact fully and keeps it in mind all throughout his first day of training. Now, although this prospective winner has done everything necessary to become a winner, he is not yet one. This is because at the current moment, he does not yet possess the characteristics of a winner. At present, he has simply *done* once that which winners do often. Therefore, his actions during the first day of conditioning are just that—merely *actions.*

It is not until he continually reaffirms his desire to be a winner and continues to perform the actions that winners perform, that his actions will become *habits.* When this occurs, and the young man continues to perform the proper actions to an even further extent, those newly formed habits become so basic and routine, that they become easier and easier to execute.

After a while, the person no longer even has to think about doing them because they essentially become automatic. The process of making decisions to perform the actions, and then carrying out those decisions, becomes so engrained in the person's psyche and behavior, that it effectively becomes a part of their existence. It becomes a part of their personality.

This person has spent enough time thinking about who he wants to become, what things he needs to do in order to become that person, and then doing those things, that such actions have become part of who he is. And now, while he still may have to reaffirm his beliefs in regard to the direction in which he is heading, most of what he does will simply be a result of him merely being himself.

So now, when Monday morning rolls around, and he knows he is supposed to train on Monday mornings for the upcoming season, that young man is going to get out of bed and go train, because that is who he is—a winner—and that is what winners do; and in order for him to remain a winner, that is what he is going to have to continue to do. If he fails to do so, then he will no longer be a "winner," since he will no longer possess the traits that winners possess.

At the same time that this is true for winners, the same is also true for those who do not wish to make the commitments to become winners. For them, the actions that they perform—or in this case, do not perform—also develop into habits. Pretty soon, after enough repetition, those habits become traits, and those traits become part of who they are as individuals.

Just like the winner does not have to think about training, because that is what he has come to do naturally, so too does a loser not have to think about training because it is simply something which he has come to *avoid* naturally.

Coach Paul Bryant knew what he was talking about when he said "The first time you quit, it's hard. The second time, it gets easier. The third time, you don't even have to think about it," and he was right.

By this third instance of quitting, a person does not even have to think about quitting because the mere notion of quitting—of not being committed and dedicated—has already become so engrained in his personality that it just flows forth from the person who he is.

The one great thing about character, however, is that it is not a static object. Character is a dynamic and ever-changing item that evolves with us. We become who we are through decisions and actions, but we do not remain that person by merely sitting still and coasting from there on out. We must constantly be making and reaffirming decisions, and acting on them in a manner that preserves the integrity of the person whom we have become. To return to the football analogy, in order to be a winner, you have to become a winner and then continue to enforce the characteristics of being a winner.

This does not mean that once you become a winner, you will always be one. Essentially, what it means is that you always have to be *becoming* a winner. Conversely, it does not mean that once you become a loser, you will always be one. There is always the opportunity to improve, and there is always the hope of becoming something greater.

~

> **We are who we choose to become.**
> **Our character is what we decide to make it.**

~

Choose A Winning Character

If being a winner is a byproduct of deciding that you want to become one, figuring out what you need to do in order to become one, and continually doing those things, then the same formula applies to being a person of good character.

No one act makes a person good or bad. No one act makes a person anything. What gives a person good character or bad character—what makes them honorable or not honorable—is the decision they make regarding who they want to become.

That realization or choice is very much like a road map, because if you do not know what your destination is, then how are you ever going to get there? If you set out on a journey with no blueprint for traveling there, you deprive yourself of any way to tell whether or not you are headed in the right direction.

That is why it is important to establish this idea of the "ideal me," and figure out who you want to be one day as a person, and what you want to do in life. The easiest way to do this is to take a close look at the people in your life who you love and the people who you respect.

First you need to identify these people. But then you need to identify *why* you love them and why you respect them. In other words, *"What qualities make them respectable?"*

Try to pinpoint as many traits as you can that make these people "good people" in your eyes. For example, someone you know or know about may be very humble, they may have an incredible work ethic, they might be a very genuine and compassionate person, they may treat everyone with dignity and respect, or they might do their best to live by their principles. Whatever the characteristics are, identify them.

The people at whom you look for some form of guidance can be people you know, or simply more prominent people who you have seen or read about in the media. For me personally, I have been very blessed to have had a lot of wonderful and noble people come into my life. I have had great parents, teachers, coaches, and friends. But I have also looked to great figures in American and world history, especially those in leadership roles.

I have heard and read about such great people as Dr. Martin Luther King, Jr., Vince Lombardi, Mahatma Gandhi, Joe Paterno, John Wooden, Paul "Bear" Bryant, Rudolph Giuliani, Eddie Robinson, and countless others. All of those men had or have numerous traits that I esteem and respect. And when I think about the person who I wish to become, it ends up being a compilation of all those traits and virtues that I admire.

Also important in this process, however, is to determine those characteristics which you do *not* want to possess, and to figure out the ways in which you do not want to live your life. No one is perfect, and you can learn something from everyone you meet. A major part of determining who you want to become is figuring out who you also do *not* want to become.

Napoleon Bonaparte talked of "conquering history," rather than simply "studying" it. What the French ruler meant by this was that instead of merely looking at past events, he sought to extract every piece of valuable information and sought to learn from it, and to apply it in some way to his own life. He learned to distinguish between what ideas and characteristics of past leaders were helpful, and which were harmful. Those which he favored, he attempted to incorporate into his personality and philosophies if possible. Those which he did not, he tried to prevent himself from developing, or eliminate the ones that already existed.

Certainly, there is no need to limit your search for knowledge to just the past, like Napoleon did. But you can also look to people of your own time, and within your own life. However one chooses to go about the process is entirely up to one to decide. What matters is that one ultimately be able to visualize the exact virtues which one wishes to possess, and that one also pinpoint the specific vices which one does not want to have.

Once this visualization is formed, it becomes what is essentially a character compass. That ever-present image of who a person wants to become begins to act like True North. By constantly looking to that destination, it forces an individual to always be thinking about the path necessary to travel upon in order to arrive there. If one can provide one's self with a specific objective, and a map by which to achieve it, then one is going to have an extremely good chance of accomplishing what they set out to accomplish.

Conversely, a person who does not take the time and effort to figure out who they should want to become and where they want to go, will be like a traveler without a map, who wanders aimlessly and is at the mercy of the winds of convenience. Therefore, there is a definite need to establish some point on the map. And there is just as great a need to plan the route to that place. Otherwise, you can know *where* you want to go, but it is highly unlikely that you are going to get there if you do not know *how* to get there.

~

To offer an analogy… Someone wanting to drive from California to Florida would not get into his car and simply start driving without first getting out a map and figuring out which is the best way to get him to the sunshine state. If he did, then how is he going to get to where he wants to go? How is he going to know when to turn onto the highway, which exits to take, and which routes to get on? He isn't, and that is the point.

You can have the best destination in mind, but if you do not take the time to figure out exactly how you are going to get there, then you are going to end up missing a turn or an exit—or many—somewhere along the way, and before you know it, you are going to be traveling northbound from California, on your way to Canada… wishfully thinking that you are going to make it to Florida.

~

"Acquiring the qualities of virtue requires a good plan and consistent effort."
~ Benjamin Franklin

We Are Who We Consciously Choose, & Allow Ourselves To Become

Who we actively seek to become as a person—the traits we seek out to exhibit and turn into personal habit—and who we actively seek to avoid becoming—the traits that we try to prevent ourselves from developing or work to correct if we have already begun to develop them—is who we indeed will become.

Who we consciously seek to become and who we consciously allow ourselves to become; and also who we consciously seek to avoid becoming… is what will determine who we ultimately are and the way we live in this world.

~

We are who we consciously choose and allow ourselves to become.

~

Once a person understands who they want to become and how they are going to go about accomplishing that objective, the only thing left to do is to actually put in the necessary work. In this case, that means beginning to act like the kind of person you want to become would act.

At the start of the process, you may be doing good acts, but you may not necessarily be a good person as of yet. And of course the opposite is true, since just because someone does bad things, it does not mean that they are a bad human being.

It is once that person has persisted in performing certain acts, that he has developed those actions into habits. And once that person executes those habits often enough—whether they are good ones or bad ones—and they become part of who he is, similar actions will begin flowing forth from that person without much thought or effort. A kind person acts kindly, because doing so is part of who he is; it is what defines him. An honest person speaks honestly, because that is who he is.

~

"The force of character is cumulative."
~ Ralph Waldo Emerson

~

The more and more a person acts in a certain way, the easier and easier it becomes to act that way. It becomes like a snowball rolling downhill. The farther it goes in the same direction, the more momentum it builds, the bigger it gets, and the faster it rolls. Once you build that momentum up for good purposes, it becomes extremely hard to do anything other than continue to increase.

It is like Newton's law of motion: an object in motion will remain in motion unless acted upon by an outside force. Well, once you get the ball rolling in regard to developing good character, it is very difficult to stop, or even to slow down. This is what Ralph Waldo Emerson meant when he said "the force of character is cumulative."

Building Good Character

Building one's good character is not an easy task. It takes hard work; it takes determination. A man's good character is not easily attained; it can only come through a persistent effort to bend it, build it, shape it, and mold it. A man's good character cannot be purchased or cheaply gained; it can only be earned through a commitment to worthy ideals, and by the perseverance to live up to and live-out those ideals.

Ultimately, building one's good character is no easy task. However, if a man invests himself—and all that he has within him… then the task most certainly will be worth it. For when a man pours his heart fully into the process of becoming a good man, he will carve for himself a great and noble character.

~

"You can't just dream yourself into character.
You must hammer—you must forge—one out for yourself."
~ Vince Lombardi, Jr.

~

It Takes Determination To Determine Your Character

A man does not become good by performing good deeds. A man becomes good because he makes a conscious decision to become good, and then he acts in correspondence with that resolution. He then makes constant decisions, each and every day, to continue along the path that he has set out upon.

In every circumstance in which a man finds himself, he must make the determination to live out his convictions. He must consistently live up to the ideals that he has chosen to aspire to, and he must do all that he can to create for himself the life he so desperately desires.

~ As a man decides himself to be, so he shall be.

The Choice Is Yours

The great thing about character is that it isn't inherited, it isn't genetic, and it doesn't have anything to do with how much money you have. The great thing about character is that it is entirely self-chosen. You get to choose your character, and you get to choose the person who you become. Make sure you are the one doing the choosing; don't let someone else dictate your life.

Take Control Of Your Life

Take control of your attitudes…
Take control of your choices…
Take control of your actions…
And take control of your life.

You Can Choose Who You Become,
and You MUST Choose Who You Become
~
What you decide to do, will determine what you become.
And what you become, will determine what becomes of your life,
Because ultimately… What you become, will determine what becomes of you.
~
You can choose who you become, and you must choose who you become as well,
because ultimately, who you become will determine what your life becomes.
~
You Must Take Responsibility for Your Own Character;
You Must Take Responsibility for Forging Your Own Character and Destiny
You must take responsibility for the creation of your own character, because ultimately,
you must take responsibility for the construction of your own destiny.
~
We are who we choose to become,
And our lives are what we choose them to be.

Character Formation Comes Through Decisions, Determinations, and Continuations

Character is not formed by one act. Rather, it is formed by decisions, determinations, and sustained commitment to living out those decisions and determinations.

Character is formed as a result of conscious thought, committed action, and continued practice. By deciding who a person wants to become, aligning his daily choices with that decision, and then by working to develop and further the habits that will take him to his ideal self… a man may choose the character which he attains; he may choose who he becomes, and therefore, he may choose what ultimately becomes of his life.

Character is formed by:
1. Deciding who it is that you want to become.
2. Determining, through positive examples or from other sources of knowledge, what characteristics that type of person possesses.
3. Continually acting in a way that corresponds to how that type of person would act.

In sports terms that means that:

One win does not make you a "winner, and one loss does not make you a "loser."

What makes you a winner ultimately is:
1. Deciding that you want to be a winner.
2. Determining what traits winners possess, and visualizing the ideal winner.
3. Continually acting in a way that is reflective of how a winner acts, and reaffirming those actions until they become a part of you and until they begin to flow from you naturally.

What makes you a loser ultimately is:
~ Not doing any of the above, at least not as of the current moment. Those people who are not winners, are not really losers—they are just people who have not decided to become winners *yet*. As was said before: the great thing about life is that you have to continually redefine or reinforce your character everyday, and that there is always reason for hope and the opportunity for improvement.

There is no such thing as a loser, only a person who has yet to become a winner.

"Where you are right now doesn't have to determine where you'll end up. No one's written your destiny for you, because you write your own destiny. You make your own future." ~ *Barack Obama*

"You may be whatever you resolve to be." ~ *General Thomas "Stonewall" Jackson*

*"You will be what you **will** to be."* ~ *James Allen*

Choose Success

Everyone Can Be Successful

Everyone has the ability to be successful. Not everyone, however, will *choose* to be successful. Whether you will be successful or not, will be determined by whether or not YOU CHOOSE TO BECOME SUCCESSFUL.

Success is not something you are born with. It is not a right. It is not a privilege. Success is a choice. More appropriately: success is a series of choices, made each and every single day, day-in and day-out. In everything that you think, say, and do—from your attitudes and your actions, to the habits that you come to form over time—you choose whether or not you are ultimately going to become successful. Each and every choice you make either increases or decreases your chances of success. Therefore, make sure that you always consider the potential impact of whatever it is that you do or not do. Every decision you make, and every action you take, will either help or hinder your chances of becoming successful. Choose wisely: choose successful actions and successful habits, and you will be choosing to become a successful person.

Choose Success

In everything that you do, you are either choosing to become successful or you are not. Every decision you make is either going to get you closer to or further away from the person you are capable of becoming. Every choice you make is either going to increase or decrease your chances for succeeding. Every decision you arrive at is either going to bring you closer to or further from your intended destination.

In everything that you do, you have to ask yourself: *Am I choosing success?*
In other words: Are the things you are doing—or that you are about to do—going to get you closer to your goals?

>If the answer is *yes*, then go ahead with it and do it.
>If the answer is *no*, then stop and don't do it. Figure out what would be more productive, determine what would be a better choice to make—or a better action to take—and then do that instead.

Am I choosing success?

   Is this going to help me succeed?
      Is this going to increase my chances of becoming successful?
         Am I **choosing** success?

   ~ If *yes*, then do it. If *no*, then don't do it.

~ Choose Success

Good Decisions + Good Situations = Good Outcomes

Good Decisions + Good Situations = Good Outcomes. The better your decisions, the better the situations you put yourself in, the better your chances for success will be.

The more good decisions you make, the more good situations you will find yourself in as a result. The more good situations you find and put yourself in, the more likely you are to be successful. This is because, when you put yourself in good situations, you literally increase your chances of having good things happen.

First of all, you make it easier and more likely to continue to make good decisions, which ultimately will increase your chances for success on its own. Secondly, when you put yourself in good situations, you increase the number of potential good things that can happen, and you decrease the number of potential bad things that can happen.

~

If you are able to continually make good decisions and consistently put yourself in good situations, you are going to be more likely to succeed than otherwise. Conversely, if you continuously make bad decisions and constantly put yourself in bad situations, you are going to be much less likely to succeed than you otherwise would be. After all, good decisions plus good situations, equals good outcomes. And *the best decisions* plus *the best situations*, equals *the best chances for success*.

~ The Best Decisions + The Best Situations = The Best Chances for Success

---

Today's Choices Are Tomorrow's Habits

Successful people don't succeed by accident. They become successful because they consciously work to develop and practice successful habits.

Today's choices are tomorrow's habits. When you make the best choices, you are not only choosing successful attitudes and successful actions, but you are also consciously choosing to practice and develop successful habits.

Success Is A Choice, and Success Is *Your* Choice

With each and every one of your choices, you are exerting direct influence over your chances for success. When you make the right choices, you set yourself up for success. When you make successful choices, you begin to create the pathway toward success: with each good choice you make, you help build the road to success, one brick at a time. **You can improve your chances for success by improving the choices that you make.**

~

Your habits form you, so form good habits.
~ *Herman Edwards*

~

Choose Greatness

Everyone Can Be Great
Within each of us lies the potential for greatness.
The opportunities are unlimited and the possibilities are endless.
Do not settle for being mediocre; do not settle for merely being good.
Dare to be great.

Choose Greatness
Just like with success, greatness is also a choice. More importantly—just like success—greatness is *your* choice to make. So how does one choose greatness?

Simple: A person chooses greatness by choosing to give his very best at all times, and to do his very best in all ways. A person chooses to become great by giving his greatest efforts to everything he does. He chooses to become great by striving to do his greatest work with anything and everything that he does.

Choosing greatness is simply a matter of making a commitment to be great.
Making a commitment is simply a matter of choosing to do so.
~
"A man can be as great as he wants to be."
~ *Vince Lombardi*
~
"Anybody can do just about anything
that he really wants to and makes up his mind to do.
We are capable of greater things than we realize."
~ *Norman Vincent Peale*

There exists a divine spark inside us all;
it is up to us to fan the flames and stoke the fire.

"Each one of us is born with a seed of greatness,
and it is our responsibility to nurture it and make it grow."
~ *Edie Raether*

Are You Willing to Become Great?
Your character is a combination of your thoughts, your habits, and your priorities. It determines the choices you make, and the choices you make determine who you become. Who you become will determine what you accomplish.
~ Are you willing to do what it takes to become special?
~ Are you willing to do what it takes to become great?

Be Great

Be Great.
Be Transcendent. Be Transforming.

~

Great individuals transcend society.
As a result, and by virtue of their transcendence,
they transform the world in which they live.

~

Do not settle for mediocrity; do not be transformed
by the low expectations of the world and of those around you.
Have the courage to always be yourself,
and dare to always be your best self.
Strive for excellence in all that you do.
Strive for greatness in all that you are.
Become everything you are capable of becoming.
Be everything you are meant to be.

~

Be Great.
Be Transcendent. Be Transforming.

~

A man can be as great as he wants to be.
If you believe in yourself and have the courage, the determination,
the dedication, the competitive drive, and if you are willing to sacrifice the little things
in life and pay the price for the things that are worthwhile, it can be done."
~ Vince Lombardi

Choose Success, Choose Greatness, and Become Excellence

The day you decide to take complete responsibility for yourself, the day you stop making excuses for yourself and stop complaining about your circumstances, the day you start to take hold of your life and everything that happens in it… that is the day you begin making your way toward success; that is the day you begin your journey toward greatness; that is the day you start upon your path to excellence.

That day—that very day in which you take hold of yourself and in which you seize responsibility for your life… that is the day you begin to become successful. That is the day you begin to become great. That is the day you begin to become *excellence*.

We make our world by the goals we pursue,
By the heights we seek and the higher view,
By hopes and dreams that reach the sun
And a will to fight till the heights are won.

~ *Alfred Grant Walton*

Become Excellence

Aim for excellence in all of your efforts
Strive for excellence in all your endeavors.
Be the absolute best you can be.
Become the absolute most you can become.

Do not settle for less than greatness.
Do not bargain for less than success.
Never settle for mediocrity.
Never settle for less.

Give your best, and give your all.
Be your best, and be your all.

Aim for excellence in all of your efforts.
Strive for excellence in all your endeavors.
Do your best, and be your greatest.
Do your most, and be your finest.

Aim for greatness, and aim for the highest.
Achieve greatness, and become the highest.
Aim for success, and aim for the best.
Achieve success, and become the best.

Strive for success, and become greatness.
Strive for greatness, and become excellence.

~

~

We must become who we wish to be.
We must become what we wish to achieve.

~

"If you want to do something special,
you must first become something special. *"*
~ Vince Lombardi

What Really Matters, What Really Lasts
Invest In What Matters, Invest In What Lasts

Invest In What Matters

When a builder sets out to build a home, he first needs to have the tools necessary to build that house. Before he can put a single block or brick in place, a builder first needs to have the wherewithal with which to do his building. Any good builder knows that the best houses are made with the best tools, and from the best materials. A good builder then, will spend his money on the finest and most precise of instruments. He will not waste his hard-earned dollars on tools that will break or be thrown away, either because they aren't made well or because they aren't important and don't matter.

Instead, a good builder will spend his money on equipment that is both strong and sturdy, equipment that is well-made and long-lasting, equipment that is significant and that matters. He invests in this type of tool because he knows that it will help him build a strong and sturdy house, a house that will be built well and that will last for a very long time as a result, a house that will be significant and a house that ultimately will matter in the long-run. Simply stated: a good builder invests in what matters.

Invest In What Lasts

When a builder sets out to build a house, he first goes out to buy the materials he needs in order to build that house. Any good builder knows that the best houses are made from the best materials. A good builder then, will buy the strongest and sturdiest materials that he can find, because he knows that they will make his house last for as long as possible. If a man is going to invest all the time and effort needed to build, then he is going to want to make sure that the house he builds lasts as long as possible.

Therefore, a good and wise builder invests in solid and sturdy materials, materials that will become the building blocks of a masterful house that will endure for a great number of years, and materials that ultimately will stand the test of time. Simply stated: a good builder invests in what lasts.

Invest In What Matters; Invest In What Lasts.

If you invest yourself in what matters, and if you invest your time and effort into what lasts, then you will build the foundation of a strong and enduring future. If you invest in what matters and in what lasts, then you will build for yourself a life and a legacy that stand the test of time.

What Really Matters

Understand What Really Matters In Life

In order to live a life that really matters, you first must understand what really matters in life. In other words, you must first realize what life truly is all about.

~ What Life Is All About ~

Life is all about being respectful, responsible, and honorable.
Life is all about showing class and having integrity.
Life is all about doing things the right way, all along the way.
Life is all about doing what's right, standing for what's right,
and standing *up* for what's right.

Life is all about making the most of your talents
and your opportunities in this life.
Life is all about making the biggest contribution that you can
make to the world around you.
Life is all about making the most of your life and your time on this Earth.

Life is all about relationships.
Life is all about how much you can love and be loved;
it is about how much you can allow yourself to love others
and to be loved by others in return.
Life is all about what you can do for others.
Life is all about the contribution you make during the course of your lifetime.

Life is all not only about your own personal success, but more importantly,
it is about your personal significance to others: it is about having an impact on other
people and being a positive presence in this world.

Life is all not only about your own personal accomplishments and reaching your own full
potential, but more importantly, it is about doing all you can to help others reach their full
potential and make the most of their lives as well.

~

Life is all about having an impact and leaving a positive legacy.

~

Live for Something Greater Than Yourself

Live for something greater than yourself. Dedicate your life to a cause that goes beyond
yourself. Create a specific and meaningful purpose for your life. Use your talents to improve
the world and to help others. Leave the world a better place because you were here.

~

Live for something greater than yourself: live a life that matters; leave a legacy that lasts.

~

What Really Matters

Life is a series of questions and answers. It consists of both the asking and the responding. The most important piece of the puzzle, however, is knowing which questions to ask, and the understanding that you not only must find the correct answers, but that you must live them out on the canvas of your own life.

How Much Do You Bench? …
And How Much Does It Matter?

"*How much do you bench?*" That might be the one question that guys and young men hear more than anything else. We hear it at the gym, at school, at practice, and pretty much everywhere else. It's like all the men in the world got together and decided that the bench press is now the official measure of a man.

Apparently, if you can bench more than the next guy, that makes you a more important person. And if not, then apparently that makes you less important…or at least that's what society tells us.

I'm not saying that you shouldn't be concerned with your personal fitness or physical appearance. What I *am* saying, is that **you should be more concerned with the things that are truly important in life.** There are so many unimportant questions out there that we constantly ask ourselves and one another, that we tend to lose sight of what really matters in our lives…and of the questions that we should really be asking—questions like:

Who are you?
What do you stand for?
What *won't* you stand for?
Who's important to you in your life?
How often do you tell those people
    that you love and appreciate them?
Do you live by your principles?
Do you treat people with respect?
Do you earn the respect and trust of others?

~

These are the types of questions we should be asking ourselves.
These are the things we should be focusing on more than how much
we can bench or how much we can squat.

~

So, how much do *you* bench?
Who cares: How much do you do for others?
Are you comfortable in that extra-small muscle shirt?
**Who cares: Are you comfortable with who you are
and with the way you're living your life?"**

What Really Matters
Things That Impress

The Things That Impress

People often try to impress others with clothes, cars, money, looks, popularity, and a number of other things that ultimately don't matter in the grand scheme of things. Rather than spending our time trying to acquire all these things—and only these things—we instead should focus on developing what really matters. Rather than concentrating on all the external things that don't really matter in the long-run in life, we instead should turn our attention to the internal things that ultimately are of greater significance.

~

Too often, we try to impress one another with the things we possess,
And not necessarily with the things that really impress.

~

Instead of trying to impress others with all the outer possessions that we can accumulate, we should try to impress them with all the inner traits that we can cultivate. Instead of trying to impress people with surface appearances and material goods, *we should try to impress people with the quality of our character.*

~

We should try to impress people with our kindness, with our respectability, with our honesty, with our integrity, with our courage, with our commitment, with our conviction, with our determination, with our fidelity, with our friendship, with our consideration, with our genuineness, with our concern for others, with our humility, with our decency, with our sincerity, with our class, with our dignity, with our virtue, with our character, and with our honor. *After all, these are the things that really matter.*

~

True success is not about what you do, but about who you are.
When it's all over, success is not about what you've done, but about who you've become.

~

Invest In What Matters. Invest In What Counts.
Invest yourself in what matters; invest yourself in what counts.
Invest in who you are. Invest in who you are becoming.
Live a great life. Live an honorable life.
Live a life that matters.

~

The Importance of Faith and Family

Faith and family are the foundation of any person's life. When hard times come knocking at the door, everything else goes out the window, except for faith and family. When difficulty arises, all we can do is lean on our foundation and rely on it for strength.

It is faith that provides us with reassurance that everything happens for a reason, and that everything in the end will work out. It is faith that tells us that we are going to be okay and that we are going to make it through whatever adversity falls upon us. In short, faith tells us that no matter how painful our despair, and no matter how deep our wounds, that there is hope. It is family that is the physical presence of that hope.

How Do You Get Through the Tough Times In Life?

There are times in all our lives when we have to go through truly difficult moments. Whether it's a difficult personal situation, something as serious as the loss of a loved one, dealing with a serious illness or personal tragedy, or maybe a situation when something doesn't work out the way you hope it would or want it to—maybe an important game that you don't win, a college you don't get accepted to, or a job you don't get—the reality is that tough times are inevitable in life. So, how do you get through those difficult moments in life? How do you whether the storm and make it through the tough times?

~

When you're going through adversity, it really weeds out the unimportant things in your life, and it forces you to realize what truly matters. When hard times come knocking at the door, everything else goes out the window. All that remains in a person's life is the foundation that they've built for themselves.

That is where faith and family come into play. Without question, faith and family have to be at the foundation of every person's life. Regardless of what someone's religious background may be, everyone has to have something in their life that gives them reason to believe that everything will be okay.

It is faith that provides us with the calming reassurance that everything happens for a reason, and that, in the end, everything will work out for the best. It is faith that tells us that we are going to be okay and that we are going to make it through whatever kind of adversity comes our way. **Faith tells us that no matter how painful our despair, no matter how deep our wounds, and no matter how hopeless (dire/bleak) our situation appears to be...there is always hope.**

It is a person's faith that offers that reassurance, and it is a person's family that provides the physical presence of that hope. When talking about the word "family," it's important to understand that family doesn't just mean the people you're related to. It means the people who are important to you in your life. Family is your relatives and your best friends, it's the people you're close to, it's your teammates, it's your mentors, it's your coaches. In short, family means the people who matter to you, and the people to whom you matter.

It is family that you can go to when you're struggling and say, "I need help right now. I need you to help me through this because I can't do it on my own—none of us can do it on our own." And it is family that rallies around you and says, "Hey, I'm here for you. Don't worry about a thing, because we're going to get through all this, and we're going to do it together."

Rely On Your Foundation For Strength

Whenever adversity strikes, the only thing you can do is turn to your faith and family, and rely on that foundation for strength. **That's what you do when you're going through the hard times—you strip away all the other things in life and you lean on what really matters.**

Being A Family

Being a family means that we are always there for each other, through good times and through hard times, for better or for worse. Being a family means that we share in each other's commitments: we take each other's burdens and we carry them as a family—together—because the strength of the family is greater than any one of its members. The strength of the bundle is greater than any of the sticks in it. We take those burdens, and we make those burdens our own burdens, because the joys of others are our joys as well, and the pain of others is our pain also.

No matter what happens in life—no matter what we have to go through—family has to always stick together. The thing to remember about family is this: if we stick together, it'll all work out. If we stick together, we'll be okay. No one can get through the tough times on his own. We need each other. We need to be there for each other.

~

For one person, the burdens of life are too heavy.
But for a family—for us—there's no obstacle that can stand in our way.

~

Being a family means that we are always there for each other. Being a family means that we always reach out to one another. It means that when your brother or sister is emotionally or spiritually tired, or when he or she is doubting their strength to carry on, you go to that person and say, "Lean on me, and I'll get you through this. Don't worry about a thing, because I'm here for you, and it's going to be alright. If you don't have the energy or the strength, I will give you mine, and we'll make it through."

~

"All I know is this: if we stick together, it'll all work out." ~ Ray Lewis

~

Being a family means that when your brother or sister is going through a difficult time and needs help, you go and you help them make it through the challenges they're facing. You go to them and you let them know that they don't ever have to go through anything in life alone. You let them know that they don't have to do it all on their own—that they don't have to fight their battles all by themselves. Family looks to one another and says, "I'm here for you. Don't worry about anything; I've got you covered; I'll take care of you. I'm here for you, and I'll always be here for you."

"We are in this journey of life together. We're in the same boat.
In this journey, there will be storms, and when these storms come—and they will—
We must weather them together."
~ Michael Turkovic

Shelter from the Storm

Dealing with adversity is a lot like dealing with the unpredictable storms that summertime always seems to bring with it. It's like when that tornado warning flashes across the TV screen, the wind starts howling, and it looks like the end of the world is coming right at you…and you think to yourself, "This can't be good."

What do you do in that situation? Well, you do what everyone is always taught to do when something like that happens: you go down to the basement of the house and you wait out the storm. You go down to the foundation—where all that thick, reinforced concrete is—because that's the strongest and most reliable part of the house. It's that foundation that is going to protect you from the high-speed winds, the torrential downpours, the thunder and lightening, and whatever else Mother Nature—and life—will throw at you.

The foundation is that safe haven you can go to for protection in the midst of the storm. It's the one part that can't be shaken by the winds of adversity. When it comes to your house, that foundation is your basement. When it comes to your life, that foundation is your faith and your family.

~

"When it comes to my priorities in life,
there's my faith and my family…
and then everything else."
~ Danny Wuerfful

~

Life Is A Team Sport, and We All Need Teammates In the Game of Life

Life is a team sport. And, just like in sports, when you're not having a good day and you are struggling through whatever it is you are doing, you need your teammates to help pick you up and support you.

In life, when you are struggling with adversity and going through the tough times, you need your family members and friends—your teammates in the game of life—to help pick you up and support you.

You need a family, and you need a team to make it through the tough times. And, just as you will undoubtedly need others to be there for you at one time or another, so too will others need you to be there for them as well when they are going through life's difficult patches.

In sports, you need your teammates to be there for you during the tough times; likewise, your teammates need you to be there for them as well. In life, you need your family and friends to be there for you during the difficult moments; likewise, your family and friends need you to be there for them as well.

~

Be there for others, support others, encourage others, care for others,
care about others, protect others, love others.

Put Others First:
Look Beyond Your Own Concerns, and Look Out For the Needs of Others

Putting others first means being able to look beyond your own concerns, and to look out for the needs of others instead. It means putting your own individual desires aside, and making other people's concerns the main focus of your attention. Simply put, putting others first means forgetting about what you can get for yourself, and learning to concentrate instead on what you can *give of* yourself. It means removing selfish thoughts about what others can do for you, and instead replacing them with self*less* thoughts of what you can do for others.

"Ask not what your teammates can do for you; ask what you can do for your teammates."
~ Irvin "Magic" Johnson

"Ask not what your country can do for you; ask what you can do for your country."
~ John F. Kennedy

"What Can I Do?"

How much better would our world be if instead of thinking about ourselves all the time, each of us thought about others, and about what we can do for others? How much better would each of our lives be if we all made it a habit to constantly ask ourselves... *"What can I do...?"*

"What can I do ...
> ... to help someone else today?
> ... to help make someone else feel better about themselves today?
> ... to help someone in need today?"

"What can I do ...
> ... to help bring hope and joy to someone else's life today?
> ... to help build someone else up today?
> ... to help make someone else's day today?"

"What can I do ...
> ... to help make other people's lives a little bit better, in some way, today?
> ... to help make my school a little bit better, in some way, today?
> ... to help make my community a little bit better, in some way, today?
> ... to help make my society a little bit better, in some way, today?"

~

"What can I do... to help make this world a better place... in any way, *and in every way*... today... and *every day*?

What can I do?

~

~ What you can do for others is more important than what you can do for yourself. ~

Another One of Sports' Great Life Lessons:
Subordinate Individual Desires for the Good of the Greater Whole

Another one of the great lessons that sports teaches is the importance of sacrifice. Essentially, it is the value of learning to put one's own personal desires aside in order to help bring about the good of something greater than oneself. In sports, this means that team needs take priority over individual desires. It means that the needs of the group take priority over the concerns of the individual.

In order for a team to succeed in its mission of winning, all members of the team—players and coaches alike—must put what's best for the team ahead of what's best for themselves. No one person is bigger than the team, and no one individual is more important than the team. Therefore, everyone on a team must do what is in the best interest of the group, at all times.

There can be no individual success without team success. And often, it is the pursuit of individual success that prohibits the attainment of team success. Everything that everyone on a team does must be about the team first: it all has to be about the team, not any one individual. It cannot be about *I*, or *you* or *me*… but rather, it must be about *US* and *WE*. It cannot be about something as small as one piece of the puzzle, but about the entire puzzle as a whole; it cannot be about one individual, one player, or one coach… it has to be about something bigger and more important than just one person. It has to be about the team.

~

Sports teach us that **we are all part of something that is larger than ourselves**, and that we have to learn to subordinate our own individual desires for the good of the greater whole. In athletics—like on a football team for example—that means making personal sacrifices for the benefit of the team. In life, it means making personal sacrifices for your family, your friends, your company, your marriage, and all your relationships.

In the game of competitive sports, you may have to sacrifice playing time or a bigger role in order to help the team win. You may have to sacrifice personal desires for fame and attention, in order to help bring about an even greater amount of glory for the team. As you go through a season, you may have to sacrifice individual wants and selfish agendas in order to be able to contribute your most to the team; you may have to give up certain activities in your personal life, prioritize your schedule accordingly, and be willing to put your thoughts of individual success aside… all for the sake of the team, and for the sake of the overall team's success.

In the game of life, you may have to sacrifice playing a sport or engaging in an extra-curricular activity during a certain season in order to get a job, take care of younger brother, or to help ends meet at home. As you get older, you may have to sacrifice some time with your friends or other fun pursuits in order to try to make a relationship work. Beyond that, you may have to sacrifice playing golf on the weekends in order to help take care of the kids while your wife puts in overtime at work, or in order for you, yourself, to work overtime in order to help pay the bills.

As you get older, you may have to sacrifice those Cowboys seasons tickets, or those Giants-Dodgers series tickets that you were able to have a shot at getting, in order to put money aside or help pay for your child's college tuition.

These are just some examples of sacrificing individual desires for the needs of something more important. When it comes down to it, a real man—a responsible and respectable man—does what he knows that he is obligated to do for the good of the group, and not necessarily what he wants to do for his own good.

~

"What's best for the team takes priority over what's best for the individual."
~ *John Wooden*

~

Understanding the essence of personal sacrifice means realizing that much of life is not about what you *want* to do, but rather it is about what you are *needed* to do. It means recognizing that there are things that are more pressing and more important than what you may *think* is important at the time. It means realizing that there are other people who are counting on you to do those more pressing and important things, rather than simply looking out for yourself and doing whatever you *feel* like doing.

When it comes to a team, or a relationship, or a family… it's not always about what you *want* to do, it's about what the greater good *needs* you to do. That is what worthwhile sacrifice is all about: putting your own interests and desires aside for the benefit of something far greater than yourself.

~

"You must be willing to sacrifice personal considerations for the welfare of all."
~ *John Wooden*

~

True commitment requires sacrifice. True commitment to others—or to put it in one simple word: *love*—requires a great deal of sacrifice.

In part, to love means to sacrifice one's self for the benefit of others. In fact, sacrificing an individual's personal interests for the good of another may very well be the greatest expression of love that there is. After all, the greatest way a person can show his love for others is to give his life for them.

We use terms like "taking a bullet for someone" and "making the ultimate sacrifice…" as sayings to show our appreciation and respect for others. Those whom we love and admire are the people who we would "take a bullet for." Those who take up the cause of their country and are willing to risk their lives for others—to "make the ultimate sacrifice"—do so out of high regard and respect for those they are serving.

In order to express commitment, and in order to express the greatest type of commitment—love—a person must be ready and willing to make sacrifices. On a team, this means that a person must be willing to put the good of the team before himself. In a business organization, it means that an employee must be willing to put the company's bottom line before his own. In a family, it means that an individual must be ready and willing to do anything, and everything, his family needs him to do. He must be prepared to put what is best for his family ahead of what is best for himself.

~

Simply put, sacrifice is about putting the needs of others before your own; it means learning to subordinate individual desires for the good of the greater whole.

~

An Essential Lesson In Life
Learning to subordinate your own agenda in order to do and achieve what is best for the team, the group, or the family… is an essential lesson in life. Being ready and willing to make the necessary sacrifices for the good of other people—to look beyond your own desires and to look out for the needs and concerns of others—is an essential part of life.

~

"Love your family members wholeheartedly; sacrifice for them whenever necessary; do everything you can in your power to help them and to let them know you love them. And to other members of humankind, just show your love to them universally, and help whoever needs your help. That is the way of love."

~ Ching Hai

A Summary of Sacrifice
Sacrifice is about putting the needs of others ahead of your own. In sports, sacrifice means putting the needs of the team before your own. In life, sacrifice means putting the needs of your family, your friends, and your loved ones ahead of your own.
Sacrifice is about forgetting about what you can do or get for yourself, and instead turning your attention to what you can do for others, and to what you can give of yourself to other people. It is about investing yourself into the effort to make a valuable contribution to something bigger and better than yourself—to the lives of others and to the world as a whole.

Put Others Before Yourself.
Be a Team Player and Be Unselfish.
Understand the importance of sacrifice: of learning to forego the pursuit of your own individual successes, in order to help bring about the success of the team as a whole. Subordinate your own individual concerns, in order to do what is best for the greater good. Set aside your own selfish desires for the sake and concerns of others.

~

We are all part of a team.
We are all part of a group. We are all part of a company.
We are all part of a family. We are all part of something
That is bigger than ourselves.

~

Live A Life That Matters
We are all part of a team, and we are all part something that is bigger than ourselves. We are all part of a larger group; and the contributions we make will only matter to the extent that they benefit the team.

We are all a part of something that is bigger than ourselves.
~ Live a life that matters.

It's Not About You
It's not about what you can do for yourself,
        It's about what you can *do for others*.
It's not about what you can gain for yourself,
        It's about what you can *give* of yourself *to others*.
It's not about the amount of wealth you can acquire for yourself;
        It's about the amount of worth you can learn to *share with others*.
It's not about the amount of value you can add to your own life;
        It's about the amount of value you can add to *the lives of others*.
It's not about the name you can make for yourself;
        It's about the *difference you can make for others*.
It's not about the success you can attain in your own life;
        It's about the *significance you can bring to the lives of others*.

~ Life is not about you; it is about others.
Life is about others, and what you can do for others.

It's not about *you*; it's about *them*."
~ *Robert Ladouceur*

"Life is not about us, but about other people and something bigger than us."
~ *Tony Dungy*

~ <u>Be For Others</u> ~

Put what's good for others ahead of what's good for you.
Consider the needs of others before your own wants.
Consider the wants of others before your own needs.

~

"Consider the rights of others before your own feelings,
and the feelings of others before your own rights."

~ *John Wooden*

It's not about what you do for yourself; it's about what you *do for others*.
It's not about what you gain for yourself; it's about what you *give of yourself to others*.

Be An Impact Player: Be A Role Model

Lead The Way: Live Your Message
When it comes right down to it, the best way—and the only way—to lead is by example. People will always pay more attention to what you do than to what you say. If you want others to be responsible and accountable, then you have to be responsible and accountable yourself. If you want other people to work hard and to dedicate themselves, then you have to work hard and dedicate yourself also. If you want others to be composed and to act with class at all times, then you have to be composed and act with class at all times as well.

Regardless of what a person says or tells people, there is one rule that always applies: **One footstep teaches more than a thousand words.** If a man's actions contradict his words, then no one will respect him, no one will trust him, and ultimately, no one will follow him. And if no one is following you, you are not a leader…you are merely a person out for a walk.

~

"Example is not the main thing in influencing others, it is the only thing."
~ Albert Schweitzer

~

The Messenger Is The Message
The message may not originally come from the messenger, but it is through him that the message gets delivered. He is the means for providing the message. Essentially, his words, his actions, and ultimately, his life, are the means by which his message is heard. So, in many regards, the messenger *is* the message.

~

The greatest way to instruct and to impact other people is by living-out your convictions. People learn by watching the examples that others set for them; and people learn by watching the example that *you* set for them as well.

~

"My life is my message."
~ Mahatma Gandhi

~

~ Be a Role Model ~

Being a role model is all about setting a positive example for others.
It is about investing in others, helping others reach their full potential,
serving as a good example of what a person can do in his life
and of what he can become in his lifetime as well.

~

Set a positive example for someone today.
Be a role model.

~ **Be A Difference-Maker** ~

Be a role model. Be a mentor. Be a leader. Be a difference-maker.
You don't have to change the entire world, in order to change a single person's life.
You don't have to change the whole universe, in order to change another person's world.

~

Be a Role Model; Be a Difference-Maker

If you look at anyone who is successful in life, the one common denominator is that they had someone along the way who was a positive influence on them. They all had a good role model in their lives: someone to look up to—whether they knew them personally, or they simply knew of them. Every successful person had someone who was a positive presence in their life, someone who cared about them and who invested in them, someone who helped teach them the lessons of life, and someone who helped them reach toward their full potential. Every successful person had that special someone in their life—someone who, through the sheer respectability of their character and the sincere concern of their interest, helped to shape the life of another.

If you want to help someone succeed, become that positive role model for him or her. Give them that blueprint for a successful life to aspire to. Go out of your way to help bring out the best in someone's life. Do your part to help teach others the valuable lessons that you have learned yourself. Be there for someone else, care about someone else, invest in someone else… Be a reason for their hope, for their future, and for their success. Be a role model. Be a difference-maker.

~

~ **Change Someone's Life** ~

Alter the course of someone's life. Steer someone in the right direction.
Reach out your hand to a fellow brother. Show the way to a better life for another.

~

Always Be Aware, Because Someone's Always Watching
Always be aware of your surroundings and even more aware of your actions.
For even when you are not, others certainly will be.

~

"People observe you when you don't even know they are watching,
and what they learn from you is your legacy to them."
~ *Charles F. Stanley*

Be a Person of Influence

The Three Things that You Need In Order to Be a Person of Influence

1. People must respect you. People must respect you for the way you carry yourself and for the way you treat others; they must respect you for what you stand for and for what you won't stand for; they must respect you for your principles and for the way that you live your life. In order to be a positive influence on others, you must first have the respect of others.

2. People must trust you. People must always know that you will keep your word and honor your commitments. They must know that you will always be truthful and forthcoming, that you will be humble and objective at all times, and that you will do all you can to become fully knowledgeable about yourself and the task at hand. People must trust that you can do what is expected of you: they must know that you are capable of doing the job that has been set before you—that you know what you are doing, that you know how to go about doing it, and that you can effectively and efficiently do it. In order to be a positive influence on others, you must first have the trust of others.

3. People must believe in you. People must respect you, they must trust you, and most importantly of all, they must *believe* in you. People must know not only that you can do something, but that you *will* do it, and they must know that you will do it to the best of your ability. People must believe in your will, character, your work ethic, and your determination. They must believe in your skill as well, and your competence; and they must also believe in your purpose and in your commitment to carrying out that purpose. In order to be a positive influence on others, you must first have the belief of others.

"If your actions inspire others to dream more,
learn more, do more and become more…
You are a leader." ~ John Quincy Adams

~ The Only Assumption You Should Ever Make ~

The only assumption that you should ever make, is that someone is always watching and learning from your example. Make sure you always act accordingly.

~

"No matter who you are or what you do, you do have influence,
and it's far beyond what you might imagine…
Someone, somewhere, is always watching.
And listening. And deciding."

~ Pat Croce

Always Set A Good Example
Realize that someone, somewhere is always watching you and learning from you. Whether it's a younger brother or sister, a cousin, a friend or teammate, or even someone who you're unaware of, there is always someone looking up to you. You have the power to set a good example or a bad one. It's entirely up to you. *Always set a good example.*

~

Always say the right thing. Always do the right thing. Always stand for the right thing.
~ Always set a good example. ~

You Are A Role Model, Whether You Like It Or Not
You are a role model, whether you like it or not. You are a role model, whether you want to be one or not. You are a role model whether you say it or not. You are a role model, whether you believe it or not.

Whether or not you think you are a role model, is irrelevant. Whether or not you want to be a role model is irrelevant. Regardless of what you say or believe, you are a role model. We are all role models.

After all, no matter who you are, no matter where you are, and no matter what you do, someone, somewhere, is always watching you.

~ You don't choose to be a role model: being a role model chooses you. ~

You Have the Power, Whether You Know It Or Not
The fact of the matter is that you are a role model… to someone, somewhere… whether you know it or not. The good news, though, is that because you are a role model, you have the power to impact another person's life.

~

"We are all role models to someone in this world, and we can all have an impact."
~ Tony Dungy

~

You Are Leaving A Legacy, Whether You Want To Or Not
"Whether you like it or not, whether you accept it or not, whether you *believe* it or not, your influence will span generations long after you've left this Earth."
~ Stu Weber

"Long after we die, the example of who we are lives on…
You are leaving a legacy—whether you want to or not. The question is, what will it be?"
~ Charles F. Stanley

No Matter What Your Position,
It Can Always Be A Position of Influence

Anyone can make a difference, anytime, anywhere. You don't have to be the most famous person in the world, or the wealthiest person in the world, in order to influence others. You do not have to stand atop the highest mountain and proclaim your message for all the world to hear, in order to make a difference.

Making a difference is not all about how much attention you can generate; it's about finding a way to create something of value for other people, and then finding a way to bring that value—to infuse that value—into other peoples' lives.

You can make a difference, no matter who you are, and no matter where you are. You can make a difference in your classroom, in your school, in your home, in your neighborhood, and in your community. You can make a difference at your local grocery store; you can make a difference in the check-out line at the local coffee shop. You can make a difference by using your thumbs to send an up-beat text-message to a friend; you can make a difference by using all of your fingers to write an e-mail.

You do not have to be the most visible and powerful human being in the world, in order to make a world of difference. What is important is that you start out by trying to make a difference where you are RIGHT NOW; what is important is that you do your best to make a difference in the life of the person you are interacting with RIGHT NOW. Don't be discouraged because you don't feel like you can change the entire world all at once.

No matter what position you are in, it is always—in some way—a position of influence. You do not have to be the most visible person in the world, nor do you have to have the most recognizable title in your profession. You can have an influence wherever you are, *who*ever you are, and in whatever it is that you do.

~

*"You have the opportunity to be a powerful influence
on the lives of other people, no matter your position in life."*

~ *V.J. Smith*

~

*"One voice can change a room, and if one voice can change a room,
then it can change a city; and if it can change a city, it can change a state,
and if it can change a state, it can change a nation, and if it can change a nation,
it can change the world … Your voice can change the world."*

~ *Barack Obama*

Be An Impact Player: Be A Difference-Maker

Make a World of Difference

Very rarely in life, people are presented with the opportunity to make a big difference. Often, however, people are given the chance to make little differences that are much smaller in scale and seemingly less important. What many do not realize though, is that when you add up all those little differences, they amount to something much larger than anyone could imagine.

~

"Greatness is a lot of small things done well.
You know, it's not just always this one great big thing."
~ *Ray Lewis*

~

Every day and every opportunity is not going to be of ultimate significance. However, it is important to realize that each situation, no matter how small or seemingly unimportant it may appear to be, has the seeds of greatness within it. Every moment, no matter how mundane, carries with it the potential for something extraordinary. What you make of that moment will determine what happens in your own future, and in the future of other people's lives as well.

~

"The future depends on what we do in the present."
~ *Mahatma Gandhi*

~

You may be able to change the world with everything that you do and say, but in each moment, you are given the opportunity to make a difference in someone else's life. You may not be able to change the whole world all at once, but you may be able to make a world of difference in another person's life.

~

"If you can't feed a hundred people, then feed just one."
~ *Mother Teresa*

~

You Can Have As Big An Influence As You Want

You can have as big an influence as you want to. You simply have to make up your mind to do so, and then get doing. Don't worry about whether other people will think you're doing too much, or that you're being annoying; don't worry about what other people will think or say. Just do what you think you're capable of doing and try to make a difference.

~

"One man can make a difference, and every man should try."
~ *Jacqueline Kennedy Onassis*

Do It... and Do It Now!

Act with kindness, and do it now. Don't think about it, don't worry about it, don't hesitate to act because you think that it'll make you look vulnerable, or because it will make you appear to be too caring or too interested. Just do it... and **Do It Now!**

Act with kindness, and do it now. Don't wait for a chance that happens to fit nicely into your schedule; don't wait for a time when it's convenient for you or when it doesn't cost you anything ... Do it NOW!

Don't let an opportunity to do something good for someone pass you by, because once it does, you won't ever get it back. The Greek philosopher, Epictetus, advised us to "never suppress a generous impulse." Therefore, if you have the desire to show some kindness or to do a good deed, then don't hold back. Act on that desire, and make sure that you not only do it... but that you do it as soon as you can.

Don't let the chance to do a good deed slip through your fingers.

Do it, and for the sake of your fellow man... Do It Now!

"I expect to pass through this world but once; any good thing therefore that I can do, or any kindness that I can show to any fellow creature, let me do it now; let me not defer or neglect it, for I shall not pass this way again."
~ *Stephen Grellet*

"You cannot do a kindness too soon, for you never know how soon it will be too late."
~ *Ralph Waldo Emerson*

~

"Do it this very moment!
Don't put it off—don't wait!
There's no use in doing a kindness...
if you do it a day too late."
~ Charles Kingsley

~

Do Something Positive For Someone Today

Each day, go out of your way to do something positive—big or small—to help improve someone's situation, to help put a little happiness into their day, to give them a reason to smile. It doesn't take a lot of time. Who cares if it costs you two minutes out of your day? Out of 24 hours... 14,400 minutes... if you don't have a few minutes to spare to make a positive impact on someone, then you're flat-out lying to yourself, or you're one heck of a selfish person.

~ Do something positive for someone today.
~ Do something positive for someone every day.

"Do something to have a positive impact on someone else today."
~ *Nick Saban*

Live Your Life The Right Way

Live the Right Way

One of my favorite quotes comes from Matthew 7:13-14, and reads:
"Enter through the narrow gate. For wide is the gate and broad is the road that leads to destruction, and many enter through it. But small is the gate and narrow the road that leads to life, and only a few find it."

~

For me, there has never been any substitute for living right. In anything a man does, there is always going to be an easy way and a right way. And almost always, the easy way is going to be the more attractive option. Despite its looks, however, this path will never lead to anywhere worthwhile. If you want to make the most of your life, then you have to make the right decisions and choose the right avenues. There is no such thing as arriving at a favorable destination without first traveling the proper journey. In many aspects, the journey itself *is* the destination, because it lays the path—one step at a time—for the road you will take to that destination.

~

"If you aren't living right, then nothing else matters."

~

Living the right way means having your priorities in the right order. It means caring about the important people in your life and doing everything you can to maintain the significant friendships and relationships in your life.

Part of valuing your meaningful relations with others, involves learning to resolve conflicts peaceably, learning to work through adversity respectfully, learning to disagree but not disagreeably. It involves learning to nip small problems in the bud, instead of allowing them to fester; and most importantly of all, it involves understanding that life is a lot more about other people than it is about you.

Living the right way means living by your principles at all times; it means treating others with respect in all ways… regardless of who they are or where they may be coming from, regardless of what they look like, regardless of what they may believe in.

Living right means staying on the straight-and-narrow. It means choosing your steps with caution, and proceeding through this world with care. It means taking yourself seriously and taking responsibility for your life, wisely weighing the decisions you make and the action you take. Living right means carefully measuring the choices you face, and treading cautiously with each stride—navigating clearly and thoughtfully through every twist and turn along the way. It means considering the magnitude of the choices you must make, and it means understanding that the decisions you make will decide and determine the path in life that you take.

~

"No man was ever lost on a straight path."
~ Indian Proverb

~

A Roadmap For Your Life

It is always important to have a roadmap for your life—some idea of where you are trying to go, and of what you are trying to accomplish during your time in this world. Every now and then, it's good to do a quick self-assessment to make sure you're on the right track and that you're headed in the right direction. Below are a few simple questions worth keeping in mind as you go through life-they are the *who*, *what*, *where*, *why*, and *how* that we should all try to answer:

~ Who ~
Who are you, and who are you trying to become?

~ What ~
What do you want to accomplish with your life, and are you making the most of the talents and opportunities given to you?

~ Where ~
Where are you going in life?... Where is that final destination—that future vision of yourself—that you are working toward?

~ Why ~
Why are you here?... Why were you put on this earth, and how will you carry out your life's purpose?

~ How ~
How do you want to be remembered? ... Are you living in such a way that your legacy will be what you want it to be?

~ I can pose all these questions *to* you, but I can't answer any of them *for* you. That part is up to you...and you can only do it by living out your answers through the decisions that you make and through the actions that you take.

~ Choose Well and Live Well. ~

Faith and Honor: A Few Things to Always Keep With You

The two most important things in a person's life are Faith and Honor. Faith doesn't have to be a religious thing, it just has to be some belief that somehow, someway, you are going to make it through the day. It can be a faith in a higher power, it can be a faith in yourself or in your friends, or it can be a faith in your family. The key is that you must believe in something, and that you must have some foundation that you can look to for hope, encouragement, and strength when times get tough.

Honor refers to how you live your life. When you pass away and people look back, they are going to look at the words you said, the things you did, and the way you carried yourself. Good or bad, that is going to be your legacy.

Some Other Important Questions To Consider

~ What will you do with your life?
~ How will you be remembered?
~ What will your legacy be?
~ What will your life's message be?

All these questions may be posed to you; however, none of them can be answered for you. The way you live your life and the legacy that you leave behind you in this world, are completely up to you to decide. Only you can determine the way you live your life and the legacy you leave behind.

Your life is what you make it. The power to live your best life and leave your best legacy is entirely in your hands. What will you do with that amazing power? The opportunity to live honorably and to leave a noble legacy is entirely up to you. What will you do with that wonderful opportunity?

~

Think carefully and choose wisely.
Then go out and live well and live right.

~

Live well, and you will be remembered well.
Live the right kind of life, and you will leave the right kind of legacy.

~

How Do You Define Success:
Success In the Game of Life Can Be Defined As...

~ Doing all you can to make the absolute most of all your talents and abilities, achieving everything that you are capable of achieving, and helping others to do all they can to reach their fullest potential: Success means reaching your absolute potential—not just improving a little bit, but improving as much as you possibly can improve, based on your own individual talents and abilities.

~ Keeping your priorities in proper order: Success means having the right priorities, and more importantly, success means making sure your life corresponds to those priorities at every moment, and in every way... each day, every day, every time, and all the time.

~ Always living by your principles: Success means having solid and noble principles, and more importantly, success means always living by your principles in everything and anything you do.

~ Always doing the right thing: Success means treating all people with respect and dignity, always carrying yourself with the utmost class, having integrity in every way, being honorable at all times and in all things, being honest and sincere in all of your dealings, being respectful at all times and being respectable in all ways, being responsible for yourself and being accountable to others, standing up for what you believe in and for what is right, attacking injustice and standing against what is wrong, and ultimately for doing all you possibly can to reach your absolute full potential in every regard.

Some Incontrovertible Laws of Life

We have all heard of the famous laws of both physics and nature—laws such as Newton's Law of Gravity, Murphy's Law of Occurrence, the Law of Supply and Demand, and many others. Additionally, there are thousands upon thousands of laws in our society, ranging from federal laws to state mandates. But when you think about it, however, how many of those laws are really needed?

After all, couldn't we simplify our legal code just a little bit? I think so. And so, along those lines, I offer a few laws of my own: they may not govern society as a whole, but perhaps they can help you govern—and live—your own life in the meantime. Here is my take on the laws that *really* matter in life… let us call them the Laws of Life:

~

1. The Law of Respect – All people are entitled to be treated with respect. All people inherently possess basic human dignity. That dignity is to be honored by respectful treatment. (Reference the Golden Rule for further explanation on practicing this law.)

2. The Law of Truth – Regardless of whether you want it to or not, the truth always rises to the top. Do good things, and good things will surface. Do bad things, and bad things will surface. The truth can never remain hidden, and the truth always has a way of straightening itself out. Like cream to the top of a glass, the truth always rises to the top.

3. The Law of Humility – At the end of the day, you are going to be humble. You can either humble yourself, or you can have someone or something else come along and humble you instead. The first of these choices is the more virtuous option, and it also is the much more pleasant path. Be humble, and stay humble.

4. The Law of Worse – No matter how bad things get in life, try to keep in mind that they could always be worse. Therefore, be thankful for the good things and the good people that you do have in your life, even if they are few and far between. Do your best to remember that, no matter what happens, there is always something to be grateful for.

5. The Law of Better – No matter how good things get, try to keep in mind that they could always be better. Therefore, never be satisfied with what you have accomplished. Keep working; keep trying to improve. Be humble, be hungry, and never be satisfied.

6. The Law of Cause and Effect – Your actions have consequences. When you choose an action, you also choose the potential consequences that go along with that action. Your decisions and actions are the cause; the consequences are the effect. Whenever you have to make a choice: stop and think things through first. Make good decisions, put yourself in good situations, and continue to make good decisions… and good things will happen.

7. The Law of Self-Worth – You are born with your self-worth. No one else can give it to you, and no one else can take it away from you. Your self-worth belongs to you, and you alone. That is why it is called your *self*-worth. No one can take it from you… unless you surrender it. No one can steal it away from you… unless you allow them to. Always understand your enormous value as a person, and do your best to always preserve and protect your self-worth.

8. The Law of Time – Time marches on… and we must learn to march with it, or else get left behind. You are going to spend the 24 hours in a day doing something. Regardless of what you choose to do—or what you choose *not* to do—you are going to trade in 24 hours worth of your life for each day that you're on this Earth. After each day is over, you will never be able to get any of that time back. Therefore, resolve to live each day to the fullest: do your best to love others as much as you can, to contribute as much as you can to the lives of others, and to enjoy your own life as much as you can… each day, and every day. Make the most of your 24 hours while you have the opportunity to. You can't get any of that time back, and you can't take any of it with you. Make the most of each day, and make each day a masterpiece.

9. The Law of Endurance – There are only two things in this world that endure: love and contribution. After everything else in this world has fallen away, it will be how much you loved others, and how much you did *for* others, that will remain as a testament to your life. Your love and your contribution are the things that will endure, long after everything else has fallen away. Therefore, love as much as you possibly can, and contribute as much to the lives of others as you possibly can.

10. The Law of Give and Gain – You will gain as much out of life as you seek to give to the lives of others. You will get out of life as much as you put into it. The more you contribute to this world, the more value you will derive from it as a result. The more you give to life, the more you will gain from life. The more you put in, the more you get out.

11. The Law of Entitlement – You are entitled to one thing in this world, and one thing only: to be treated with respect and dignity, for the sole reason that you are a human being—and all members of the human family deserve to be treated in such a way. That is the only thing you are entitled to; everything else you must earn.

12. The Law of Earnings – You may not always get what you want in life. But, you will almost always get what you deserve. Ultimately, what you deserve will be directly correlated to how much you are willing to earn. Everything worthwhile in life has a price. The greater the rewards you seek, the greater the price you will have to pay to attain them. It is that simple. Do not expect success to be given to you, but instead, expect to achieve whatever success you are willing to work for. Do not expect to be given anything, but instead, learn to expect only what you will earn. While you may not always get what you want in life, you will always get what you pay for. You will get what your hard work deserves; you will get what you are willing to earn. As former United States president, Theodore Roosevelt, once said: "In this life we get nothing, save by effort."

13. The Law of Investment – When it comes to life—whether it is in regard to your relationships, your career, your goals, or your pursuits—one thing is for certain: you get out however much you put in. The greater the investment, the greater the return will be. The more you do for the lives of others, the more your own life will be enriched. The more meaning you seek to create, the more meaningful your own life will be. The more you contribute to this world, the deeper and more valuable your own experience in it will be. Regardless of what aspect of life it is in, the equation always remains the same: the greater the investment, the greater the return.

14. The Law of Hardship – Life is hard. Life is a constant struggle. There are no days off, and the only easy day was yesterday. But, if you can come to grips with the fact that life indeed is hard, then you can begin to prepare yourself for the daily challenges that you most certainly will face. Once you understand that life is a struggle, then you can begin to ready yourself for the battle—and, what is more important, you can prepare yourself to win the battle. Life is hard, and there are no days off from the struggle. Your life will have its share of hardship. But, if you can accept that adversity is a natural part of life, then you can begin to ready yourself to not only meet your adversity head-on, but also to overcome that adversity.

15. The Law of Progress – Achievement is progress-dependent, not time-dependent. In other words: simply because you work at something for a certain amount of time—or simply because you do something a certain number of times—does not mean that you will get better at it or that you will achieve what you set out to achieve. What matters is not the amount of time that you invest; what matters is the amount of quality time you invest. It is not the quantity of what you do, but the quality of what you do that counts. It is not how much you do, but the excellence with which you do it. Therefore, always invest your best and fullest efforts. Do not merely go through the motions, and do not simply toil away aimless. As the legendary coach John Wooden, once said: "Never mistake activity for achievement." Work hard, work smart, be proactive, and be productive. Improvement and achievement are progress-dependent, not time-dependent.

16. The Law of One – You only get one life, and you only get one chance to live that life. Make sure you do the absolute most that you can to maximize your life, and to do the most with your life as well. Live the best way you know how, and do your best in everything and anything that you do. Seek to become your best in every regard, and always strive to make the most of every opportunity that comes your way. You only get one life, you only get one chance to live it, you only get one opportunity to live each moment within that life, you only get one opportunity to live your life to the fullest, you only get one chance to enjoy your life as much as you can, and you only get one chance to have as big of a positive influence on the world as you possibly can. You have to understand this basic fact, you have to take advantage of each and every chance that you get, you have to make the most of each and every opportunity that you are given, and you have to do all that you possibly can to maximize your time in this world and the one life you get to live in it. You only get one life, and you only get one chance to live it. Live your life with a sense of urgency, and make sure that you make full use of your one opportunity on this Earth. You only live once. But, if you live right and if you live well… then once is exactly enough.

17. The Law of Gratitude – At any given time, there is always more to be grateful for than you perhaps might realize. At any given time, there are always more blessings in your life than there are problems. At any given time, there are always more than enough good people and good things in your life to be thankful for than you perhaps might realize. If you look closely enough, you will always find something to be grateful for.

If you look hard enough, you will always find something to be thankful for. Therefore, always seek to find the good things and the good people that you have in your life, and always seek to express your gratitude to them and for them. Live your life with an attitude of gratitude.

18. The Law of Always-and-Never – Always do good things, and never do bad things. That is simple enough. The time is always right to do what is right. The time is always wrong to do what is wrong. In other words… There is never a wrong time to do the right thing, and there is never a right time to do the wrong thing. Practice good things at all times, and practice bad things at no time. Virtue always, vice never.

19. The Law of Proper Order – Keep your priorities in proper order, and your life, in turn, will be kept in proper order. If you mess your priorities up, it will mess you up. Therefore, always keep your priorities in proper order.

20. The Law of Karma – What goes around, comes around. Therefore, always be careful what you make "go around." Do good, and good things will happen. Do bad, and bad things will happen. Always remember that, eventually, it all catches up to you. Send goodness out into the world, and goodness will return into your life. Send evil and rottenness out into the world, and those same things will return to you. Sow seeds of good deeds, and you will reap the ripened fruits of goodness. Sow seeds of ill-favor, and you will reap a rotten harvest as a result. Send love and kindness into the lives of others, and those same things will return into your own life. Send ill-will into the lives of others, and again, those same things will return into your own life. What goes around, comes around. Whether it is good or bad, in the end you will get what you deserve (… either in this world or the next.) Therefore… Do good, be good, and all will be good.

~

~ Live right and live well. Live by the laws of life. Live by the book. ~

~

Leave A Legacy

Live Your Best Life; Leave Your Best Legacy

Strive to live your best life, and do all you can to leave your best legacy. Live a life that matters: you only get one opportunity in this world, so make it count and make it matter.

Be Your Best, And You'll Have No Regrets

Charles F. Stanley once said: "One of the most horrible things I can think of is coming to the end of life and looking back with regret, thinking, *What difference have I made?*"

Don't let such a thing happen to you.
Do all the good you can do in this life,
and do it all the very best you can do it.
Make your life count. Make your life matter.
And let there be no doubt about it.
Most people spend their whole lives
wondering if they've made a difference …
Make sure you never have that problem.

Leave This World Unmistakably Better

Make the most of yourself.
Make the most of your time on this Earth.
Make the most of your influence.
Make the most of your impact on this world.

Make your life count. Make your life matter.
Live right and live well.
Leave this world unmistakably better.

~

Live A Life That Matters …
And Let There Be No Doubt About It

Live a life that matters … and let there be no doubt about it.
Make the most of yourself, and make the most of your life.
Maximize all of your talents and all of your abilities.
Make the most of every one of your opportunities
to impact the lives of others in a positive way.

~

Live a life that matters … and let there be no doubt about it.
Believe in something. Stand for something. Live for something.
Make a difference. Make an impact. Make your mark.
Live your life and leave your legacy.

~

The Value of Your Life

The Value of Your Life Is Measured By Actions, Not Possessions

The value of your life is measured by your actions, not by your possessions. The type of car you drive, the kind of clothes you wear, and the amount of money you make have nothing to do with what kind of a human being you are. Having a flashy car, wearing expensive clothes, and carrying a large stack of dollars does not make you any more or less important than anyone else; nor does it make you any more or less of a man than anyone else. Ultimately, you will be judged by your actions and your contributions, not by your possessions.

The Value of Your Life Is Measured By What You Do For Others, & Not Yourself

The value of your life is measured by what you do for others, not by what you do for yourself. The personal accomplishments you achieve, the individual accolades you accumulate, and the various distinctions of personal glory and conquest have absolutely nothing to do with what kind of a human being you are. Living selfishly and looking out for only yourself does not make you any more or happier of a person than anyone else; nor does it make you any more important of a person than anyone else. Ultimately, you will be judged by your contributions and by what you do for others, not by what you do for yourself.

~

"We make a living by what we get.
We make a **life** by what we **give**."
~ *Winston Churchill*

How Much Have You Loved And Served Others?

"At the close of life, the question will not be …

How much have you gotten,
But how much have you given;
Not how much have you won,
But how much have you done;
Not how much have you saved,
But how much have you sacrificed;
Not how much have you been honored,
But how much have you loved and served others."

~ Nathan C. Schaeff

In The End, Each Of Us Will Be Judged…

"In the end, each of us will be judged…
By our standard of life, not by our standard of living;
By our measure of giving, not by our measure of wealth;
By our simple goodness, not by our seeming greatness."

~ Author Unknown

~ You'll Never See A Dollar Sign On A Tombstone ~

No one has a dollar-sign carved on their tombstone. In other words: the value of your life is measured by what you do for others, not how much money you can make for yourself. The value of your life is measured by how much you can give to others, not how much you can get for yourself.

~

Make Your Mark

Focus on making your mark, not on making a name for yourself. Focus on making a difference, not on making a dollar.

It's amazing how much you can accomplish when you don't care who gets the credit. It's incredible how many lives you can touch when you don't care how many dollar signs are involved. It's amazing how much good you can put into the world when you don't care about how much you put into your pocket.

It's amazing how much you can raise the level of good will and kindness in the world, when you don't care about how much you can raise your level of status. It's amazing how much you can increase the amount of goodness in this world when you don't care about how much you can increase your reputation.

~

"From what we get, we can make a living;
what we give, however, makes a life."

~ *Arthur Ashe*

~ Make Your Mark, and Forget About Making A Buck ~

"Focusing your life solely on making a buck shows a certain poverty of ambition: it asks too little of yourself. Because, it's only when you hitch your wagon to something larger than yourself, that you realize your true potential." ~ *Barack Obama*

Make Your Mark On the Hearts of Others

We all make a name for ourselves in the end… after all, that is what an epitaph is for. Make sure you leave more than just your name on a piece of granite. Make your mark on the lives of others, and forget about making a name for yourself. Have an impact on the world in which you live, and forget about making a quick buck here and there.

Don't worry about making the most of your profits. Instead, focus on making the most of your life. Maximize your talents, your opportunities, and the impact that you can have on others. Make your mark on the hearts and souls of those with whom you share this journey through life.

~

Not What You Gain, But What You Give

It is not about what you *gain for yourself*—but about what you *give of yourself*—that really matters.

It is not about what kind of name you can make for yourself—but about what kind of *difference you can make for others*—that really matters.

"It's about the journey—yours and mine—and the lives we can touch, the legacy we can leave, and the world we can change for the better."
~ *Tony Dungy*

Be an Adder, Not a Subtractor...
Be a Multiplier, Not a Divider

Be an adder, not a subtractor.
Add something positive to other people's lives.
Be a positive presence in the lives of others,
and make a positive contribution to the world in which you live.

Be a multiplier, not a divider.
Multiply your influence in this world
by using your talents and opportunities to impact others.
Be a source of significant change in the lives of others
and make a lasting contribution to the world in which you live.

When it comes down to it...

It's not what you do for yourself, but what you *do for others*;
It's not what you gain for yourself, but what you *give of yourself to others*...

... that really matters.

~

*Do not focus selfishly on what other people can do for you.
Concentrate instead, on what you can do for others.*

~

A Worthy Question, and One Worth Answering

Live your whole life trying to answer the question...

~ *How much good can one man do?*

~ Do all the good you can, for as long as you possibly can... and do your best to make your life an answer to the question: *How much good can one man do?*

~

"Wouldn't it be a beautiful world if just 10 percent of the people
who believe in the power of love would compete with one another
to see who could do the most good for the most people?"

~ *Muhammad Ali*

Where Is Your Applause Going to Come From?

At the end of your life, you're going to get a round of applause. The major distinction, however, is not going to be how loud that applause is, how long it lasts for, or even how many people there are clapping. Instead, the major distinction is going to be *where* that applause comes from.

You see, when it's all said and done, your applause is going to come from one of two places: it's either going to come from all the people who are still here in this world, who are happy to see you go because you were a bad person or because they didn't like or respect you … OR, it's going to come from all the people in Heaven, who are applauding you because you lived a good life—an honorable life—and who are happy because they're getting a good one to join them up there.

In the end, it's totally up to you to decide where your applause is going to come from. Fortunately, and ultimately, it all depends on the way that you live your life.

So ... I ask you this … ***Where is your applause going to come from?***

~

> **"When we leave this world,**
> **how much we have loved will be our true legacy.**
> **It is the only thing we will leave behind and carry with us."**
>
> ~ Anne Siloy

~

> *"Success in life has nothing to do*
> *with what you gain or accomplish for yourself:*
> ***It's what you do for others.****"*
>
> ~ *Danny Thomas*

How Will The World Speak Your Name?

"When a man sees his end, he wants to know there was some purpose to his life.
How will the world speak my name in years to come?"
~ The character of Marcus Aurelius, from the movie *Gladiator*

~

"And when you speak of me… speak well."
~ Kevin Costner, in the movie, *Bull Durham*

~

Make sure you give them a reason to.

Your Legacy's Final Place

1. Where Your Legacy *Won't* Be Found

Your legacy won't be found in your bank account. Those funds will
be transferred into someone else's name and bank account,
or worse yet, be given to the IRS or the State.

Your legacy won't be found in your closet. Those clothes and accessories will be
given away, or worse yet, thrown away.

Your legacy won't be found in your garage. That car of yours will be given, or worse
yet, sold in the newspaper to the very first bidder.

Your legacy won't be found in your casket. That body of yours will soon fade away;
those good looks and big muscles will soon wither away;
those organs and body parts of yours will soon be given away,
or worse yet, be left to rot in some obscure box.

~

2. Where Your Legacy *Will* Be Found

Your legacy will be found in the hearts of others: in the lives of those you leave behind. If
you have invested in other people, if you have loved and served others, if you have devoted
yourself to improving the conditions of the world around you, and if you have dedicated your
life to enhancing the lives of those who surround you… then rest assured that your legacy
will be found in the most wonderful of places, and in the greatest number of faces.

~

If you live your life with honor, and if you live your life for others,
then do not worry about where your legacy will end up.
Rest assured, no one will have any trouble finding it.

"A good character is the best tombstone.
Those who loved you and were helped by you
will remember you when 'forget-me-nots' have withered.
Carve your name on hearts, not on marble."
~ Charles H. Spurgeon

~

Live In Such A Way
That You Will Always Be Remembered

You only live once, but, if you live right… then once is enough.
Live well and live right. You only live once.
But, if you live well and if you live right,
then once is exactly enough.

~

Make a Difference In the Lives of Others
Make a difference. Live to love, and love to serve.
Learn the importance of putting others before yourself.
Learn the importance of serving others ahead of yourself.
Base your thoughts and actions on the question, *"What can I do for you?"*
Try to leave the world a better place because you were here.

~

Make a difference. Or, as a famous bumper sticker slogan reads:

"Make a dent in the universe."

~

~

~ Invest In What Matters ~
Invest in what matters. Invest in what lasts.
Live a life that matters. Leave a legacy that lasts.

~

"The depth of our footprints is defined by our love."

~ Tomas Karkalas

~

~

The Splendid Deeds of Those
"Let me sing the splendid deeds
Of those who toil to serve mankind,
The men who break old ways and make
New paths for those who come behind.
And face their problems, unafraid,
Who think and plan to lift for man
The burden that on him is laid…"

~ Edgar A. Guest

~

**"True glory consists in doing what deserves to be written;
in writing what deserves to be read; and in so living as to make the world
happier and better for our living in it."**

~ Pliny the Elder

The Roadmap to Happiness: A Set of Directions for Living a Worthwhile Life

I have thought deeply about what constitutes real happiness—true, genuine happiness. I have tried to simplify these thoughts as much as possible into brief, straightforward guidelines, that hopefully will serve you well for many years to come. What follows is my best personal opinion of how to go about creating a truly worthwhile and happy life. It is a "roadmap to happiness" of sorts… and hopefully it steers you in the right direction.

~ Be good, and do good. That is simple enough.

~ Know what is right, and do what is right. (Again, that is simple enough.)

~ Live each day in such a manner that, when you go to sleep each night, you do so with a clear conscience. This will come from making every effort that you can to live the life you know you *should* be living.

~ Live your life the best way you know how.

~ Never do something you won't be proud of.

~ Never become someone you won't be proud of.

~ Do not search for riches, fame, or material wealth. Live your life the best way that you can, and if you do, you will attain the most valuable possession there is: peace of mind.

~ Realize that there is no substitute for being a good person.

~ Work hard at developing meaningful, genuine relationships. As legendary coach, John Wooden, said: "Make friendship a fine art."

~ Contribute to the lives of others.

~ Help make other people's lives a little better and more pleasant than they might otherwise be.

~ Have a positive impact on other people. Care for others as much as you can, and show appreciation to the important people in your life as often as you can.

~ Leave a legacy of love and respect.

~ Learn to forgive, and actually practice forgiveness.

~ Learn to ask for forgiveness.

~ Learn to control your emotions. Learn to think before you speak and act.

~ Learn to control your anger, or else it will control you.

~ Never judge anyone. Be kind and respectful to everyone; you never know what someone might be going through.

~ Keep an open mind. Accept the fact that you may not always be right.

~ Keep an open heart. Understand that what you want in life, and that what you are called to do, may change as you gather more knowledge and experiences.

~ Do not fear change. Embrace the exciting opportunities that come with the future.

~ Always be positive. Remember: you can be realistic and positive at the same time.

~ Enjoy the life you have, because it's the only one you're going to get.

~ Don't always take yourself too seriously. Learn to laugh at yourself and at your circumstances. Find ways to make the arduous and tedious things enjoyable.

~ Don't waste time complaining. Find something to be thankful for, and make the most of the good things you have in your life. Focus on the positives, and you will find that everything else seems to disappear from view.

~ Appreciate what you have. Pursue what you want.
~ Do not be contented with the work of yesterday. Keep moving forward,
and keep striving toward something worthwhile.
~ Always do your best. If your best is good enough, then enjoy the rewards.
If your best isn't good enough, then keep working and keep giving your best
until one day it is.
~ Be humble; it is better to be humble of your own choosing than to be humbled by other
people or by circumstances.
~ Never be satisfied with any accomplishments, but instead, resolve to continue to do
your best every single day.
~ Find out what you have a passion for, and then do it. And don't just do it for your own
benefit; find a way to use your gifts and your passion to help others.
~ Do two things with your life: simplify it, and maximize it.
~ Hold on tightly to your sense of self-worth and your dreams. They belong to you, and
you alone. No one can take away any of those things unless you allow them too.
~ Learn to value your integrity. You come into this world with it:
make sure you do all you can to leave this world with it as well.
~ Don't just go through the motions in life.
Make the most of yourself and your time in this world.
~ Don't wish for better circumstances. Go out and make them.
~ Make the most of your talent and your opportunities, and find a way to do it in service
to something that is greater than your own immediate self.
~ Leave your mark on this world. Leave a piece of your spirit behind in the hearts
and minds of everyone you meet.
~ Let the world be a better place for your having been here.
~ Realize that we are all part of something larger than ourselves,
and that we are called to do as much good in this lifetime as we possibly can.
~ Live with honor, live a life that matters.

~ Live in such a way so that at the end of your life, you will be able to say—
in the words of Henry David Thoreau…

"My life has been the poem I would have writ.
But I could not both live and utter it."

… In other words: **Make your life a masterpiece.**

~ *Live a life that matters. Leave a legacy that lasts.* ~

The Only Things That Endure

In The End, It Is Love That Endures

The most important thing that I have learned in life is this: nearly everything fades away. Money fades away over time; material possessions get taken from you or passed on to those who succeed you in this world; fame and glory are fleeting, and don't last for very long; your looks most certainly fade away; and so too, undoubtedly, does your health. Moments rush by you—not even their memories stay with you forever, as they too fade away as the years pass you by; and even most of the people you come to know in this life eventually fade away, in one fashion or another; and finally, life, itself, one day slips away. This is the inescapable nature of our mutual destiny. Though we would wish it not so, in the end, nearly everything fades away.

However, life has taught me that there is one thing that lasts, that there is one thing that endures forever. Though the world may be filled with all sorts of objects of every shape and size, and though it may be overflowing with an abundance of sights and faces, and moments and places, and though it may be drenched in the light of beautiful memories too numerous ever to count … sadly, all these things give way.

For, in the end, only love endures. Everything else may fade away, but not love. **Love endures.** At the end of our walk through this wonderful world, if we have lived as we fully were intended to live, we will realize that love is all that endures… love… and the manifestation of that love, in the form of positive contribution.

The contribution we make to the lives of others is what we will leave behind us in this world, as a sign that we were here, that we mattered in the grand scheme of things, and that we made a difference in other people's lives.

~

Nearly all things fade away in the end.
Yet, life has taught me that there is one thing that lasts…
Everything else may fade away, but not love.
Love endures.

~

All these things will fade away. But, life has taught me that there is one thing that lasts: everything else may fade away, but not love. ***Love endures.***

~

"Ultimately, love is everything."
~ M. Scott Peck

Love & Contribution

There are only two things in this world that endure: love and contribution.
After everything else in this world has fallen away, it will be how much you loved others, and how much you did *for* others, that will remain as a testament to your life. Therefore, love as much as you possibly can, and contribute as much to the lives of others as you possibly can. Your love and your contribution are the things that will endure, long after everything else has fallen away.

Love, and the contribution that springs forth from that love, are what living really is all about. When you put life into perspective, you will find that it all comes down to love and contribution. It is about how much you love others, and how much you do for others.

In the final analysis, it will not be about how much money you made, how many cars you owned, how many material possessions you had, what your bank account read, or what your stock portfolio was… because if those things were all that you focused on in your lifetime, then none of those things will have added up to any meaningful success.
In the end, there are only two things that stand the test of time… ***How much you have loved others, and how much you have done for others.*** In the end, only Love and Contribution endure.

Love and contribution are the only things that endure. They are the only things that last. Ultimately, it is how much we love others, and how much we do for others, that will remain in this world as a testament to the life we have lived.

A New Principle for Living: The Enduring Principle

I offer a new principle for living: perhaps we may call it the Enduring Principle—for, it lays out the things that we should do to make our influence in this world as enduring and endless as possible…

If love and contribution are the things that endure…
Then we should love and contribute as much as we can.

~ *We should love as much as we can, and we should contribute as much as we can.*

A Sense of Permanence

We are temporary in nature, but we have the potential to have an impact that will be permanent. Though our lives may be temporary, our influence may live on forever.
While your body might be temporary, do all you can to make sure that your impact is as permanent as you can make it.

~

"All earthly things disappear: first the bodies of men, and in time the memories of them. Seek what is eternal, and there you will find true peace."

~ *Marcus Aurelius*

Make Your Contribution

Your contribution is all about what you do for others. It is the mark you leave on this world. Your contribution is the proof that you helped make other people's lives and the world better while you were here; that you impacted the world in a positive way.

~

"After the cheers have died down and the stadium is empty,
after the headlines have been written, and after you are back in the quiet of your room,
and the championship ring has been placed on the dresser and all the pomp and fanfare
have faded, the enduring thing that is left is the dedication to doing with our lives
the very best we can to make the world a better place in which to live*."*
~ Vince Lombardi

Contribute to the Lives of Others;
Contribute to the World In Which You Live

Contribute something to the lives of others and to the world around you. Do something for someone else. Go out of your way to be of service to another person. Find a way to make someone else's day… today, and every day.

At the end of each day, you should be able to look back at it and feel that you have done something worthwhile with the 24 hours you've just been given. You should know that you exchanged that time for something of significance—that you contributed something to someone other than yourself.

You have lived a worthwhile day when you can look back over it and know that you did something meaningful with the time you were given: that you made the most of every hour and every moment, that you made the best of every chance and every opportunity, that you did your best and that you gave your all to everything you did, and that you made a positive impact on the lives of others and on the world around you…
that you did something that mattered.

~

"I am certain that after the dust of centuries has passed over our cities,
we, too, will be remembered not for victories or defeats in battle or in politics,
but for our contributions to the human spirit."
~ John F. Kennedy

~

~ Love as much as you possibly can. ~
Contribute as much to the lives of others as you possibly can.

Love As Much As You Can…
Contribute As Much As You Can… & Enjoy It All As Much As You Can
If you do your best to love others as much as you can, to contribute to others and to the world at large as much as you can, and do your best to make a difference in this world, then you will find true meaning and fulfillment in this lifetime. You will get the most out of your life, because you will have given the most to it. In the process, you will have positively impacted other people's lives, brought joy and hope to others, and found true significance and enjoyment in your own life as a result.

"I arise in the morning torn between a desire to improve the world and a desire to enjoy the world." ~ *E. B. White*

~ *Why not do both?*

~

~

Life, Love, and Contribution
What really matters in life is who you are, who you love,
and what you do for others.

~

~

Invest In What Matters. Invest In What Lasts.
Invest in what matters: invest in who you are; invest in who you are becoming.
Invest in what lasts: invest in your relationships; invest in your contribution to this world.
Live a great life. Leave a great legacy. Live a life that matters.
Make a contribution that endures.
Leave a legacy that lasts.

~

~ Live beyond your years. ~
Live a life that matters. Leave a legacy that lasts.

Focus On Your Contribution

I remember walking through the locker room prior to a game once, seeing the various members of the team getting suited up and preparing themselves for the mental and physical struggle that lay ahead.

Inevitably, there are always one or two student-athletes who can be found standing squarely in front of the mirror making sure they look good—making sure they "looked the part" of a play-maker. You know: they're the ones checking themselves out and flexing in front of the locker room mirror, checking to make sure their eye-black is applied just right, making sure their brand-name wristbands and armbands are pulled on just right, making sure their tape-jobs look good and straight, and making sure they look all big and puffed up... so they can impress everyone who comes to see them play... especially the ladies and all the fans in the stand. (Although, it bears asking: do you think the opposing strong safety or middle linebacker really cares how well-dressed you are, or how tight and legit you look... as he's getting ready to lay you out? Somehow, I don't think he cares.)

As a coach, I realize that—as many of the others in the locker room also do—that what really matters is the production on the field, and not what anyone looks like when they are on the field. In other words: it is not about how you look, or how big you look; it is not about how much you talk, or about how big a game you can talk... ultimately, it is about what you can contribute. And it is about what you actually *do* contribute.

All the name-brand wristbands in the world don't mean a thing if you can't catch a football. All the eye-black in the sporting goods store won't matter an ounce if you can't block or tackle. All the apparel and accessories won't make a difference... if you, yourself, can't make a difference.

~

Looking like a play-maker doesn't mean a thing.
It's *being* a play-maker that means everything. Anyone can talk a big game—anyone can talk about making a contribution. What really matters, though, is what you do when the lights come on. It's not who talks about making a contribution: it's about who actually steps up and makes that contribution when it counts.

~

A lot of times, we get so caught up in the surface things—the things that we think are important: things like our looks, our clothes, our image, our reputation, what other people think about us or say about us, and so on. However, none of those things are what really matter.

Now, do not get me wrong: sure it's nice to look good, it's nice to be able to dress well, it's nice to have people say good things about us, and it's nice to have a good reputation. But, just as is the case with competitive sports, what ultimately matters *the most* is the contribution we make.

~

"A player is a success only when he does his best in service to the team."
~ John Wooden

~

Contribute. Contribute. Contribute.

Life is much more about the substance of how we live, rather than the style with which we live. To borrow from a popular cliché: the substance is more important than the style.

We all spend a ton of time working on our appearances and on our images. Most of us invest unnecessary amounts of time on the surface aspects of life—things such as the looks, the clothes, the cars, the jewelry, and so on.

However, when it is all said and done, the most important part of our lives will not be how many hours we went to the gym for, what kind of clothes we wore to certain events, what kind of car we pulled up in at someone's house, or how many attractive people flocked to our arm when we arrived and walked through the door. When it is all said and done… *the most important part of our lives will be what we have contributed*.

~

At the end of your life, all of the surface things—the looks, the muscles, the cars, the clothes, the sneakers, the jewelry, the money… all those things are going to be gone. All of those things, and you, yourself, will eventually be gone.
What are you going to leave in their place?

What are you going to leave in their place?
What are you going to leave in *your* place?

Use your time and your talents in this world wisely. Invest your time, invest your energy, and invest yourself into the lives of others, and into what you can do for the lives of others. Whatever you decide to do in this lifetime, always remember that you will be trading your life for, and always keep in mind that whatever you do in this world, you will leave in your place after you are gone. Make sure it is something worthwhile.

Make Your Contribution; Leave Your Mark

Do not be so focused on the *style* aspect of life that you forget about the *substance* part of it in the process. Do not just concern yourself with the shallow, surface things of life: instead, concern yourself with the significant and substantial components of life— in other words… the things that matter, and the things that last.

~

Be less concerned with the *stylish* things in life, and more concerned with the actual *substance* of living.

~

Focus on your contribution…
and your legacy will take care of itself.

~ *What will your contribution be?*

CONCLUDING POINTS

Are You For REAL?

Are you a *REAL* Man? ~ The Search Continues

More than two thousand years ago, a Greek philosopher by the name of Diogenes of Sinope set out to find what he called a *good man*. Diogenes was a cynic, meaning that he doubted the natural goodness of this world and of those who lived in it. He dedicated his life to finding evidence to the contrary.

Diogenes was known to have wandered through the streets of Athens in broad daylight, holding up a lantern to each man he passed, shining the light on him and asking: *"Are you a good man?"*

Diogenes' quest to find a man who was both wise and honest—a man who was fair and just—apparently never produced what the philosopher was looking for. Nearly two thousand years ago, it seems as though a good and decent man was hard to find.

And so it is today, as the case remains very much the same. Sadly, we live in a society with a desperate shortage of honorable men. The world needs more *real* men… men who are respectful and respectable, men who have principles and who live by those principles, men of honor and integrity, men who are willing to invest in this world, and men who are willing to make a positive and lasting difference in the lives of others.

And so now, I—a modern-day Diogenes of sorts, holding up my proverbial lantern as I wander through this world of ours—have one very important question to ask *you*: **Are you a _REAL_ Man**?

~

Are you for REAL?
Do you have what it takes?
Will you stand up and be a REAL Man?
Will you stand tall and make a REAL
Difference in the world?

~

~

"The question is not can you change the world around you.
The only question is will you decide to do so."

~ Jeffrey Marx

~

Spread The Message

Help spread the REAL Man message

Help spread the message of what it means to be a REAL man. Get the word out—through your words and your deeds—that being a REAL man is all about the way you live your life, the way you treat other people, and ultimately, what you do for others and for the world around you.

Don't let the world continue to accept mediocrity from its men; go out and be a source of change in your school, in your community, in your workplace, in your neighborhood, in your home, and in your world. Be a REAL Man, and be the source of REAL Change.

Be the Change You Wish to See In the World

If any man wishes to change the world,
He first must seek to change himself.

~

If any man desires to transform the people around him,
He first must work to transform himself.

~

In this way, such a man may become the change
He wishes to see in the world.

"If you want to change the world, the place to begin is with yourself."
~ Stephen R. Covey

Be the Source of REAL Change

The world needs REAL men, and
The world needs *you* to be a REAL man.
Only by becoming a REAL man can you help become
The source of REAL change.

A man must be the change he wishes to see in the world.
A man must be the change he wishes to see in others.
It is not enough to talk about being a REAL man.
One must actually go out and… BE a REAL Man!

*"I don't believe in standing back and talking, but in changing things.
Go out and change it and make your contribution."*
~ Eddie Robinson

Make A REAL Difference

Be a REAL Man & Make a REAL Difference!

The famous poet Edwin Markham once said: "A man is either a hammer or an anvil: he either molds society or is molded by it."

~

What the late writer essentially meant by these words, was that there are two types of people in the world: there are those who are content to be the absolute minimum of whatever society allows them to be, and then there are those who have the strength, courage, and determination to seek greatness in their lives. The weak and timid souls who lack the will to be themselves never accomplish anything worthwhile in life. As a result, they allow society to shape them into average, ordinary souls who never know the fulfillment that comes with reaching their full potential.

The bold and the honorable, however, live their lives with a confidence and a conviction that is unmatched by those around them. They live with commitment, and they live with courage. They have a strong belief in themselves and an incredible sense of purpose in their lives. As a result of their strong mind and determined attitude, such people rise above the confines of a mediocre society and transform the world in which they live into a better, more respectful, and more honorable place.

Be a REAL man!
Make a REAL difference!

"If we are afraid to be different,
then how can we make a difference?"
~ Reverend John I. Jenkins

~

Only those who would dare to be different can ever
truly hope to make a difference.

~

A Final Challenge

My special thanks to you for picking up this book, and with those sentiments of gratitude, I will also issue a personal challenge to you as well: read the book, take to heart its message, but more importantly, *live out* the notion of what it means to be a REAL Man. Do not just read about being a real man; do not just talk about being a real man. Live it out.

The World Needs More REAL Men

The world needs more REAL men…
Men who are both respectful and respectable…
Men who have principles and men who live by those principles…
Men of honor and men of integrity…
Men of courage and men of will…
Men who will stand up for what they believe in…
Men who will speak up for what is right…
Men who will be a guiding light and beacon of hope for others…
Men who will make a difference in this world.

~

The world is calling, and greatness awaits.
Will you answer the challenge?
Do you have what it takes?

~

Accept the challenge and rise to the occasion.
Others are looking to you; the world is counting on you.

Answer the Call:
Stand Up and Stand Tall.
Be a REAL Man!

Answer The Call: Stand Up and Stand Tall!

Go out and be a REAL Man: A man who will …

+ *Respect all people,*
+ *Especially women.*
+ *Always do the right thing.*
+ *Live a life that matters.*

The question is not whether you will be a man.
The question is… ***What kind of a man will you be?***

Be a **REAL** Man!

About REAL Man Inc.

About REAL Man Inc.
REAL Man Inc. is a not-for-profit LLC, founded by a high school coach and mentor, in 2009. It currently is in the process of establishing complete 501(c) non-profit status. The purpose of REAL Man Inc. is to provide young men, and anyone in a position to influence them, with the guidance and resources to help them develop into men of substance, men of principle, men of honor, and men of will.

Above all, the organization is committed to helping today's boys become REAL men: Men who *respect all people, especially women*; men who *always do the right* thing, and men who *live a life that matters*.

The overarching mission of REAL Man *Inc.* is not only to educate and spread a valuable message, but to have people receive that message and **to *incorporate* it into the fabric of who they are**. It is to spread the message of what it means to be a real man; to breathe life into that message by encouraging people to take it to heart and to live it out in their daily lives; to raise up the next generation of young people across the country and around the world; and to ultimately help make the world a better place in which to live.

REAL Man Inc. is committed to spreading the message about what it means to be a real man, through word-of-mouth and a variety of other methods. REAL Man Inc. uses an educational website (www.RealManInc.org), a book and other educational materials—such as signs, wallet cards, awareness wristbands, and flyers—to help spread its message.

The ultimate goal is to get the "REAL Man" message into the hands of every football coach in America, and eventually into the hearts and minds of every man in this world.

Stand Up and Stand Tall:
Be a REAL Man!

About REAL Man Inc.

The mission of REAL Man Inc. is to promote an important message that is very much needed in our society today. It is designed to help boys and men of all ages to develop an understanding of what it truly means to be a *real* man.

About the "Inc." ~ What does it mean?

Why the *Inc.*? ~ It stands for "incorporated," but not in the way you might think. The mission of REAL Man Inc. is not only to get boys and men to read the message, but to reflect on and *incorporate* that message into their daily lives.

Becoming a *real* man is not something that you can merely pay lip-service to. It is something that you must believe in, and more importantly, it is something that you must live out: in your words and in your actions. Making a commitment to being a *real* man is not merely a decision; it is a way of life.

About the Paw Logo ~ What does it represent?

Why the paw logo? ~ There are two reasons for the paw print logo. Firstly, the paw logo has been the symbol of several of the football programs in which I have had the opportunity to coach over the years. It also is a very popular logo for many high school athletic programs throughout the country. Given my personal experiences, and also the coincidence that there are both four fingers in a paw and four letters in the word "real," the paw-print logo only seemed like a natural fit.

Secondly, the paw is a symbolic image. As is the case with a footprint, a paw-print is a visible sign that someone or something was here. It is an imprint: an impression left when one has passed through a particular area with a certain amount of weight. The paw-print is symbolic of having an impact and of leaving one's mark on the world in which one lives.

One of the components of being a REAL man is to *live a life that matters*. This means living respectfully, responsibly, and honorably. It means dedicating yourself to a life of personal excellence and social significance.

Living a life that matters is about going above and beyond the individual confines of your own life, in order to reach out and help enhance the lives of those around you. It is about positively affecting the lives of others and leaving your mark on the world in which you live.

~

Make an impact and make an impression.
Leave a legacy and leave your mark on this world.
Walk through life with depth and gravity
and leave your footprint… or in this case …
your *paw* print … on the world through which you pass.

~

"You will be known forever by the tracks you leave."
~ Dakota Saying

About Coach DiCocco

About Coach DiCocco

Coach Frank DiCocco has worked with young men and women throughout the country, serving as a coach and mentor to hundreds of young people at the high school and middle school levels. He has coached both football and strength & conditioning within various athletic programs, and has also served as an administrator and department head as well.

Coach Frank DiCocco has been blessed to serve our nation's youth in a number of cities over the past several years. He has accumulated extensive leadership experience in the process, coaching the sport of football in some of the nation's most prominent and well-respected high school programs. He currently coaches at William T. Dwyer High School, in Palm Beach Gardens, Florida.

Coach DiCocco's career includes additional stops at some of the nation's most prestigious schools and prominent athletics programs, including Godby High School in Tallahassee, Florida; the Rindge and Latin School in Cambridge, Massachusetts; the Fessenden School in West Newton, Massachusetts, Paul VI Catholic High School in Fairfax, Virginia; and South Point High School in Rock Hill, South Carolina.

Coach DiCocco graduated from Boston College in 2006, earning a Bachelor of Arts degree in Communications, as well as a Minor in General Education. He is also a 2002 graduate of the Avon Old Farms School, located in Avon, Connecticut. At present, Coach DiCocco is working to complete a Master's degree in Physical Education & Athletic Administration from Winthrop University. Although originally from Connecticut, Coach DiCocco currently maintains a residence in the South Florida area.

~

In addition to his coaching career and website, Frank DiCocco writes a weekly inspirational column espousing life lessons and other important pieces of advice, which he sends to many of his student-athletes, fellow colleagues, friends, and personal associates. The "Thought of the Week" column is sent out via e-mail to hundreds of people across the country each week.

To contact Coach DiCocco, or to be included on the weekly e-mail list, please send him a message at fdicocco@gmail.com. You may also reach Coach DiCocco via telephone, at the number (860) 543-9683.

~

Live in such a way that you will always be remembered.
Live in such a way that a part of you lives on.

~

"To live in the hearts of those you leave behind is not to die."
~ Robert Orr

BE A REAL MAN
MAKE A REAL DIFFERENCE

RESPECT ALL PEOPLE

Show respect to all people, at all times, in all ways.
Treat others the way you would want to be treated.
Respect yourself and always carry yourself with class.

ESPECIALLY WOMEN

Treat women with the utmost respect.
Be a gentleman at all times. Be respectful in all ways.
Accept women. Respect women. Protect women.

ALWAYS DO THE RIGHT THING

Have the courage to do the right thing.
Always be yourself. Always keep your word.
Live by your principles. Honor your commitments.

LIVE A LIFE THAT MATTERS

Live with honor. Live with excellence.
Live with purpose. Live with determination.
Be a role model. Make a difference in the lives of others.
Leave a legacy. Live for something greater than yourself.

Stand Up and Stand Tall:

~ **Be a REAL Man!** ~

6878322R0

Made in the USA
Charleston, SC
19 December 2010